Origins of a Spontaneous Revolution

Economics, Cognition, and Society

This series provides a forum for theoretical and empirical investigations of social phenomena. It promotes works that focus on the interactions among cognitive processes, individual behavior, and social outcomes. It is especially open to interdisciplinary books that are genuinely integrative.

Editor: Timur Kuran

Editorial Board: Sheila Ryan Johansson

Advisory Board: James M. Buchanan
Albert O. Hirschman
Mancur Olson

Titles in the Series

Origins of a Spontaneous Revolution: East Germany, 1989

Karl-Dieter Opp, Peter Voss, Christiane Gern

Ann Arbor

THE UNIVERSITY OF MICHIGAN PRESS

English translation copyright © by the University of Michigan 1995
Originally published in German by Klett-Cotta, Stuttgart
All rights reserved
Published in the United States of America by
The University of Michigan Press
Manufactured in the United States of America
⊗ Printed on acid-free paper

1998   1997   1996   1995   4   3   2   1

A CIP catalog record for this book is available from the British Library.

Library of Congress Cataloging-in-Publication Data

Opp, Karl-Dieter.
   Origins of a spontaneous revolution : East Germany, 1989 / Karl-
Dieter Opp, Peter Voss, Christiane Gern.
      p.   cm. — (Economics, cognition, and society)
   Includes bibliographical references.
   ISBN 0-472-10575-2 (alk. paper)
   1. Germany (East)—Politics and government—1989–1990.
2. Opposition (Political science)—Germany (East).   3. Social
movements—Germany (East)—History.   4. Political culture—Germany
(East).   5. Germany—History—Unification, 1990.   I. Voss, Peter.
II. Gern, Christiane.   III. Title.   IV. Series.
DD289.065   1995
943.1087'8—dc20   95-8860
                                                                                      CIP

Preface

There is an enormous number of newspaper and magazine articles, radio and TV programs, scientific articles and books about the revolution of 1989 in the German Democratic Republic (GDR). Why, then, write yet another book on this subject? Is there really anything new to be said or written?

Most of the literature on the GDR revolution *describes* the events that took place in 1989. We find books with pictures of the demonstrators in Leipzig, eyewitness accounts from participants in demonstrations, statements from former officials of the Ministry of State Security (Stasi) or their victims, chronologies of events, documents such as speeches given during the peace prayers in Leipzig, and political statements by opposition groups.

No one would deny that the documentation of the events of 1989 is necessary in order to understand the revolution. A question of equal, if not more, importance to be asked is: *Why* did a revolution occur in the GDR in 1989? There are indeed a number of explanations that have been put forward to answer this question, and the reader may certainly have his or her own explanation for the revolutionary events. Yet, though many of those explanations appear to be plausible at first glance, doubts surface after closer analysis of them. It is often said, for example, that the growing dissatisfaction of citizens in the GDR was a major factor in the origin of the protests. Why, then, weren't there any large-scale protests earlier? A high level of dissatisfaction existed long before the massive protests of 1989. The politics of Mikhail Gorbachev are also often viewed as catalysts for the protests, yet why did the protests begin only in 1989, four years after Gorbachev's rise to power? Furthermore, how could Gorbachev's political program cause individual GDR citizens to take part in demonstrations such as the one on October 9 in Leipzig and risk their lives? Even if these and other explanations seem plausible, how do we know that they are actually correct? Simply because events such as Gorbachev's political reforms occurred prior to the demonstrations does not mean that they were indeed the causes of the protests and the collapse of the GDR.

It is therefore not at all clear what the causes of the revolution in the GDR were. This book is the first comprehensive attempt to *explain* the revolution in the GDR. It focuses on the following questions: How could the mass protests arise in the fall of 1989 despite high personal risks? Why did the protests remain peaceful? How was it possible that the protests emerged spontaneously, that is, without having been organized? What was the role of opposition groups, the church, and personal contacts between the citizens for the development of the revolution? Why did the communist regime finally resign, without bloodshed?

The first basic idea of this book is this: Because the revolution was "made" by the citizens of the GDR, an explanation of "the" revolution must explain the behavior of the citizens. In other words, the explanation must focus on the individual GDR citizens. Many readers may consider this self-evident, yet most explanations of the GDR revolution do not proceed in this way. This issue will be explored in detail in chapter 2.

Although our procedure appears acceptable at first glance, it may be fraught with the following problem: It may seem that events such as Gorbachev's reforms or the political changes in countries such as Poland and Hungary are not included in explanations focusing on individual actors. The contrary is true. Placing the individual citizen at the focal point of the analysis, the question of how Gorbachev's reforms or the liberalization in Poland and Hungary affected the revolution in the GDR can be answered in a new way. If these events indeed influenced the revolution in the GDR, then they must somehow have motivated the individual citizens to act. How this happened will be addressed in this book.

Although the individual citizen is the focal point of this book, the other side—the government and the security forces—cannot be neglected. The question of why the communist regime of the Sozialistische Einheitspartei Deutschlands [Socialist unity party of Germany] (SED) acted as it did will be addressed in chapter 11. Why, for example, did the SED regime not choose a "Chinese solution"—that is, why was there not even an attempt made to put down the protests?

The second basic idea of this book is that we are using a general theory that has proven useful in the social sciences: the theory of rational action. We apply a version of this theory that uses "soft" incentives and individual perceptions as explanatory factors, and that is less controversial than a narrow neoclassical economic model of man. This theory leads us to select the factors that help explain the GDR revolution. Our theoretical approach will be spelled out in chapter 2.

The present book is not confined to theoretical speculations. If an explanation is claimed to be correct, it must be supported by facts. If the revolution in the GDR is to be explained on the basis of the decisions of individual actors, data supporting such an explanation must refer to single individuals. In other words, those who took part in the revolution must be heard. In November and December 1990, we conducted a representative survey of 1,300 citizens of the city of Leipzig. This is the only representative survey referring almost solely to the events of 1989. We further interviewed 209 members of opposition groups in Leipzig. Finally, we had informal talks with 19 Leipzig citizens—16 face-to-face conversations (qualitative interviews) and one group discussion with three citizens. The interviews and the discussion dealt with the events in the GDR in 1989 and at the beginning of 1990. These are unparalleled data about one of the most important epochs in German history.

Along with these data we also included all available material relevant to our topic. This material includes documents such as those made available to us by opposition groups, programmatic statements of opposition groups, jokes and slogans that were presented during the Monday demonstrations, Stasi (security forces) reports about opposition groups, autobiographies of Politburo members, and publications with reports by participants of the demonstrations.

Our findings do not just confirm what is already known. Many widely accepted assumptions were not in line with our data. For example, our data analyses indicate that economic discontent was not a cause for participation in the demonstrations. Another finding is that some of the goals for which citizens demonstrated, such as introducing a market economy in the GDR, hardly changed after October 9. What changed was the expression of goals in public. Our book contains many other interesting and new findings.

Let us look at the contents of the book more closely. In order to analyze the revolution in the GDR, it is useful to begin with a description of the forms of resistance against the SED regime throughout the history of the GDR (chapter 1). In chapter 2 we will then present the general theoretical approach that we will apply throughout the book.

Because the citizen protests were goal-directed actions, we ask what their goals were (chapter 3) and to what extent these goals gave rise to the protests (chapter 4). In chapter 5 we examine whether moral incentives played a role for participating in the protests. Is it possible to explain the nonviolent character of the protests by means of the citizens' general moral views (chapter 6)? In chapter 7 we focus on the extent to which opposition groups or personal networks of friends and coworkers promoted participation in the protests. The role of the church will be analyzed in chapter 8.

One of the most fascinating and puzzling features of the revolution in the GDR is the fact that the citizens took action in spite of the danger involved. How can it be explained that a single citizen, who certainly cannot influence the process of history, takes part in the demonstration in Leipzig on October 9, 1989, although one had to face the risk of a bloodbath? Why was repression ineffective in stopping the revolution? These are the questions addressed in chapter 9.

An analysis of demographic characteristics of protest participants and nonparticipants is included in chapter 10. For example, were the protest participants younger than the nonparticipants, and did demonstrators and nondemonstrators differ according to their education—as is typically the case in Western democracies? Next we turn to the "other side" (chapter 11): One of the still most debated questions today is why the SED regime did not react tougher against the protesting citizens.

The preceding chapters contain, so to speak, the building blocks of our explanation. These blocks are then combined to an explanation of the processes of the revolution (chapter 12). In this chapter we also address another typical feature of the GDR revolution: The protests emerged spontaneously, that is, without any organization by groups. How was it possible that the demonstrators came together spontaneously without any form of organization?

It is often said that social scientists spend a lot of money to find out what everybody knows already. To examine this claim, we analyze the extent to which commonsense explanations of the partners in our qualitative interviews were concurrent with our own explanation (chapter 13).

The last two chapters go beyond the topic of the GDR revolution. In chapter 14 we address the question of the *general* conditions for the emergence of spontaneous peaceful revolutions. The last chapter (15) focuses on our own theoretical approach. In the social science literature there are several theories that claim to offer a general explanation of revolutions. We investigate the extent to which the revolution in the GDR may make a modification of other theoretical perspectives necessary.

The appendix contains first an account of the history of the research project from which this book emerged. We then address in more detail the questions that were addressed in the introduction. In particular, we describe the construction of the scales. The appendix is intended for those readers who have knowledge of empirical social research.

This book is no technical monograph for a small group of social scientists but, rather, is intended for a broad audience of economists, historians, political scientists, sociologists, and the interested reader with some social science background. Technical details such as the results of statistical analyses or scale construction are addressed in footnotes or in the appendix.

The chapters of this book have been written by the author(s) indicated after the title of each chapter. However, this book is a joint effort: each version of a chapter was intensively discussed by all three authors, and the discussions always led to extensive revisions.

The German names of streets, squares, and churches have not been translated. Thus, Grimmaische Straße (street), Karl-Marx-Platz (square), or Nikolai Kirche (church) have been left unchanged. The German letter ß referring to a sharp "s" (as in "assets") has not been changed, either. All quotations from German sources were translated into English by the authors.

This book was made possible by a grant from the German Research Association (Deutsche Forschungsgemeinschaft). We are particularly grateful that the decision for support was made in a short period of time, considering the urgency of research projects about the GDR. We would also like to thank the ZUMA (Zentrum für Umfragen, Methoden und Analysen [Center for surveys, methods and analyses]) in Mannheim for its valuable help in modifying our questionnaire and choosing the research institute—the USUMA (Unabhängiger Service für Umfragen, Methoden und Analysen [Independent service for surveys, methods and analyses]) in East Berlin, which also deserves our thanks, in particular Mr. Rainer Schwarz. Prof. Detlef Pollack from the University of Leipzig, who read parts of the manuscript, provided us with valuable comments. We would especially like to thank our respondents who took the time to answer our questions.

Contents

Introduction

Christiane Gern and Karl-Dieter Opp

This book includes findings from several sets of data: in particular, from a representative survey of the population of Leipzig that was conducted in autumn 1990. This introduction will provide the reader with some information about this survey and the other data. Topics that require a knowledge of statistics will be addressed in the appendix of this book.

The Data Used

In November and December 1990, one year after the decisive events for the collapse of the GDR, a representative sample of 1,300 citizens of the city of Leipzig was taken. The major part of this survey dealt with the events of autumn 1989. A second sample consisted of 209 citizens who described themselves as members of the opposition movement. These data are mainly used in chapter 10. Both surveys were administered by the survey institute USUMA, East Berlin.

A third set of data consists of detailed, largely spontaneous conversations with 19 citizens who played a particular role in the autumn 1989 events. These qualitative interviews were conducted by the authors themselves and mostly covered the same topics as the survey. We will continually use quotes from the qualitative interviews to illustrate our hypotheses. Detailed information about the sets of data and the survey institute are presented in the appendix.

The Questionnaire

The questionnaires for the representative sample and the sample of the opposition groups were identical and contained, with one exception, solely standardized—that is, preformulated—questions and answer categories, which the interviewer read aloud to the respondent. The exception was a self-administered questionnaire that was filled out by the respondent. After completion, the respondent put the questionnaire in an envelope and returned it to the interviewer. This method is used when the topics are considered delicate and face-to-face answers thus may be unreliable. We used the self-administered questionnaire to ascertain participation in political activities, such as in the Monday demonstrations in Leipzig; the political goals respondents wanted to achieve with their participation; and the respondents' closeness to political parties.

Questions were posed in reference to two periods of time: The first and larger part of the questionnaire refers to the period up to October 9, 1989. This date was chosen because it was the turning point in the development of the GDR in autumn 1989. The smaller, second part of the questionnaire refers to the time between October 9, 1989, and March 18, 1990, the date of the first free elections for the national parliament, the Volkskammer [people's chamber]. The self-administered questionnaire also was structured in this manner. The reference period was mentioned in the interview questions continuously so that respondents could not confuse the time periods. It took respondents an average of 67 minutes to fill out the whole questionnaire.

Problems of the Survey

Why Leipzig?

The Monday demonstrations in Leipzig contributed to the emergence of protests in other cities of the GDR and to the collapse of the regime. Explaining the revolution of the GDR therefore requires explaining the Leipzig protests. This is the major reason we limited our representative survey to the city of Leipzig.

Respondents were selected randomly from the population of Leipzig (see the appendix for more details), yet this does not mean that our findings are limited to the citizens of Leipzig. All citizens of the GDR were subject to the economic and political order of the GDR, and the citizens of the GDR were probably very similar in regard to the characteristics we use to explain the protests. Such is the case, for example, for political dissatisfaction and the extent to which citizens believed themselves able to change the political situation by means of protest.

Even if the *extent* of dissatisfaction and other factors differed in various regions, this in no way means that the factors also had different *effects*. There is no evidence that different factors contributed to the emergence of the protests in Leipzig than elsewhere. But let us assume a reader contends that Leipzig is a special case. We would then argue that Leipzig is the place where the revolution in the GDR began, and that we are therefore at least able to explain its origin.

Validity of the Data

Problems may have occurred because the survey took place in the end of 1990, while questions for the most part referred to the time before October 9,

1989. Furthermore, respondents had to switch reference periods because some questions referred to the period between October 9, 1989, and March 18, 1990.

Such a survey can create two key problems. First, events may not be dated exactly, and attitudes and opinions may not always be clearly remembered. People tend to remember past events in accordance with present opinions (Strube 1987). Second, recollection of events may be distorted by discussions with people who have other opinions or who acted differently. In regard to the chronology of events, there is a tendency to remember events that lay farther in the past as more recent and events that are more recent as farther in the past than they actually are (Strube 1987, Schwarz 1990).

To minimize these problems, we tried to make it easier for respondents to recall past events by asking the following question at the outset of the interview: "What comes to your mind spontaneously when you think back to the time between May 1st and October 9th, 1989?" We attempted to counteract false dating of events and attitudes by choosing dates that were associated with well-known events and were continually mentioned in public (Strube 1987, see also Schwarz 1990). The first demonstration that was not crushed took place on October 9, 1989, and the day of the first free election was March 18, 1990. We are confident that most respondents recalled these dates.

Findings from psychological research show that people remember events particularly well if these events are unique, consequential, unexpected, and emotion provoking (Brewer 1986, 44). The events in autumn 1989 were definitely unique: a comparable uprising occurred on June 17, 1953, but was crushed with the help of Russian troops. The events in autumn 1989 were consequential because they were of utmost importance in changing the lives of the GDR citizens. The events were unexpected and associated with very strong emotions. To be sure, it may be difficult for respondents to remember all details or exact dates, such as when exactly the New Forum was founded and when exactly Egon Krenz replaced Erich Honecker, but they will certainly be able to remember their personal reactions to and attitudes toward these and similar events and various characteristics of the situation of this time.

This psychological research is in agreement with what many citizens of the former GDR told us in personal conversations when we prepared the questionnaire. Many citizens told us they will never forget what happened in autumn 1989 nor their hopes, fears, and grievances after about 40 years under a repressive communist regime. Thus, memory failures should have been less of a problem than is usually the case in retrospective research.

Nevertheless, answers to some survey questions may be fraught with distortions. In particular, we distinguish between two types of retrospective bias. An *outcome effect* refers to the tendency of respondents to adjust their cognition of an event to its outcome—in this case, the protests' immense success. Second, a *hero effect* may have occurred: In view of the celebrated upsurge of the population—a writer even called Leipzig "city of heroes" (Heldenstadt)—citizens may have overstated their role in the revolution, in particular their extent of participation and the risk that accompanied their participation.

We have ascertained the extent of each respondent's *perceived personal influence* to contribute to changes by participating in protest actions. People may be unwilling or unable to admit that they did not anticipate the outcome of the large-scale protests that changed history (outcome effect). However, isn't it much more heroic, in particular for a participant in the demonstrations, to say one did not believe the protests would be effective? Thus, the outcome effect would lead to an overstatement of perceived influence, whereas the hero effect would prompt respondents to understate their perceived influence. These countervailing effects probably led to correct answers to items about perceived influence in 1989. Furthermore, many published personal reports about the revolution indicate that in autumn 1989 the success of the protests was unexpected and that it is therefore socially acceptable to say so. Yet, many citizens say they expected the protests to lead to reforms, but not to an overthrow of the system. Thus, it is unlikely that respondents' reports of their influence are grossly distorted.

We asked a number of questions about the *repression* respondents expected when they participated in protest actions. The outcome effect implies that respondents would express a low likelihood and a low fear of repression because, both October 9 and later, the regime did not impose repression. The hero effect would lead respondents to say that they regarded bloodshed as highly likely and that all who attended the demonstrations were very courageous. In public discourse about the revolution, people often admit to a fear of possible repression, whereas others say they did not anticipate severe sanctions. In our qualitative interviews, both views were expressed quite clearly. The high average values on the repression scales (see the appendix) indicate that the outcome effect can be safely ruled out in this case. The hero effect is not relevant either, because respondents' answers to the various repression items probably reflect the high level of repression that in fact existed in the GDR.

As to *protest norms*—that is, feelings of obligation to participate in protest actions—a hero effect probably did not operate. An outcome effect may have led to a rationalization: *having* participated in a successful event may prompt respondents to believe they *should* have participated. However, pressure to rationalize behavior according to a norm occurs only if the behavior is considered morally wrong. Perhaps some nonparticipants have a bad conscience, but these individuals should then develop some sort of antiprotest norms. Those who participated in the protest actions did the "right thing," so they need not invoke some normative justification. Because the majority of our respondents are nonparticipants, and the mean of the protest norms scale (see the appendix) is relatively high, a significant amount of rationalization probably did not occur. The framing of the questions referring to norms is also not conducive to rationalizations because we did not simply ask whether respondents felt an obligation to participate. Instead, we presented respondents with descriptions of situations—high risk, expected success, and so forth (see the appendix)—and asked them to indicate the extent to which one should participate in such situations. It is implausible that respondents would develop such complex rationalizations after the fact. In public discourse about the revolution, there is no general conception that citizens had or did not have a duty to participate. In our qualitative interviews, respondents stated quite different views regarding the duty to participate.

In summary, these arguments do not support a consistent distortion or bias regarding specific factors that we used in our explanatory arguments.

In regard to participation in demonstrations and other forms of protests before October 9, 1989, a hero effect may have occurred: The demonstrations of 1989 were viewed positively; therefore, respondents may have overstated their participation. To circumvent this problem, questions referring to participation in protests were part of the self-administered questionnaire. There was thus no incentive to exaggerate participation to the interviewer.

One interview question, in our opinion, is the most decisive test for the existence of bias in the direction of social desirability: membership in the SED, the ruling Communist party. Party membership was strongly stigmatized after the collapse of the regime. If respondents gave socially desirable answers, few respondents would have admitted membership. However, the percentage of SED members in our sample corresponds exceedingly well to the SED membership in Leipzig (see the appendix). This result seems especially important because the respective question was not posed in the self-administered questionnaire.

Another precaution taken against the two effects mentioned was that interview questions were carefully phrased so that quite diverse answers would seem acceptable to the respondent.

The interviewers evaluated each interviewee, and their ratings indicate that in general there were no problems. In regard to the willingness to answer the questions, 1,073 or 83 percent of the respondents (out of 1,300) received the highest rating, and 115 or 9 percent the second highest out of five possible ratings. Further, 1,173 or 90 percent of the interviews were rated as generally reliable, 88 or 7 percent as generally less reliable. Results of regression analyses, which included our most important variables, for respondents who received the highest ratings on willingness to answer and reliability of responses were almost identical to results of analyses that included all respondents.

We also asked respondents how well they generally remembered the events in autumn 1989. Of the 1,287 respondents with a valid answer, 57.3 percent said that they could remember things exactly, 41 percent indicated that they had forgotten some things, and only 1.6 percent said they could not remember the events at all. In assessing these answers, we must take into account that respondents did not know what questions we were going to ask. Whatever the case, the answers in no way indicate that the respondents generally could not recall the events well.

We carried out statistical analyses to examine whether the results were different for those who said they "remember exactly" and for those who said that they had "forgotten some things." We disregarded the third group (1.6 percent) because of the low number of respondents. The results of these analyses are very similar (for details see the appendix).

General Protests and Demonstrations before October 9, 1989

We distinguish between two forms of protest: general protests and demonstrations (see the appendix for measurement details and standard statistical indices). Mainly two reasons motivated us to differentiate between participation in general protests and in demonstrations: (1) the demonstrations were decisive for the collapse of the GDR and (2) we presumed that different incentives may be important for participating in either type of action. The latter assumption was confirmed by the data, as we will see later on.

Questions on the performance of political actions were part of the self-administered questionnaire. *Participation in general protests before October 9* consists of four activities:

(1) participation in or founding of an opposition group; (2) refusal to vote or casting an invalid vote; (3) refusal to become a member of the SED, union or similar political groups; (4) participation in peace prayers (Friedensgebete) and similar church activities.

For each action, respondents were assigned code 4 when they took part several times and code 3 for participating once. Respondents were assigned code 2 when they "considered" participation, but didn't carry it out, and code 1 when they said the activity "was out of the question." The values for each respondent were added and then divided by four. Respondents who had not even considered one of the four forms of protest received a value of 1 accordingly, and respondents who took part many times in all activities received a value of 4.

The participation in *demonstrations* before October 9 was ascertained by asking respondents if they had taken part in one or more of the demonstrations on September 25, October 2, October 7, and October 9. The scale *participation in demonstrations before October 9* refers to the frequency with which respondents took part in the four demonstrations. The scale ranges from 0 (did not participate in any demonstration) to 4 (participated four times). The name of the scale should be more exactly, "participation in demonstrations before *and on* October 9." For the sake of simplicity, we will say "before" October 9.

CHAPTER 1

Citizens against the State: Political Protest in the GDR

Peter Voss

Protest in the GDR Prior to 1989

Political protests as extensive as those in autumn 1989 had taken place only once before in the German Democratic Republic—and this was in 1953. The peaceful protesters of the 1989 revolution in the GDR who were younger than about 45 had only read of the public uprising of June 17, 1953, in schoolbooks published by the Communist party SED (Sozialistische Einheitspartei Deutschlands [Socialist Unity Party of Germany]), and they painted no rosy picture of this event. The older citizens in particular remember their powerlessness in view of the violent intervention of Soviet tanks. Therefore, most of the citizens began their autumn 1989 revolution without ever having taken part in a protest. What they knew about demonstrations against the government they had seen in reports on Western TV.

Nevertheless, the time between 1953 and 1989 was not protest free. When Stasi (Ministry of State Security) and court files are opened to the public, one will find a detailed documentation of the political resistance against the SED regime. Yet this resistance did not occur in public. State information policies covered up every uprising or twisted the truth if a cover-up was impossible. The "unity" of people and party was not to be doubted.

Did the people therefore have absolutely no memories of political conflict? This is one of the questions we tried to answer with our qualitative interviews. Because we interviewed citizens of Leipzig, the responses primarily referred to events that occurred in this city. Many citizens of Leipzig still remember the Battle of Leuschner Platz. In 1965, the music preferred by young people did not conform to socialist values. SED officials believed that the Beatles were becoming too popular. Young people listened to the music groups instead of working for the FDJ (Freie Deutsche Jugend [Free German Youth]) school year, an educational measure of the FDJ wherein participation was a duty. Therefore, a number of popular music groups were suddenly banned. Several hundred young people demonstrated peacefully in downtown Leipzig against the prohibition of their music. They were provoked by a massive police action, and rioting began. Erich Loest wrote about this event in his book *Es geht seinen Gang* [Everything takes its course]. Those who were 16 years old at that time made a startling discovery. The state of workers and farmers had police dogs for all those who did not accede to its opinions:

> Before the "Battle of Leuschner Platz" everything in the world had its orderly place for me. The enemy was to the West. The Americans bombed Vietnam and Kiesinger [a German chancellor] was a fascist. Now one of our dogs was biting me when it should have been biting an American bombing Vietnam. I wasn't attacking with napalm. A GDR dog had no reason to be biting me, for God's sake. (Loest 1979, 29)

At the same location in downtown Leipzig three years later, an event occurred that remains in the minds of the citizens and even had a longer-lasting effect because of its tragic symbolism: the destruction of the Universitätskirche (University Church) on May 30, 1968. The church did not fit into the socialist architectural design of downtown Leipzig. The political conflict surrounding the church pervaded the atmosphere in Leipzig for approximately 10 years (1959 to 1968). SED head Paul Fröhlich, backed up personally by Walter Ulbricht—the first head of the GDR—ignored the public outcry against the church's blowing up. The ideological indoctrination of the allegedly democratically elected city parliament at that time already can be seen from the fact that only one city official voted against the church's destruction: Pastor Hans-Georg Rausch from the Leipzig suburb of Probstheida. Cabaret artist Bernd-Lutz Lange recalled the situation in one of our qualitative interviews:

> Well, the Universitätskirche was blown up in 1968. The city of Leipzig and its inhabitants never forgot that feeling of powerlessness, of helplessness. . . . We older citizens—say, the ones around 40 and certainly those over 45 like me, and the senior citizens—never got over the fact that our system suddenly created this terrible powerlessness among its citizens. For me, this was something unforgettable over the years. It is the only church which was not damaged in World War II. To demolish it just because some SED party head didn't want a church standing on a Karl Marx Platz, together with Walter Ulbricht, who was from Leipzig himself and was not fond of the church as an institution, was an atrocity. It was a late Gothic church consecrated by none other than Martin Luther himself. There were demonstrations back then, and that was something very unusual in 1968.

During the mentioned protests, a large number of security forces and police were deployed and numerous arrests were made. Leipzig citizens lived with the trauma of powerlessness against legalized state violence for a long time. Political protest in the streets died for the next twenty years. Nevertheless, the protests in 1965 and 1968, and afterward others that are not recorded in any chronicle so far, certainly had an impact on the events of autumn 1989. We spoke with Jochen Läßig from the Neues Forum [New forum], and he confirmed that this was the case: "Although the protests were different, they always kept a consciousness that there is something there, that there are those who do not accommodate to the current state of politics."

The decade-long absence of an opposition in the GDR cannot be understood without the events of June 17, 1953. These events silenced the opposition for a long time. On June 17, workers used the forms of fighting that were normal prior to 1933 to achieve economic and political changes: strikes and demonstrations. They thought that a state of "workers and farmers" would not deny them democratic rights. Russian tanks taught them that they were living in a one-party dictatorship and not in a democracy.

Within the socialism practiced in the GDR, there was neither a legal parliamentary nor any other legal opposition. Every public form of political pluralism was immediately and forcefully put down. "The company" (Stasi, the Ministry of State Security) was in charge of illegal opponents. The massive Stasi apparatus had only one task: to suppress any opinions deviating from party ideology. The so-called "block parties," the elections to choose "people's representatives," and the toleration of church activities were only facets of a pseudodemocracy.

Political opponents in the GDR could not organize themselves under such conditions. Protest actions before 1988 consisted therefore only of actions by single individuals or some small groups (see Rein 1989). There are no reliable data on the exact numbers of members in these groups. Pollack (1990, 18), for example, estimates total membership between 10,000 and 15,000.

If one takes a look at the historical development of the various opposition groups, one continuously encounters an East Berlin group named Die Umweltbibliothek [The environmental library], founded in 1986. This group met in rooms of the Zion community and was a thorn in the eye of the Stasi from the beginning. The Umweltbibliothek supported in particular the work of many environmental groups by providing them with material usually not available to the public. In one of our qualitative interviews, Jochen Läßig described the group as "the information center of the GDR opposition groups" and commented further, "They were really constructing a political organization." On the night of November 24, 1987, state security forces occupied the offices of the Umweltbibliothek, confiscated their entire material, arrested seven young adults, and accused them of producing illegal publications. That ignited a wave of protests which spread throughout Berlin and even beyond the GDR. After this time, the protest movement grew.

The Initiative für Frieden und Menschenrechte [Initiative for peace and human rights], also founded in East Berlin in 1985, was probably the oldest opposition group in the GDR. In the minds of the Stasi, this was a group "not rooted in organizational structures of the church, that aimed at undermining the socialist state and societal order under the protection of the protestant church" (Mitter and Wolle 1990, 68). A Leipzig group by the name of Gerechtigkeit [Justice] had been operating since 1988 and had close connections to the groups in Berlin. The Neues Forum [New forum] stemmed originally from the IFM (Initiative für Frieden und Menschenrechte) in 1989. Yet in contrast to the groups mentioned before, the Neues Forum was rather a mass movement. Christian Müller, a Neues Forum member, commented on this point in one of our qualitative interviews:

> . . . the call [to found the Neues Forum] came on September 10th. By the end of September, approximately 8,000 had signed up for membership. By the end of October, there were 50,000. By mid-November, 200,000 individuals signed up, indicating that they sympathized with or would like to become active members of the Neues Forum. To organize this mass of people in about one and a half months and do something with them was impossible. It was rather symbolic that public statements were made sometimes by some small groups, which in turn created greater solidarity, and that there was something that could be a guide.

Sociologist Detlef Pollack agrees. During a personal interview, he said that in his opinion, groups such as the Neues Forum were "points of crystallization through which mass protests could find an orientation." The opposition groups neither initiated nor led the peaceful revolution, but that makes their role no less important, he stressed. "Not the Neues Forum initiated the mass protests but rather vice versa: The masses put the Neues Forum at the top of their movement."

Opposition in the GDR did not develop according to the well-known snowball effect, in which a small number of revolutionaries sparks a mass movement. The few "revolutionaries" in fact remained among themselves also in autumn 1989. The crowds took to the streets spontaneously. The opposition groups did not trigger the revolution. Bernd Okun commented in an interview with us:

> The opposition movement was actually a very small movement. It was the Western media which made it appear so large. Bärbel Bohley [one of

the well known figures of the opposition movement] appeared—I'm exaggerating—once a day on the West German TV station ZDF. There was thus only an impression of a strong movement. The opposition movement, in reality, did not represent even 1 percent of the population.

SED leaders were aware of this and thus didn't take their opponents seriously, but, rather, treated them as criminals (Schabowski 1990, 18f).[1]

Forms of Political Action

Theater

Theater in the GDR had always criticized the current social situation. Classic pieces as well as contemporary drama by playwrights such as Ulrich Plenzdorf, Volker Braun, Christoph Hein, and Heiner Müller were used for this purpose.

What makes theater so attractive that people are willing to stand in lines for hours to get tickets? The answer is simple. People stand in lines when themes are addressed on stage which they never found in newspapers. While the media is busy glorifying the current conditions, as usual, theater focuses on societal contradictions, is concerned with questions about the past, and takes the opportunity to design its own utopias. (Menge 1990, 73)

It was particularly the numerous cabarets in the GDR, along with the theaters, that exposed many social grievances—although always censored.

On October 4, 1989, the actors and cabaret performers gathered in the State Theater of Dresden for the first time, then read the following proclamation:

We're stepping out from behind our roles. Under the current conditions in our country, we have no choice. A country which cannot keep its youth jeopardizes its future. A government which does not speak to its people is not trustworthy. A party leadership which does not adapt its principles to new realities is doomed to fall. A people forced into silence will begin to become violent. The truth must be told. We have built this country. We won't let this country be destroyed.

---

1. The role of the opposition groups for the emergence of the revolution will be dealt with in more detail in chapter 7.

The effect of this appeal on the audience was overwhelming. By the next day, the news had spread around the city and then around the whole country. Government officials threatened the theater management and actors. But on October 5, they reiterated their appeal on stage after the evening performance. They continued every night after the show.

Rock Music

Like theater, various rock music groups used their unique artistic means to express political protest. Youths in particular have always identified with this form of expression. On September 18, 1989, rock musicians made their own appeal to the public for the first time. The appeal was signed by members of groups such as Pankow, City, Silly, and Karat and included this passage:

> We, the signers of this document, are worried about the current situation in our country, about the massive exodus of many peers, about the crisis of the meaning of this societal alternative and about the unbearable "ignorance" of our government and party leadership, who dismiss the present contradictions as trifling and hold an inflexible course into the future. The issue is not "reforms intended to destroy socialism" but, rather, reforms that will enable socialism a continued existence in this country.

This resolution was read at a number of rock concerts and other entertainment events. Its publication was prohibited by the government. Its authors and sympathizers were faced with massive public criticism and threats.

The appeals by the actors of the State Theater of Dresden, by the rock musicians, and many other declarations and appeals had one thing in common: They had no intent of replacing the existing socialist order with a capitalist one. What they wanted was a democratization of the existing socialist system in the GDR.

The Biermann Syndrome

Five years after the rise of Erich Honecker to power in 1971, the Politburo already had to deal permanently with rebellious artists and authors. The leading Polit-bureaucrats had, as Joachim Walther put it, "a rather disturbed, if not somewhat neurotic relationship to art and literature at all times" (*Protokoll eines Tribunals* 1991, 7). Therefore, they viewed the work of artists with great skepticism and immediately regarded every critical comment as directed against the socialist state.

There was a controversy surrounding songwriter Wolf Biermann. His refusal to assimilate provoked people to take sides. Sharp conflicts arose among artists and writers themselves, and it came to confrontations with the bureaucracy in charge of culture. After Biermann's expatriation in 1976, the emigration of major artists and writers began. In summer 1979, the association of GDR writers ousted nine of its members, including Stefan Heym, under pressure from the SED. Strong protests arose, not only from other countries, but from within the GDR as well.

> How much the functionaries of the association [of GDR writers] valued the opinion of the reader in the "promised land" of reading shows how the mail referring to these protests was handled: It was put into a large, unmarked brown paper package untouched for ten years. (Joachim Walther in *Protokoll eines Tribunals* 1991, 17)

The Biermann syndrome—that is to say, the suspicion and surveillance of those who showed solidarity with him and were thus considered dissidents—had an enormous impact. SED reactions became grotesque. For example, scientist and opposing philosopher Robert Havemann, a friend of Biermann, was placed under house arrest so as to prevent any contact to Biermann. Biermann (1990, 62) recalls:

> His house at the Möllensee (Möllen Lake) in Grünheide was kept by the Stasi like a fortress until he died in 1982. The small street where he lived was closed off by army trucks for years. About 200 spies guarded a man sick with tuberculosis night and day. Infrared spotlights were placed around his property. They even positioned a military boat on the lake at Havemann's property—a kind of battleship "Dshierzynski."

The Gorbachev Cult

When Soviet premier Mikhail Gorbachev introduced perestroika in 1985, there were winds of change blowing for the critically thinking artists and intellectuals in the GDR. Glasnost created an incredible attraction. For the first time, people in the GDR voluntarily read the speeches given by the General Secretary of the Soviet Communist party! People became more receptive toward Soviet literature and new Soviet plays and films. The trite slogan "Learning from the Soviet Union means learning to win!" took on new meaning. It was not unusual for the SED to be criticized by use of Gorbachev's quotations. SED head Erich Honecker tried in vain to shelter the GDR from this wave of "New Thinking." "Gorbachev was a tabu subject in the Politburo. If it was addressed at all, it occurred in passing when Honecker made some sarcastic remarks about Gorbachev" (Schabowski 1990, 36).

Publications about the policies of perestroika in the Soviet Union were systematically banned by the SED media authorities. The publishing of Gorbachev's book *Change and New Ideas for Our Country and the Entire World* (translation of the German title) was continuously postponed by the publisher (Dietz) and then printed only because of pressure from the lower reaches of the party in a very limited edition. Plays written by Soviet playwrights were removed from theater programs. Soviet TV and cinema movies were banned. The icing on the cake was the banning of the popular magazine *Sputnik* in November 1988, which was a personal decision of Honecker. This decision led a number of party members to leave the party, indeed the most pronounced form of protest within the party.

Groups of youths developed a real "Gorbi" cult. T-shirts with Gorbi portraits were imported from Hungary and then worn publicly in the GDR. Stasi members ripped Gorbi stickers from youths' T-shirts during the demonstrations on May 1, 1989, in Berlin. Yet such anti-Gorbachev actions were not very successful; in fact, they produced the opposite effect. When Gorbachev came to Berlin on the occasion of the fortieth anniversary of the GDR, people shouted "Gorbi! Gorbi!" and "Gorbi, help!"

Activities of the Church

Political opposition in the GDR grew primarily under the auspices of the Church (for details see chapter 8). To a great extent, citizens used forms of action that had proven successful within the realms of the Church for many years. These include so-called "symbolic activities" (Elvers and Findeis 1990, 100), such as peace decades, prayers for peace, vigils, human chains, fasts, and the like. The purpose of these activities was to reach the public, often with the support of Western media. Other church-based activities took place around church conventions. Other activities were organized such as the "Pleiße River memorial walk"[2] and the Street Music Festival in Leipzig, which attracted the attention of the public.

Private Niches

Withdrawal into private niches was a widespread, although a barely visible or spectacular, form of political protest—that is, activities that were in any way related to politics were avoided. This behavior was so widespread that Günter Gaus, a West German journalist, coined the term *niche society* to describe the

---

2. The "Pleiße River memorial walks" were environmentally focused activities in commemoration of the "burial" of the Pleiße River, which was cemented over. Today, alternative groups still call for the reopening of the Pleiße River in Leipzig.

GDR. It is difficult to say when this withdrawal, which was sometimes a complete refusal to participate in any societal events, began in the history of the GDR. In the first years of the GDR, it was not yet a typical phenomenon, but the enthusiasm for this new system lost its luster after a while. "The early eighties created a permanently discontented and angry GDR citizen, who simply withdrew into the private sphere" (Förster and Roski 1990, 33).

There were many kinds of niches: a profession in which party membership and political activity were not necessary; a hobby not controlled by colleagues or supervisors, such as a cottage or small garden; a house on the outskirts of the city (Datschikistan); the family as a space free from ideology; escape to sickness or disability; alcohol abuse. The destructive impact of these niches was greater than one might think. A society in which the citizens simply dwell in their own niches cannot develop. To be sure, everything seemed to work in an orderly fashion but it was actually an enormous facade.

Escape and Emigration

During the 40 years of the GDR's existence, the dominant form of passive political protest was escape, which was relatively easy before the building of the Berlin Wall in 1961. The wall stabilized the flood of refugees, but the 1970s saw a renewed wave of refugees to the West. The Helsinki conference and the conferences that followed strengthened the pressure on GDR leaders to allow an increasing number of visits to friends and relatives for humanitarian reasons. Thousands never returned. Finally, the government gave its citizens the opportunity to apply for legal emigration at the beginning of 1989. The applicant numbers skyrocketed, and the government used various tricks and chicanery to hinder this flood of emigrants. The arbitrariness and lack of human concern that accompanied applications in turn sparked an even greater desire to emigrate among other citizens.

When the opportunity came to leave the GDR through Hungary to Austria, the exodus of hundreds of thousands could not be stopped. Many more crossed the borders into West Germany after the wall fell on November 9, 1989. Because of its dimensions, this emigration from West to East Germany cannot be compared to the emigration from other European countries. GDR citizens knew that if they crossed the border, they could count on the full support of the Federal Republic of Germany (FRG) authorities. There were no language or cultural barriers, and most emigrants received support from relatives and friends as well.[3]

---

3. For a detailed analysis of the connection between "exit" and "voice" in the history of the GDR, see Hirschman 1993. For the emigration wave, see also chapter 12.

Demonstrations before 1989

GDR citizens were used to demonstrations. On every occasion possible, those "at the top" organized demonstrations. Routine demonstrations took place each year in January in memory of the murders of Karl Liebknecht and Rosa Luxemburg; on the first of May (Labor Day); in September for the victims of fascism and militarism; and in October commemorating the foundation of the republic. Participation in these demonstrations was more-or-less mandatory for working citizens. Exact records were kept regarding nonparticipation, which carried with it the risk of being denied possible bonus pay or a reservation for a vacation. Schoolchildren, apprentices, and students had to attend the demonstrations as groups. Marches past the representatives of the party and government often lasted over five hours.

In later years, participation took on an increasingly formal character. One had to participate, but time of attendance was cut down to the very minimum: One came, was seen by authorities, and left again immediately. Because firms had strict instructions to have their employees attend, bonuses were often paid for those who showed up. Only those who knew this system and had adapted to its rituals were able to appreciate the radical change when thousands voluntarily took to the streets in September and October 1989.

In early 1988, critical citizens of Berlin attempted to enunciate their own demands at the Liebknecht-Luxemburg demonstrations. The governmental authorities referred to their call of freedom for "people who think differently" as an "infamous provocation," and the demonstrators were given hard punishments as a result (see Schabowski 1990, 18).

Looking back today, the events surrounding the LL demonstration, as the Liebknecht-Luxemburg demonstrations were called, in January 1988 resembled a test for autumn 1989. This scenario of opposition was repeated in January 1989 in Leipzig and not in Berlin, due to the fact that there was an immense Stasi presence in Berlin and opposition activity hence was not possible.

> On the commemoration day of the murders of Rosa Luxemburg and Karl Liebknecht, a Leipzig group called "Initiative für demokratische Erneuerung unserer Gesellschaft" ("Initiative for democratic renewal of our society") announced a separate rally. The members wanted to stand up in public for the freedom of expression, freedom to convene peacefully and to form groups, freedom of the press, and to speak out against the banning of the magazine "Sputnik" and Soviet films. Western media had reported that the initiators of the demonstration had already been arrested on Thursday and Friday, and that in the rally in downtown Leipzig on Sunday about 800 people had taken part and that about 1/4 of them had been arrested, but released later. (Menge 1990, 36)

Demonstrations in 1989

The first large Monday demonstration took place on September 25, 1989, in Leipzig. About 5,000 people demonstrated along the inner ring of the city, following a prayer for peace in the Nikolai Kirche [Nicholas Church]. From that point on, mass demonstrations became a preferred and effective means of political protest.

Mass demonstrations spread throughout the entire country in a matter of days. After the peaceful demonstration by about 70,000 citizens on October 9 in Leipzig passed its test, the numbers of participants grew and grew. Suddenly expectations developed: When will those in the north wake up? Hasn't Suhl (a city in the south of the GDR) demonstrated yet? The available data on participant numbers were compared, competitions arose, and records were noted. A complete overview of all demonstrations that occurred between September 1989 and March 1990 is not available. Because most of the demonstrations were not officially allowed, there are also no official statistics. The Stasi probably stopped counting at some point. The opposition groups themselves counted the participants at their own events. In figure 1, we summarized the participant numbers of different cities (including Leipzig). The dates

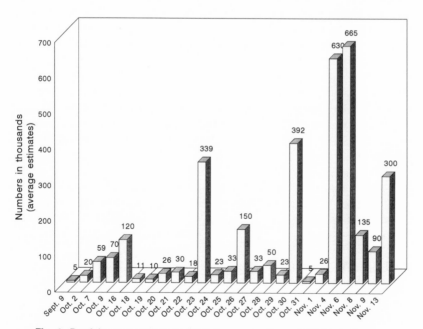

Fig. 1. Participant numbers in GDR demonstrations, 1989 (data from Neues Forum Leipzig 1990, Schneider 1990, and Tetzner 1990)

of October 16, 23, and 30 and November 6 and 13 were Mondays with particularly high rates of participation. The Leipzig Monday demonstrations seem to have had an impact on other cities. Smaller demonstrations were held on other days as well, but with the exception of October 26 (100,000 participants on a Thursday in Dresden) and November 4 (500,000 participants on a Saturday in Berlin), Mondays became the high points of protest. After November 13, participation rates dropped everywhere. Many demands of the citizens had been granted. On November 17, Hans Modrow gave a declaration on the goals of his newly formed government, and the Volkskammer assured the temporary government its confidence.

The political mass demonstrations proved to be the most impressive form of protest. As soon as concessions were made and demands met, new ones developed immediately. Honecker's fall, the Politburo's resignation, the Stoph government's capitulation, the opening of the borders: these were the successes of continuous political protest. Finally, Egon Krenz (Honecker's successor) and his entire cabinet stepped down in early December 1989. The peaceful revolution had won.

Participation of GDR Citizens: Survey Findings

Figure 2 shows participation (once or several times) in the four protest activities *prior to* October 9, 1989. It is striking that the refusal to vote or to become a member of the SED or related organizations were the most frequent forms of protest (33 percent and 40 percent, respectively). Participation in peace prayers or other church activities was also quite frequent (27 percent). Working in opposition groups, in contrast, proved to be much less frequent (5 percent). Furthermore, we found a high percentage of respondents for whom working in an opposition group was out of the question (74 percent).

For the time *after* October 9, 1989, we ascertained only participation in peace prayers and working in opposition groups (fig. 3), because pressure to become an SED member or to vote no longer existed. Working with opposition groups hardly changed. As to participation in peace prayers, participation rates dropped slightly, and more respondents reported that this activity was out of the question after October 9 than before this date. We presume that this is a result of the newly created freedoms for legal political protest that were initiated after October 9.

The Leipzig Monday Demonstrations

The Monday demonstrations in Leipzig were the beginning and the motor of the revolution in the GDR (for details, see chapter 12). They developed into a political institution that was used by different groups for the achievement of

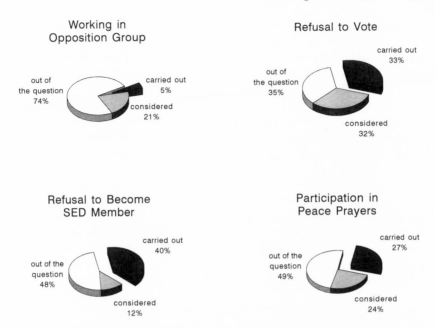

Fig. 2 **Participation in protest actions** *before* **October 9, 1989**

their political goals. Twenty-three Monday demonstrations took place between September 25, 1989, and March 12, 1990. Their political spectrum changed notably over time. The topics ranged from demands for legal freedom of travel to the loud call for German unity.

Why did the demonstrations take place on Mondays? Since 1982, peace prayers had taken place in the Nikolai Kirche on Mondays. The peaceful

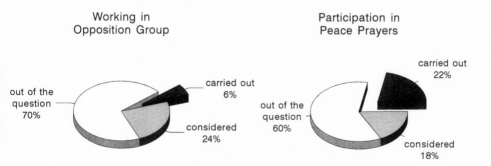

Fig. 3 **Participation in protest actions** *after* **October 9, 1989**

revolution in the GDR had a strict timetable: Monday, 5 P.M., prayer for peace, followed at about 6 P.M. by gathering at the Karl-Marx-Platz, and finally a march around the city on the Ring to the new city hall, break up, and return home. There were probably never more regular demonstrations in the history of revolutions.

It is interesting to note that in the beginning, this scenario was not given. It developed within the protest process and became a ritual that was not forgotten even after a year's break. Leipzig radio journalists Lutz Löscher and Jürgen Vogel remember their first Monday demonstration:

> It was a Monday later, the 25th of September. It is clear. Today we will be at the Nikolai Kirche. At five o'clock, for the prayer, it is crowded, as it happens for the Mondays before. We wait outside with many others in the church courtyard and still others wait in the Grimmaische Straße. There is a feeling in the air; a peculiar feeling of inexplicable unity. There is a grim joy in meeting friends, who are almost all young people. Open inspection of one's neighbor was typical for the Stasi, and one could tell by their haircut. Lines of police in the side streets, vans filled with police; what an effort. The church bells ring at 6 P.M. End of the mass. People leave the church. A few are singing something about God. The song "We Shall Overcome" is more clearly heard. Incredible, those punks sing the "Internationale." Typical GDR, only singing the refrain. No one knows the whole song. At about 6:45 P.M. the core of the crowd starts moving into the pedestrian zone of the Grimmaische Straße. You couldn't tell who was leading the march on the way to Karl Marx Platz between the Gewandhaus and opera house. And all of a sudden there are a few thousand people, lookers-on line up and the streets are overflowing. Cars must stop. An old tram tries to drive through the intersection, an old No. 16 or 28, honks its horn and brakes for the crowds. There is shouting and whistling, the doors are opened, and the driver storms out of the car, wildly gesticulating, and discusses with the people. The tram stands still, the demonstrators put the driver on their shoulders. (Löscher and Vogel 1990, 130)

There were three large demonstrations in Leipzig before the decisive Monday demonstration on October 9, 1989: on Monday, September 25, with approximately 5,000 participants; on Monday, October 2, with approximately 20,000 participants; and on Saturday, October 7, with approximately 10,000 participants. In each case there were clashes with the security forces. The police and Stasi tried to disperse the demonstrators, and many were taken into custody. The security forces were particularly nervous on October 7, the national holiday in the GDR, for which many state ceremonies and celebrations of the fortieth anniversary were organized.

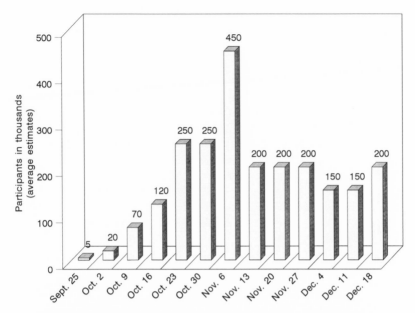

Fig. 4. Participants in Leipzig Monday demonstrations, September–December 1989 (compiled from Neues Forum Leipzig 1990, Förster and Roski 1990, Schneider 1990, and Tetzner 1990)

On the following Monday, the ninth of October, the entire city waited with bated breath for something terrible to happen. After the events on October 7, people thought that demonstrations would lead to hard clashes in Leipzig and elsewhere in the GDR. The critical point had been reached. Either the SED leaders would resort to a "Chinese solution" or they would simply allow things to take their course. Why the SED chose to take the course of action it did will be analyzed in chapter 9.

On the evening of October 9, the peaceful revolution had won. Leipzig sent the message to the rest of the country: It is possible to change the existing system by peaceful means! The call, "We are the people!" brought increasingly more people into the streets of Leipzig (see fig. 4).[4] Up until November 6, the number of participants in the Monday demonstrations grew constantly. After this date the number oscillated around 200,000.

The Monday demonstrations were not organized. Bernd-Lutz Lange expressed this aptly in one of our qualitative interviews:

---

4. The sources used for figure 4 differ from those in Opp 1991b. Figure 4 is based on the numbers that are most often mentioned in this literature; we thus use the modal value. This method has the advantage of not taking extreme estimates into account.

There was no head of the revolution. The head was the Nikolai Kirche and the body the center of the city. There was only one leadership: Monday, 5 P.M., the Nikolai Kirche.

This does not mean that every participant went to the demonstrations alone. A question in our survey read: "When you first participated in a demonstration before October 9, did you attend on your own or did you go with others?" Only 33 percent indicated they went alone.

Where did the demonstrators come from? According to the GDR yearbook of statistics, Leipzig had a population of 530,010 at the end of 1989. This means that every second citizen, and on November 6 every six out of seven, had to have taken part. However, perhaps only about half the demonstrators were from Leipzig. The Monday demonstrations gained force from tens of thousands of commuters who lived in the surrounding areas of Leipzig or from cities farther away.

How Many Citizens Demonstrated?

How did the estimates of the number of participants in the demonstrations originate? It is striking that we have found no information about who made these estimates or about the way these estimates were obtained. For example, how can it be ascertained whether on October 9 in Leipzig 70,000 citizens, the generally accepted figure, actually demonstrated? To explore how many participants may have been on the Karl-Marx-Platz on October 9, 1989, the first two authors paced off its area and the adjacent street, Grimmaische Straße, where demonstrators also gathered. This area comprises 41,500 square meters. Photos of the October 9 demonstration show that people stood close together. Assuming four persons per square meter yields a total of 166,000 participants. If there were only three persons per square meter, which is certainly an underestimate, we get 124,500 participants. The alleged number of 70,000 reported in all publications is certainly false. The official figures probably reflect only the relative sizes of the demonstrations.

Protest Symbolism

Each revolution has its own symbolism: buildings, squares, flags, songs, or the actions of the revolutionaries. The storming of the Bastille, the cruiser *Aurora*, the Leipzig Nikolai Kirche—these are all symbols of revolutionary events. Symbols, whether material objects or actions, make the identification of participants with the common cause easier.

Protesting citizens resisted the state symbols by creating their own. The symbols originated from church traditions and from the civil movements of the West. The lighted candle was *the* symbol of the peaceful revolution in autumn 1989. Hence, Jörg Swoboda named his book about the role of the Christians in the revolution in the GDR *Die Revolution der Kerzen* [The revolution of the candles]. Those who took part will never forget the incredible scenes of thousands of candles in front of the Nikolai Kirche, on the Leipziger Ring, and around the Stasi offices. The candle symbolized peace and silent protest. Peace prayers, vigils, fasts, human chains, and songs were used for the purpose of political protest as well. Songs ranged from the soft "Dona nobis pacem" in the churches to the self-assured "We Shall Overcome" in front of the church doors and finally to the angry "Internationale" in front of the police lines. People carried the symbol of the Easter march movement and raised their hands with the victory symbol of the American civil rights movement.

Flags played a special role. Initially, one only saw GDR flags with the "worker and farmer" state symbol cut out. Then came the black, red, and gold flags of West Germany and later the state flags of Saxony and Thuringia, as well as the almost completely unknown flags of the different cities and regions. Even the traditional SPD (Sozialdemokratische Partei Deutschlands [the party of Western social democrats]) flags and those of many associations banned after the founding of the GDR waved in the demonstrations. Whoever drove through the GDR between December 1989 and March 1990 was astounded to see that people everywhere voluntarily raised flags. Even in state-owned companies, the flag of the Federal Republic of Germany was hoisted!

Until the end of November 1989, no symbols of violence could be found at the demonstrations. Even accusations and calls for resignation occurred without aggression and were often presented humorously. There were no gallows to hang Honecker, and no dolls were burned. Radicalism and violence first started spreading after right-wing extremists took advantage of the demonstrations for their own purposes and the representatives of the civil movement withdrew.

It was a widespread phenomenon for people to carry their own slogans. One in ten of our respondents admitted to having had slogans, banners, flags, and the like with them. An exhibition of these demonstration objects was shown in the Nikolai Kirche in autumn 1990, showing the unbroken political creativity of people even after 40 years of state-ordered slogans.

Summary

The revolution in autumn 1989 was a *spontaneous revolution*. Protesting citizens had next to no experience in protest. What they knew about forms of protest they learned from the Western media, and many were not appropriate under GDR conditions. But long before the impressive mass demonstrations in the GDR in 1989 occurred, there existed various kinds of protests, particularly by artists and under the roof of the church. At the hottest phase of the revolution, the protests finally moved to the streets. Symbols and rituals typical for the GDR developed.

CHAPTER 2

How Could It Happen?
An Explanation of the East German Revolution

Karl-Dieter Opp

The revolution in the German Democratic Republic was a complicated social process consisting of many different events. Before we begin with an explanation of these events, we must first decide which of these events we want to explain. This is the first topic of this chapter. We will then show why explanations of the collapse of the GDR presented by journalists, politicians, and social scientists are insufficient. Finally, we will present our own explanatory approach.

What Is to Be Explained?

Looking back at the events from the autumn of 1989 to early 1990, it is astounding that such a large portion of the population in the GDR took part in the protests. Compared to the GDR in the autumn of 1989, participation in Western countries was and is considerably lower. Therefore, the first question that must be answered in explaining the revolution in the GDR is:

1. Why did a relatively large portion of the population take part in the protests?

The protests in the GDR began with relatively small numbers of participants, then evolved with explosive force. Accordingly, an explanation of the revolution of the GDR must answer the question:

2. Why did the number of protests (after September 1989) first increase dramatically and then slowly decrease before disappearing completely?

Many observers were surprised that the citizens did not use violence. When citizens are confronted with a hated government, can it not be expected that these dissatisfied citizens become violent? A third question should therefore be asked:

   3. Why did the citizens protest peacefully?

The protests in the GDR were particularly surprising for another reason: The SED regime had practiced repression for over 40 years and kept opposition at bay. Why did this suddenly not work in 1989? A question to be answered thus is:

   4. Why didn't state sanctions hinder the protests in 1989?

Demonstrations and other protest activities in Western countries are usually well organized. For example, a group sets a date for a demonstration, makes the date known to the public authorities, and both accord about where and when the demonstration will take place. Countercultural networks often help spread information about time and place of the demonstration. The protests in Leipzig were not organized (see chapter 1) but, rather, developed spontaneously. How was that possible? How is it possible for about 70,000 people to gather at the Karl-Marx-Platz in Leipzig on October 9, 1989, without any form of organization? This indeed is an important question that has to be dealt with:

   5. How could the demonstrations in the autumn of 1989 emerge without
      having been organized?

The protests did not occur throughout the GDR simultaneously. Leipzig played a vanguard role. This is another puzzle of the revolutionary events in the autumn of 1989 that has to be tackled:

   6. Why did the protests first take place in Leipzig?

The protests in autumn 1989 led to the resignation of the government, to radical changes in the economic and social order, and to the extinction of a state. Thus, it was one of the very rare revolutions "from below" in world history (Tullock 1974, 1987). It has to be explained why the protests in 1989 had these far-reaching consequences, in other words:

   7. Why did the SED regime not react differently to the protests of the
      citizens?

There are certainly other interesting questions that could be asked about the revolution in the GDR, but these seven questions are most commonly asked when the revolution of the GDR is debated and, in our opinion, are also the most interesting questions. We will therefore focus only on those issues.

Was the Collapse of the GDR a Revolution?

There are no right or wrong answers to this question. The term *revolution* has many different meanings. Whether one of those meanings is chosen or a new definition is proposed, is a question of usefulness. For example, *revolution* is sometimes defined as violent actions of a group in order to change the social order as a whole. If we apply this definition, then the events in the GDR in 1989 are not a revolution. But if we define *revolution* as a change of the social order as a whole, when the change is not achieved by political elections, then the events in the GDR should be called a revolution. A decision must be made about which concept is to be chosen.

Because we have made clear what we are going to explain, it is not useful to enter into a debate about whether one should label those events a *revolution*. Everyday language suggests we call these events a revolution, thus we will adopt this usage. We choose the following definition: *revolution* is a change of the social order as a whole that did not occur by means of political elections. No matter what the exact meaning of "change of the social order as a whole" may be, there can be no doubt that such a change took place in the GDR. The reader may choose to use another definition. If she or he decides to do so, she or he may simply replace the word *revolution* with another term she or he prefers.

Incomplete Explanations

We have already mentioned that there are currently a number of explanations of the revolution in the GDR and that these explanations are flawed. We will now present some of those widely accepted explanations and discuss the problems associated with them.

Factor Explanations

Many explanations of the revolution in the GDR select one or more components of the political and economic situation of the GDR or other countries, and call it or them a cause of the revolution. For example, a widespread explanation points to the high level of dissatisfaction in the population as a cause of the revolution. One writer claims that "the indignation from denied rights, crumbling and defective economic and environmental policies" caused the upheaval (Staritz 1990, 15).

One of the problems with this explanation is that dissatisfaction with the social and economic order did not suddenly develop in 1989, but was present long before 1989. Why did dissatisfaction lead to massive protests only in 1989? Adherents of this explanation will probably advance a "boiler" theory: Discontent became so unbearable that the top of the boiler finally blew off. The problem with this explanation is that it remains unclear when discontent reaches the point at which the top of the boiler blows off. As long as this problem is not resolved, the boiler theory cannot be disproven. Whenever a revolution occurs, one could maintain that dissatisfaction had reached its boiling point so that a revolution became inevitable. We will return to other deficiencies of a discontent explanation later on.

This explanation and many others have one thing in common: They fail to provide any evidence showing why the selected factors caused a revolution. Such explanations are incomplete. How difficult it is to find arguments for the validity of simple causal statements becomes evident if we would assert that the Wimbledon victories of Steffi Graf and Boris Becker in June 1989 were the causes of the protests in the GDR in 1989. Certainly no one would accept such a proposition. But why is this explanation not acceptable? Simply because another explanation appears more plausible does not prove it wrong. Different people regard different explanations as plausible.

Macrolevel Explanations

There are two types of factors that are used to explain the revolution in the GDR. One focuses on the characteristics of individual actors who took part in the revolution. Our previous example illustrates this type of factors: It is maintained that those *people* who were highly dissatisfied took part in the protests. The second type of factors refers to collective entities, in particular to *societies*. For example, it is claimed that the liberalizations of the Soviet Union, Hungary, and Poland were the causes of the GDR revolution. This type of explanation shares the weakness of the types of explanations focusing on individual actors: It is a factor explanation. But macrolevel explanations are burdened with an additional problem. The protesters were single individuals. If societal factors are put forward as explanatory factors, it remains unclear how these factors prompted the individuals to take part or not to take part in the protests. How, for example, could the liberalization in the Soviet Union lead hundreds of thousands of Leipzig citizens to demonstrate in October 1989? Macrolevel explanations thus fail to provide the links between the societal and the individual level.

Partial Explanations

We have seen that "the" revolution was a complex event and that each of the questions mentioned previously should be answered in explaining "the" revolution. Many attempts to explain the revolution in the GDR fail to accomplish this. For example, if it is only explained why citizens took part in the demonstrations in October 1989, we do not know why the other events being part of "the" revolution occurred. We call such explanations partial explanations because they focus only on particular phenomena, rather than on the entire set of questions mentioned before.

Preferences and Constraints: A General Theory of Human Behavior

We pointed out that factor explanations are incomplete because arguments for singling out (at least) one factor as the (or a) cause of the revolution are missing. What could such an argument look like? For example, what arguments could be adduced against the assertion that the Wimbledon victories of Boris Becker and Steffi Graf caused the revolution in the GDR? One would have to possess general propositions in the sense of lawlike statements with two characteristics: They should imply that sporting events in general (or in certain kinds of situations) have no impact on people's participation in political protests, and those general statements would have to be confirmed by results of empirical research. If such statements exist, we could adduce them as arguments against the claim that the two Wimbledon victories were causes of the revolution in the GDR.[1]

To avoid the sort of problematic explanations of the revolution in the GDR that we have outlined, we will apply a general theory of action, which will now be presented. The protests of the population were the actions of many individuals. Therefore, in explaining these protests, the individual is our starting point. This may be obvious for those readers who do not have a background in the social sciences. However, placing the individual at the center of an explanation—that is, using an individualistic approach—is controversial in the social sciences. It is common to explain phenomena such as revolutions by making the society or groups the units of analyses.[2] In this chapter, we will not discuss such a collectivistic approach—this will be done in chapter 15—but, rather, present our own explanatory model.

If we choose to focus on the citizens of the GDR as the units of our analysis, we best apply a theory of social action that is already used by a great

1. The previous criticism of incomplete explanations is based on results of the philosophy of science about the logic of explanation. See, for example, Hempel 1965 or a philosophy of science textbook such as Chalmers 1982. We are aware of the fact that there is a continuing debate about the adequate procedure of explaining singular events. In our opinion, however, the critics of the so-called covering law model have not provided any convincing alternative procedure of explaining singular events.

2. This is also the typical approach toward explaining the revolution in East Germany. An example is Pollack's (1990) attempt to explain the revolution in the GDR from a social system perspective. See also the collection of essays in Joas and Kohli 1993.

number of social scientists: the rational actor model, also called rational choice theory. It can be summarized in three hypotheses.[3] The first proposition asserts that human behavior is goal oriented—that human beings act in order to reach their personal *goals*. These goals may range from the desire to own certain goods to the need for having rights such as freedom to express an opinion or to travel to other countries.

Human behavior cannot simply be explained by goals. There are various limitations to reaching goals. For example, an available income is a constraint for buying goods. If GDR citizens wanted to criticize the SED prior to October 9, 1989, they had to reckon with state penalties, such as occupational disadvantages. Thus, fulfilling the desire to speak freely would adversely affect the achievement of other goals such as professional advancement. Accordingly, the second proposition of the rational actor theory asserts that beside the goals of an actor, opportunities or constraints individuals are faced with affect their behavior. *Opportunities* are events that expand the possibilities of individuals to attain their goals, whereas *constraints* are events that reduce the possibility to attain one's goals.

The third proposition specifies *how* human beings behave if they cannot reach their goals—that is, when they are faced with behavioral constraints. The rational actor model maintains that people act in order to realize their needs to the greatest possible extent, given the restrictions they are faced with. This hypothesis is often referred to as the principle of utility maximization. The concept of *utility*, as used in this theory, does not refer only to material gain but, rather, has a broad meaning. For example, if one enjoys giving a friend a gift, then one "gains" something from the act of giving.

Utility can be positive or negative. Positive utilities are often called *benefits*. Negative utilities are often called *costs*. State repression, for example, would be a negative utility because individuals are prevented from realizing certain needs. Thus, costs do not refer only to material or monetary losses. Something that results in positive or negative utility is often termed a (positive or negative) *incentive*.

This explanatory model has already been used to explain a great number of social phenomena, including political protest and revolutions.[4] We believe that the version of the rational actor model that we use in this book is a promising approach to explain the revolution in the GDR in 1989.

---

3. For more detailed accounts see, for example, Alchian and Allen 1974, chapter 3; Becker 1976, chapter 1; Brunner 1987; Coleman 1990, chapter 1; Frey 1980, 1992; Kirchgässner 1980; Meckling 1976; Weede 1992.

4. This is also true for a variant of the rational actor model, value-expectancy theory. See Ajzen 1988; Ajzen and Fishbein 1980; Feather 1982. For the application of the rational actor model in regard to protest behavior and revolutions, see Chong 1991; Klandermans 1984; Muller 1979; Opp 1986, 1989; Opp and Roehl 1990b; Finkel, Muller, and Opp 1989; Taylor 1988; Tullock 1974, 1987.

The Application of the Theory

How can the rational actor model be used to explain the revolution in the GDR? Because revolutions are the result of individual decisions, we first must ask who the participants in the revolution were. Among the actors were first of all the citizens of the GDR. The citizen protests were influenced by the state, as well as the security forces, whose decisions depended in turn on the citizens' protests. Furthermore, decisions of other countries were presumably also a deciding factor for the citizens' decisions to participate, as we will see later on. The actions of other countries also appear to have influenced the GDR government's decisions regarding measures against the emerging protests. For example, the Soviet Union's decision not to send in troops during public disturbances probably influenced the GDR government's decisions about sanctioning dissident citizens. We thus differentiate between three kinds of actors: the GDR citizens, the GDR regime, and third countries. We will see later that it is useful to differentiate even more between these groups (see also chapter 12).

In order to explain the behavior of these actors, the rational actor model prompts us to assume that each of those actors was attempting to maximize his or her utility. What were the concrete costs and benefits that influenced the behavior of each actor?

The revolution was a social process—that is, the actors changed their behavior over time. According to the rational actor model, a change of behavior is the result of changes in preferences or constraints or both. When attempting to explain the *development* of the revolutionary events, we must determine which incentives changed over time.

Another important question is *why* a change in incentives took place. We have already seen that actors' decisions were interdependent: certain actions of actors were constraints for the actions of other actors or expanded their opportunities. Explaining the revolution in the GDR requires therefore ascertaining how the decisions of particular actors changed the incentives of other actors.

Thus, to explain a complex social process such as the revolution in the GDR by applying the rational actor model, we must address the following questions:

1. Who were the actors who participated in the revolution?
2. What were the costs and benefits—that is, the types of incentives that influenced their actions?
3. How did these costs and benefits change over time?
4. Which actions of which actors changed the costs and benefits for the actions of other actors?

At the beginning of this chapter, we criticized explanations using macro-factors. We said that if factors such as the liberalization in the Soviet Union were alleged as causes of the revolution in the GDR, the question would arise about how these factors prompted individuals to take or not take part in the protests. Such factors are actions of particular actors, such as citizens who leave the GDR or politicians who open the borders of their country for GDR citizens. How can these factors lead individuals to participate in the protests? The basic idea is that *macrofactors are only relevant for individual participation in protest actions if they influence the costs or benefits of individual actors to participate*. In other words, macrofactors may have an *indirect* effect on protest participation: they may change the incentives, which in turn directly influence protest participation. For example, the emigration wave—a macrofactor—may have led the citizens to believe that the SED regime was now forced to accept reforms, and the probability of this would be increased if the citizens themselves took part in protests.

The relationship between macrofactors on the one hand and individual incentives to protest on the other must be determined empirically. In explaining the revolution, it is important to formulate and empirically test hypotheses about such relationships.

Our considerations show how the rational actor model solves the problem of *incomplete explanations*: The model directs attention toward certain factors, which are singled out as causal for social action. These factors are, as was noted before, preferences and constraints (or opportunities). If a reader asks why these factors are considered causal, the answer is that the rational actor theory implies the causality of these factors and that this explanatory model has been relatively well corroborated empirically. We can therefore assume that the kind of behaviors this book focuses on can also be validly explained by means of the costs and benefits of this behavior. But we will not be content with postulating the validity of our explanation; we will also test it empirically.

Conditions for the Citizen Protests

In this section we will propose hypotheses about the kinds of costs and benefits that may be relevant for the emergence of the protests in the GDR. In subsequent chapters we will provide data to test these hypotheses.

Dissatisfaction as a Cause of the Revolution:
The Free-Rider Problem

One of the oldest hypotheses used to explain political protest maintains that the more discontent citizens are with economic or political conditions in their country, the more politically active they become.[5] This hypothesis is also widely applied to explain the protests in the GDR: most of the time the increasingly deteriorating economic conditions, the high level of environmental pollution and the political restrictions in the GDR in 1989 are mentioned as the major causes for the protests and the collapse of the GDR.

Apart from the problems of a grievance proposition mentioned before, it is further not in line with the results of empirical research. It is not true that discontented individuals protest particularly frequently.[6] Further, the discontent proposition cannot explain why protests often rise when a population's or group's dissatisfaction *de*creases. Alexis de Tocqueville ([1856] 1978) noted this phenomenon in his analysis of the causes of the French Revolution in 1789. We can also observe this phenomenon in the GDR. After the demonstrations on October 9, 1989, political freedom was expanded, whereas the economic situation did not change. If the discontent proposition is valid, a decrease in the protests would have been expected. Yet the opposite occurred.

There is another argument against the discontent proposition. If the politically active citizens reach their goals, those who were not active would still reap the benefits. Thus, the new economic and social order that evolved out of the GDR revolution also holds for those who did not participate in the protests. In other words, the goals of protests are normally *public goods*. These are, by definition, goods that are at each group member's disposal when they are provided, even if a particular member made no contribution to their production. For example, citizens enjoy protection against crime even if they don't pay taxes. The provision of public goods is burdened with the free-rider problem: When a person knows that she or he can enjoy a good without contributing to its production he or she won't invest any resources to provide the good but rather will hope that others produce it.

The incentive of enjoying the fruits of others' efforts is particularly strong if a public good can be obtained only through the contributions of many people. The single individual, in this case, is a tiny particle in a large mass and her or his participation will not influence the production of the good. An individual must further reckon with opportunity costs when she or he participates. This means that one must give up the benefits of actions that could have been taken instead of contributing. For example, instead of participating in a demonstration that aims at the provision of public goods, one could go for a walk or to a movie.[7]

---

5. An informative overview of variants of and problems with this hypothesis can be found in McAdam 1982, 6–19.

6. Piven and Cloward (1977) in particular found that it is more the exception than the rule that the lower social classes, who are deprived to a great extent, take part in protests.

7. These ideas are presented in more detail in the literature on the theory of collective action. The standard reference is Olson 1965; see also Hardin 1982.

Although the aforementioned arguments disprove the discontent proposition, it would be absurd to maintain that dissatisfaction played no role in the protests in the GDR. It appears that dissatisfaction only increases protest *under certain conditions*. What are these conditions?[8] We mentioned earlier that the single individual within a large group has no influence on the provision of the public good at which the group aims. This may be true, but a single person's decision to take part in a demonstration does not depend on whether this person will *really* be influential, but rather on whether she or he *perceives* that her or his participation makes a difference. Empirical research has shown that there are many people who believe that their individual political action, whether voting or protesting, is influential. Furthermore, individuals differ in regard to how strongly they believe their actions will have an impact.[9]

If we assume that there are always individuals in a group who believe their activity does make a difference, then political dissatisfaction also has an effect on protests in large groups: Given a certain amount of political dissatisfaction, the likelihood that a person will become active increases in accordance with the extent to which she or he believes it to be politically efficacious. People who are very dissatisfied and who simultaneously perceive their actions as very influential are apt to become politically active to a high extent.

These arguments only hold true if individuals are also convinced that the group's activity as a whole will be successful. If a citizen believes that a group's demonstration is useless, even a high amount of personal dissatisfaction won't be an incentive for protest.

Let us assume a person believes that she or he would *personally* have no influence if she or he participated in some political action, but nevertheless believes that the *group as a whole* would attain the political goal. Would this be an incentive for participating in some political action? The answer is no, as the free-rider problem presents itself here quite clearly: If someone believes that the group will be successful, why should she or he become active? The reason is that the group's action will bring success even if the person does not take part. Thus, the expected success of the group alone is not an incentive for participation. Yet if a person believes herself or himself to be personally influential and also expects the group to be successful, she or he will have a particularly strong incentive to participate.

Dissatisfaction can influence protest in yet another way. If a politically active person is told that his or her participation is actually useless because he

---

8. For the following argument, see particularly Finkel, Muller, and Opp 1989; Opp 1992b.

9. See in particular Moe 1980; Muller and Opp 1986; Opp 1985, 1988a, 1989.

or she as a single individual is not able to make a difference anyway, the reaction is usually: "If everyone thought like that, protests would never take place." In other words, the belief is, "each person is important for the success of a group," or "we are only strong if we act jointly." If one accepts this *unity principle* and further believes that the group will be successful, then political dissatisfaction will promote participation.

The unity principle is a cognitive belief; that is, people believe that a group can be successful only if everyone participates. In addition, a moral conviction may develop: if groups can be successful only when everyone participates, each person therefore has a *duty* to participate. Such a duty, however, will not be accepted under all conditions. If one believes that the group will not be successful—that is, that only a few people will take part—then one will not believe in the duty to participate.

To summarize, the free-rider problem can be solved if one of the following conditions is given:

a. high perceived personal influence and perceived group success, or
b. strong belief in the unity principle and high perceived group success, or
c. a sense of duty to participate and high perceived group success.

If these conditions and discontent are present to a relatively high extent, this means that there is a strong *public goods motivation*: a motivation or willingness to participate in the provision of a public good. In chapters 3 and 4 we will state some additional hypotheses about the effects of discontent, and we will examine the extent to which these hypotheses are in line with our data.

State Sanctions, Moral and Social Incentives

Let us assume that a person's public goods motivation is very high. Nevertheless, this person may not participate in any protests to provide some public good. If, for example, a student is in the middle of studying for an exam, then he or she might be afraid that time spent protesting would take away valuable time for achieving a good grade. In this case, public goods motivation is high, but other incentives may be so strong that the person will not participate in the protests.

On the other hand, it is possible that people take part in a demonstration even if their public goods motivation is low. For example, if friends persuade a person to join a demonstration, then this person will probably come along even if she or he—in the extreme case—has no idea what the protest is about.

Thus, other incentives may *in addition to* or *instead of* a public good motivation influence participation in political protests. Among these incentives the following are of particular importance.[10]

State Sanctions

According to the explanatory model used in this book, expected state sanctions (or, equivalently, repression) are behavioral constraints, or costs. Accordingly, increasing state sanctions will lower the sanctioned behavior—assuming that other incentives for this very action do not change.

We distinguish between two characteristics of sanctions. First, the more a citizen expects a sanction to occur—that is, the higher the *subjective probability* that sanctions will be carried out—the less frequently a person will engage in the respective behavior. Second, the more severe the sanctions—that is, the greater the *fear of sanctions*—the more a person will refrain from the respective behavior.

These hypotheses imply that state sanctions have a *deterrence effect*: high likelihood and fear of repression suppress sanctioned behavior. However, empirical research also has shown that state sanctions often have a *radicalization effect*. For example, it has been found that opponents of nuclear power demonstrate more often when they are faced with relatively severe state sanctions.[11] How can this be explained? If protesters expect or experience severe state repression, positive incentives for the respective behavior often increase. For example, if citizens view harsh police actions at a demonstration against environmental pollution as unjustified, then participants having been exposed to sanctions experience sympathy and support from their family and friends: one has protested for a good cause and unjustly incurred severe punishment. Thus, repression increases social incentives to protest. The precise conditions under which state repression has a deterrence or a radicalization effect will be described in more detail in chapter 6.

Moral Incentives

For many of our everyday actions, rules—or equivalently, *norms*—exist. For example, we are generally expected to greet people we know when we meet them, or eat with a knife, fork, and spoon in restaurants. If we do not conform to such norms, we might have a bad conscience. In this case sociologists say that a norm is *internalized:* a norm becomes a motive for action. Violating norms leads to sanctions by other people or institutions, such as the police or the courts.

---

10. The following incentives are discussed in various writings. See in particular Baumgärtner 1991; Chong 1991; Finkel and Opp 1991; Klandermans 1984; Muller and Opp 1986; Opp 1986, 1989, 1990b; Opp and Roehl 1990a; Tullock 1971, 1974; Uhlaner 1989.

11. For details see Opp and Roehl 1990a, 1990b. These writings contain specific hypotheses about the effects of sanctions and the results of empirical research, with further references.

Norms also play a role in political action, and in protests in particular.[12] Why do many people take part in political elections? The duty of being a good citizen is certainly a motive for this. If one does not take part, one might get a bad conscience and have to face the negative reactions of friends and relatives.

Norms apply only under certain circumstances. People will feel no duty to protest when they are relatively satisfied with governmental policies, or perhaps also, if participation is very risky. The role of norms for the emergence of protests in the GDR will be dealt with extensively in chapters 5 and 6.

It is controversial whether norms can be viewed as a certain kind of incentive and thus as a variable of the rational actor model. We use a broad version of the model in this book, in which norms can be possible incentives for action (for details see Opp 1989, chap. 2).

Social Incentives

Empirical research has shown that protest participation depends largely on incentives from the social environment.[13] Such incentives include *expectations of reference persons*, individuals whose opinions have particular importance, such as family members and friends. If such people believe that one should become politically active, it is certainly an incentive to follow these expectations.

Among the social incentives there are further *positive sanctions,* such as social support, approval, recognition or prestige from friends and relatives because of participation in political protest. Political groups are often sources of such incentives. The social environment also provides *negative sanctions* for being politically active. For example, participating in a demonstration as a form of political activity is despised in some social groups.

We have seen how state sanctions, their probability and severity, affect participation in political protest. This idea is also valid for sanctions from the social environment. If positive sanctions appear probable and are highly valued, they become strong positive incentives to protest; if individuals anticipate negative sanctions and are frightened of them, it is likely that they will abstain from political action.

The occurrence of sanctions depends on certain conditions. For example, most of the population generally values violent forms of protest negatively. These kinds of actions will therefore be sanctioned negatively. If the costs for participation (in the form of state repression) are very high, the social environ-

---

12. See Marwell and Ames 1979; Muller 1979; Opp 1986, 1989; Riker and Ordeshook 1968, 1973.

13. See, for example, Klandermans 1984; Knoke 1988; Opp 1986; Finkel, Muller, and Opp 1989; Mitchell 1979; Muller and Opp 1986; Tillock and Morrison 1979; Useem 1980; Walsh and Warland 1983.

ment will not encourage participation but, rather, sanction it negatively. Chapters 7 and 8 will deal extensively with the role of social incentives for the emergence of the protests in the GDR.

The Distribution of Incentives

Citizens differ according to the extent to which they are faced with the incentives mentioned earlier. To explain the development of protest within a group or society, the *distribution* of the incentives is an important factor. For example, let us imagine that 3 people in a group of 100 have a high level of all those incentives. In this case, only those 3 people will perhaps organize a small protest and persuade others to join. If the level of incentives of the other 97 citizens is low, the 3 activists will not be able to raise the incentives to such an extent that more participants will join in.

In the social science literature, the role of *political entrepreneurs* for initiating political action has been emphasized.[14] Political entrepreneurs are defined here as individuals with high incentives for political action. Political entrepreneurs are important for the initiation and development of protest because they bear part of the costs of protests, such as the organization of demonstrations or group meetings. We will address the role of political entrepreneurs in the GDR—that is, the role of opposition groups and the church—in greater detail later (see chapters 7, 8, and 10).

"Exit" and Forms of Political Protest

One of the questions we wish to address in this book refers to the conditions for *nonviolent* protests—that is, protests in which people incur no physical harm and objects are not damaged. We will answer this question here only briefly—a more extensive discussion is provided in chapter 7. The choice to engage in nonviolent protest actions first depends on the extent to which people believe these actions will be more successful than violent political action. Second, people will decide to choose nonviolent participation if less severe state repression is expected for nonviolent activities. Third, the nature of the internalized protest norms influences the kind of political activity: if the citizens of a country generally view only nonviolent forms of political activity as morally justified or even necessary, this form of activity will occur more often than if violence is an accepted kind of political action. Finally, the choice of nonviolence depends on social incentives: if the social environment

---

14. See Frohlich, Oppenheimer, and Young 1971; Frohlich and Oppenheimer 1978, chapter 4; Popkin 1988; White 1988.

provides a high level of positive sanctions for nonviolent activity and negative sanctions for violent activity, the choice for nonviolence will occur more often.

Citizens of the GDR expressed their discontent not only by participating in protest actions, but also by moving to West Germany. This exit was possible by application or by legal travel into other Eastern bloc countries after May 1989, and from there to West Germany. Exit, however, was costly. It was never known whether and when a decision would be made after application, and one had to face various repressive measures during the long application process. Because of the high level of border security, direct emigration to West Germany without state approval meant putting one's life at risk. In any event, in the case of emigration, GDR citizens had to break off all social ties and had to hand over to the state all objects of value at the time of exit. Because of these high costs, emigration was not an alternative for most GDR citizens. It therefore seems justified that we do not explain why citizens chose exit instead of voice, but we will address the *effects* of emigration on protest and state reactions in the GDR.[15]

Revolutions as Social Processes

Our previous considerations imply that if incentives for protest in a country are high, individuals will then choose some specific form of protest. We would then observe at different locations all over the country some people who carry signs, some who gather in front of city halls or party headquarters to verbally express their discontent. Yet this is not what happpened in the GDR in 1989. On the evening of October 9, 1989, in Leipzig, for example, about 70,000 people gathered at Karl-Marx-Platz. That is to say, the actions of the GDR citizens were *coordinated*. We differentiate among four possibilities of coordination.

The Organization Model

Protest actions such as demonstrations may be organized by a person or a group. This group decides where and when protest activities should take place and circulates various calls to participate. Many demonstrations in Western countries arise this way. We will see later that this organization model does not apply to the protests in the GDR.

---

15. The conditions for the choice of exit and voice are dealt with in detail by Hirschman (1970). See also his analysis of the relationships between both forms of reactions during the revolution in the GDR (Hirschman 1993).

The Micromobilization Model

A group may first choose a time and place to hold a demonstration. This group then passes on information about its plans to other people or groups. They are also asked to inform other people or groups about the time and place of the demonstration, and tell the others to pass the information on, and so forth. This process corresponds to a micromobilization model: many persons or groups mobilize other persons or groups, who in turn mobilize other people or groups. This process is like a *snowball system*: each person who receives a message passes it on to others.

The micromobilization model and the organization model have in common that political action is planned. Yet they differ in that information processing occurs decentralized within the micromobilization model, whereas information is passed centrally or through a hierarchy—that is, from one group to another—in the organization model. In the micromobilization model, however, the protests are not organized. For example, no buses are chartered to transport participants to the demonstration place and back, and no negotiations are made with the authorities or police in regard to helping the group carry out its protest.

Compared to the organization model, the micromobilization model is very cost-effective per person. The effort of informing others and organizing the political action is not expended by a single group, but, rather, by a larger number of groups. Costs, therefore, are divided more evenly among the individuals. Later we will see that the micromobilization model also cannot explain the protests in the GDR.

The Threshold Model

The threshold model assumes that if single individuals carry out particular actions, then carrying out these actions becomes less costly for others. If, for example, a person expects only a few others to participate in a demonstration, he or she may be afraid of negative reactions from onlookers or may think that he or she might be injured by the police. On the other hand, if a person expects many people to take part in a demonstration, she or he might not have the aforementioned fears, and friends may encourage her or him to participate.

This expectation indicates how participation according to the threshold model may come about. First, people participate whose (net) benefits of participation are very high. Their participation lowers the costs of participation for a certain number of others to such an extent that their participation "threshold" is reached. These others also will take part in the next demonstration. This larger number of participants in turn causes the participation threshold to be reached for another group of people, and so on.[16] The threshold model thus describes a *chain reaction*: certain people react in a certain way, triggering reactions from others; and the behavior of these people in turn triggers still more people to react in the same way, and so forth.

The threshold model contains a number of assumptions. For example:

1. Citizens estimate the number of participants.
2. The (net) benefits of citizens are distributed in a specific way: if a certain number of individuals participate, there is always a group of other participants whose threshold is reached—that is, whose costs of participation decrease to an extent that they participate, too. This in turn causes another group to reach its participation threshold, and so on. In reality, however, there may be gaps: after a certain number of participants is reached, the costs of participation for others do not decrease to an extent that additional individuals become active.
3. The model presumes that the protests must be coordinated somehow by the members of the first group of people who participate. If this is the case, it must further be assumed that the following groups (whose costs are lowered by means of the preceding protests) carry out exactly the same kind of protest as the previous group. Thus, the threshold model cannot explain the *coordination* of protests, as we will demonstrate in chapter 12.

The Spontaneous Cooperation Model

The model that is best suited to explain the coordination of protests is termed the *spontaneous cooperation* or the *spontaneous coordination* model. Identical behavior of a large number of people is often the result of the same decisions they make, although largely isolated from each other, because they find themselves in a similar situation. The result is a coordination of behavior without arrangement, organization, or mobilization (Schelling 1960, 54–58).

Let us look at an example. On the evening of November 9, 1989, Günter Schabowski announced that GDR citizens had the freedom to travel to the West; the ordinance was valid that same day. This announcement was spread immediately by the media. As a result, thousands of GDR citizens gathered at Bornholmer Straße in East Berlin. This situation occurred because many citizens wanted the same thing (freedom of travel to the West) and because all of them had been informed about Schabowski's announcement. Many people certainly adapted themselves to the behavior of others on their way to the

---

16. See in particular the ideas developed by Mark Granovetter; for example, Granovetter 1978, 1986. See also Prosch and Abraham 1991; Karklins and Petersen 1993.

Bornholmer Straße—they presumably noticed others heading toward Bornholmer Straße—yet the fact that a large number of people went to the Bornholmer Straße simultaneously demonstrates that they had all made decisions that were not dependent on the behavior of others. This does not mean that a group of people (such as a married couple) could not have made a joint decision about whether to go to the Bornholmer Straße or not, but the decisions of all participants were not interdependent.

What conditions are necessary for a protest to be brought about by spontaneous cooperation? First, the citizens must be willing to take part in a particular kind of political action, such as nonviolent protests, within a certain time period. In terms of the explanatory model used here, this means that the net utility for *any* kind of protest of a particular class of protests is larger than for other kinds of protests or for nonactivity. For example, it presumably didn't matter to the citizens of Leipzig if the demonstrations had taken place on Tuesdays rather than Mondays or if the protests took the form of a human chain or a rally. Second, the citizens must assume that no group or institution will organize collective protests. If a citizen expects others to organize protests in which she or he may participate, then there are strong incentives to wait until others do the work. Third, it must be too costly for citizens to organize the protests themselves.

Citizens are thus faced with a dilemma: on the one hand, they would like to express their discontent by some form of action; on the other hand, opportunities for doing so are lacking. They could solve this dilemma by going to a certain place at a certain time, say, to the center of a city where they expect to find many other citizens willing to protest.

If citizens take this solution into account, two problems arise. First, where and when will a sufficient number of people convene who are willing to express their discontent? Because many citizens are faced with the same problem, a *coordination problem* arises. Second, will a sufficient number of citizens gather so that the gathering will be viewed as a protest by the regime? How high will the costs of participation be for the citizen if the costs depend, among other things, on the number of other participants? This is the *problem of the critical mass*. Whether spontaneous coordination emerges depends on the extent to which the citizens are able to solve those two problems.

The coordination problem will be solved if citizens decide to go to the same place at the same time simultaneously, which occurs if each person presumes that many others will gather at the same time and place. How can such an expectation arise? It may be known that an event is to take place at a certain place and time, perhaps on a regular basis. Such an event doesn't necessarily have to be connected to protests. For example, concerts may be held regularly in public and certain citizens hold signs demanding reforms during the concerts. Other citizens who know about this activity and who are interested in airing their dissatisfaction may come when the next concert takes place. They may assume that such protest actions will be repeated or that mere citizen attendance would be seen as protest. The form of protest that occurs will in part depend on the situation. For example, someone may sing a protest song or shout a political demand to the point where many people begin singing or speaking in chorus. It is important that the protesting citizens believe that their activity will be viewed as protest by political decision makers.

Anniversaries of events, where blatant regime repression was exercised or citizen protests occurred in the past, were opportunities for many citizens to gather at central places. An example is the anniversary of Jan Palach's protest by setting himself on fire, when many people gathered at Wenzel Square in Prague. Such events generate expectations that many other people will gather at central places of a city.

Expectations to meet others at a particular place and time often also occur if a critical event takes pace. An example is the coup against Gorbachev in August 1991. When the coup had become known, a great number of citizens gathered at public places in Moscow, without any prior organization.

For the solution of the critical mass problem, the number of people expected to attend an event at a particular time and place will play the following role. If only a small group of people is expected, risks of state sanctions are very low because a small gathering will not be viewed as a protest. Yet the larger the number of people, the more the gathering will be considered a protest, and the less will be the personal risk a participant expects. In any case, citizens can say at the time of arrest that they were just walking through the city. Thus, if citizens decide to go to a certain place at a certain time, they will assume that state sanctions won't happen.

Yet this is true only if state sanctions are not dependent on the number of participants in a protest. If state sanctions increase according to the number of participants, participation in large demonstrations will probably be accompanied by relatively high costs.

The spontaneous cooperation model does not imply that each citizen decides completely on his or her own to go to a particular place. A micromobilization may occur to some extent in that a person asks friends to join her or him in going to the meeting place. There are thus cases where spontaneous coordination is supplemented by processes that are described by the micromobilization model.

Processes described by the threshold model may also play a role. If a certain number of citizens are active at a certain time, this may lower the costs of the protest for other people who find out about it. Yet, as we mentioned earlier, spontaneous coordination cannot be explained by means of this model alone.

Readers who are informed about the revolution in the GDR will surmise that the citizen protests in the GDR can best be explained by means of the spontaneous cooperation model. We will demonstrate this in detail in chapter 12.

The Dynamics of the Revolution

An important question has not yet been answered: What social processes led to the protests, and ultimately to the resignation of the SED regime in 1989? We mentioned that it is necessary in this regard to examine how and why the mentioned incentives changed. We will address this question in more detail in chapter 12.

The Reactions of the State

Is it possible to apply our explanatory model to explain the reactions of the SED regime in autumn 1989? The answer is a definite yes. The rational actor model explains human action. The members of the SED regime are human beings, so the model can be used to explain their behavior, with their preferences and constraints as the determinants of their behavior. Furthermore, members of governments maximize their personal utility—that is, they try to realize their goals to the highest possible extent. To be sure, the kinds of goals and constraints they consider differ from those of average citizens, but nonetheless preferences and constraints are the factors that determine action of the members of a government. We will deal with the behavior of the SED regime in detail in chapter 11.

Summary

The first step in explaining the revolution in the GDR is to determine what exactly is to be explained. We said that "the" revolution—see our definition—is a complex social event which must be divided into several components. These components are the subject of the explanation. Let us summarize those components in the form of questions to be answered:

1. Why did a relatively large percentage of the total population in the GDR take part in the protests?
2. Why did the protests increase dramatically, starting at the end of September, and then decrease before disappearing altogether?
3. Why did the citizens protest nonviolently?
4. Why didn't the threat of state sanctions stop or prevent the protests?
5. How can the spontaneous emergence of the demonstrations in autumn 1989, without any group organization, be explained?

6. Why did the protests first occur in Leipzig?

7. How can the SED regime's reactions to the protests be explained?

We began by criticizing some widely accepted answers to those questions. Many of those explanations are incomplete because they simply mention some factors, such as economic discontent, without adducing any arguments showing why the alleged causes and no other factors—such as the Wimbledon victories of Boris Becker and Steffi Graf in 1989—are relevant.

To avoid this problem, we apply a general theory of human behavior in this book, which helps us to determine factors that are relevant in explaining the revolution. In short, individuals act in order to reach their goals (preferences) to the highest extent possible, taking into account the constraints and behavioral opportunities they face. We then showed how this theory—the rational actor model—can be used to explain the revolution in the GDR.

On the basis of earlier research, we described the incentives that are relevant for the emergence of protests. These incentives include the amount of dissatisfaction, the effect of which depends in particular on the degree to which individuals believe themselves able to make political changes by means of their actions (perceived personal influence), state sanctions, as well as moral and social incentives.

Yet this does not explain how the protests occurred spontaneously, without any form of organization. We discussed various possibilities of coordinating individual actions and stated conditions under which spontaneous gatherings of citizens could take place at particular locations and times. In conclusion, we showed that our model also can be used to explain the process of the revolution and the reactions of the state.

In this chapter we developed the basic hypotheses relevant to the explanation of the revolution. We will expand on these hypotheses in the following chapters and test them with empirical data.

CHAPTER 3

The Goals of the Revolution

Peter Voss

In this chapter we will describe the goals underlying the protests and protest movements of GDR citizens. As we saw in the preceding chapter, discontent with the existing situation is an important condition for oppositional action. One condition for people to become dissatisfied is that they have the chance to compare their situation with that of others and find out that the others are better off. This is termed *relative deprivation*. To prevent relative deprivation, dictators attempt to shield those under their rule from outside information. Yet this is becoming harder and harder in the era of modern mass media. In the case of the GDR, this undertaking proved unsuccessful despite the wall, travel restrictions, and interfering transmitters. For the vast majority of GDR citizens, Western media were accessible.

Yet citizens do not become dissatisfied only if they compare their situation with that of others. One can simply become dissatisfied if one cannot achieve something that one desires. Even if one believes that people in every society must stand in lines in front of stores, one can nevertheless be discontent with standing in lines. This form of dissatisfaction is called *absolute deprivation*.

The Situation in the GDR Prior to October 9, 1989

In 1989, the provision of private and collective goods was visibly deteriorating. The GDR economy was almost bankrupt, which had an effect on each individual citizen's economic situation. The shortage of goods and services was sometimes grotesque. For example, one had to wait three months for an umbrella to be repaired and there was a waiting period of years for bath tiles. The massive migration aggravated the situation even more. The situation was particularly precarious in the areas of health care, social services, transportation, and food delivery for restaurants. A vicious circle began: continually worsening supply led to increased legal and illegal exit out of the GDR, especially by young workers, and the lack of workers in turn aggravated the crisis further.

Yet most of the "applicants"—SED bureaucrat jargon for people who applied for legal exit—were not economic refugees. Pastor Christian Führer had dealt with such individuals in a discussion group named Hoffnung [Hope] in the Nikolai Kirche of Leipzig long before the revolutionary changes. He said in one of our qualitative interviews:

> Those who wanted to leave were more frustrated by work-related problems, such as not being able to get ahead professionally because they were not members of the party, or were tired of shuffling papers year after year, rather than motivated by thoughts of economic wealth. This hidden unemployment accompanied by an SED bureaucracy and claim to power simply overran people. At one point or another people just couldn't take it anymore. And each person had his/her own "point of no return" where he/she just didn't want to or wasn't able to continue living under these conditions, and said to themselves: "Get out before they crush you completely."

What exactly were the forms of discontent and their causes?

The Causes of Dissatisfaction

To find seemingly unbiased information on the factual living conditions of a country's population, one has to look at official statistics. In the GDR the state even had a monopoly on the statistics. In concrete terms, only data congruent with party ideology were published. Furthermore, statistics were often glossed over from above. GDR leader Erich Honecker's economic secretary, Günter Mittag, developed his own system of "information" for the GDR economy. An expert on Mittag's tactics commented:

> Mittag's information monopoly over the economy allowed him to manipulate the alarming image of the GDR economy in the media by means of a well-contrived system of palliation, made up of reports, analyses and publications. (Schabowski 1991, 126 f.)

The situation was similar in other areas, such as in health care. The SED manipulated medical statistics for its own interests and then used them for propaganda purposes. Certain numbers were kept secret, such as data concerning suicide, abortion, child abuse, and alcoholism. In a brochure published shortly before unification, entitled "40 Years of Health and Social Services in the GDR-Statistics and Facts" such data are missing. The brochure maintained that efforts of the SED health and social service policies were successful in improving the health conditions of the population. Increased general life expectancy is presented as proof of their policies' success. However, this notable development was primarily a result of decreased baby and infant mortality rates. Yet if we look at the life expectancy of men and women in specific age categories, no improvements can be found. In fact, middle-aged men showed a tendency toward lower life expectancy. Statistics also do not mention that the GDR population ranges in the lower third in regard to life expectancy among European countries. In comparison to the leading nations of the world, the GDR population even had a life expectancy of six years less (see Arnold and Schirmer 1990, 78 ff.).

Because the GDR citizens were informed about only the positive aspects of the socialist health system, and because their own experiences within it were limited, they could not have a realistic picture about the quality of medical care for themselves. As a result, they simply accepted the health care system as it was and didn't express any great dissatisfaction with it. Yet the deficiencies in medical care weren't so great that they alone would give rise to a coup against the government.

Objective living conditions and citizens' subjective perceptions do not necessarily coincide. Another example of this is the so-called full employment of the GDR population. The GDR's economy suffered from a chronic lack of workers. Increases in production were generally the product of a redistribution of workers. To achieve this, either propaganda activities were begun or the wage-scale system was arbitrarily manipulated. For example, in view of the continuing shortages of workers in the chemical and the coal industry, wages were raised as incentives without being based on increases of productivity. If a person did not work, she or he was labeled as "asocial" and often incurred legal penalties. Yet such measures did not increase productivity, and the gap to the leading capitalist countries continued to grow. Despite this fact, the majority of citizens viewed the employment policies of the socialist system as an enormous advantage over capitalist systems and valued them highly as social achievements.

In this chapter, we would like to address the factors that influenced the citizens' dissatisfaction. We primarily make use of two statistical publications that appeared *after the fall of the GDR* (1989). The first is the *Sozialreport '90* [Social report '90] by Gunnar Winkler (final editing on February 2, 1990) and the (last!) *Statistisches Jahrbuch* der DDR [Statistical Yearbook of the GDR] (final editing in June 1990). Written on the basis of data never before published, these publications attempted to describe the conditions in the GDR more objectively than ever before. Yet because the analyses of trends also made use of older material, this was only possible to a limited extent.

The Political Situation
Until autumn 1989, no one seriously believed that the GDR would crumble. Its sovereignty was recognized in foreign affairs; domestically, most citizens had come to terms with their state. Those who argue today that the people in

the GDR thought of nothing else but how they could get rid of the SED government and be unified with West Germany lack sufficient factual knowledge. Physician and psychotherapist Hans-Joachim Maaz (1990, 14 f.) made the GDR citizens' opportunism public:

> Ninety-nine percent of the population went along with the phony elections. Millions of people regularly took part in the big jubilant parades, the majority of us being members of the Young Pioneers, going to the Socialist Youth Initiation of the FDJ, and acting against our own interests as members of the Free Federation of German Trade Unions. More than half a million people are believed to have taken part in the degrading snooping practices of the state security service. And no one can argue that she or he did not look on, personally experience or participate in the outright poisoning and destruction of our environment, the decaying of our cities, the cynical mendacity of the media, the public disclosures, the absurd political slogans, the decaying morals and the destruction of human relations by means of corruption, spying, denunciation, toadyism and "chumming up" to those in power. The most striking symptom is rather the fact that we were tolerant, silent, and simply looked away.

There was nevertheless also widespread political dissatisfaction in the GDR. In the second half of the 1980s, the situation escalated. Despite being confronted with the ideas of glasnost and perestroika, SED leaders were clearly not intending to introduce any reforms. The old "Politburo gentlemen" clung furiously to their positions of power. They either controlled or led all areas of society through their party machine. The government was simply made up of marionettes in the hands of the *nomenklatura*. The Stasi became a state within a state. Every form of "pluralism of opinion" was condemned from the beginning. "People with opposing opinions" were disdained, expatriated, and often sentenced in political trials.

Upbringing and education were dominated by Marxist-Leninist ideology. Rituals, national holidays, medals, and honors were intended to promote GDR citizens' identification with their state. A clever system of pseudo-democracy pretended to let citizens participate in important decisions. The winners of the elections were always chosen beforehand.

The German question of unification was considered forever solved, and the GDR was viewed as a guarantee of stability in Europe. To keep everyone from believing anything else, GDR citizens were not allowed to travel to the West.

Migration
In the 40 years of its existence, the GDR lost a large amount of its population. The population dropped from 18.892 million in 1949 to 16.614 million in

1989. At the time of the GDR's fall, 12 percent fewer people lived in the GDR compared to the time of its founding. Those who left were usually young and highly skilled.

The population decrease was essentially caused by three factors:

1. A continuing decrease in the birth rate as a result of the adverse demographical situation, the free distribution of contraceptives, and legal abortions. (From 1980 to 1989, 884,124 legal abortions were registered in the GDR; that is 43 abortions for every 100 births).
2. Migration, particularly into West Germany. From 1980 to 1989, 767,242 citizens left the GDR. These were cases of legally approved migration. Total (including illegal) migration is estimated to have been much higher.
3. An extremely low number of immigrants.

In the year prior to the GDR's fall, legal and illegal exit out of the GDR took an enormous increase. In jokes the DDR (the German abbreviation for GDR) was called "*D*er *d*oofe *R*est" [the stupid ones who remain]. Discussions probably took place in every household about whether "bearing with existing socialism" was still worth it.

Environment
Dissatisfaction with the environment was not a mere concern for the ozone layer, but, rather, for concrete working conditions and personal health problems. It had to do with the local forests, lakes, and rivers, which were necessary for relaxation because one could not flee from the destroyed environment into the vacation paradise in the West.

Data concerning environmental conditions were top secret in the GDR. Official propaganda maintained that capitalism was responsible for the world-wide environmental catastrophes and that only socialism could provide humanitarian environmental policies. To maintain this image, the SED government (as well as governments of other socialist countries) kept the real environmental situation a secret. Yet dying forests cannot be covered up like a bad investment in the economy. In Saxony's overcrowded areas, the people suffered from the continuously smoggy air, although the government denied its existence. Therefore, many of the demands made by demonstrators in autumn 1989 called for the solution of these problems.

The data currently available show that the GDR was on its way to becoming an environmental crisis area. Sulfur dioxide emissions before the GDR's fall totaled 5.2 million tons, or 312 kg per inhabitant and 48.1 tons per square kilometer. The GDR's emissions were the highest in all of Europe. This was also the case for dust emission. More than a quarter of the population was affected by inadmissible dust emission: 132 kg of dust fall per inhabitant was recorded to have fallen. The case is similar for other air-polluting substances.[1] More than 60 percent of the flowing water in the GDR was heavily polluted. The proportion of highly damaged forests rose from 28.8 percent in 1986 to 54.3% in 1989.

The enormous environmental pollution in the GDR was known only to specialists. Many companies, communal farms, and armies (of the GDR as well as of the Soviet Union stationed in the GDR) contaminated huge areas for decades. Although asbestos warnings were made throughout the world, the GDR continued high production and structural installation of asbestos products. Until the fall of the GDR, 14 million square meters of unprotected asbestos mats were installed, especially in room interiors. The conditions at dumping sites were indescribable.

Working Conditions
Working conditions deteriorated for most of the population in the 1980s, due to:

1. Increasing corrosion of industrial machinery and deterioration in the construction of buildings.
2. Increasing utilization of workplaces hazardous to the workers.
3. Insufficient usage of modern technology for comprehensive rationalization.

This situation led to massive health problems among the population. Work-related diseases ranged from 20 percent to 40 percent of the cases even before the deterioration in the 1980s. In 1989, one out of four employees (one out of three for workers in the production of goods) was exposed to pathogenic work conditions. The general working environment deteriorated so much that widespread health-threatening effects resulted in unmotivated workers. Much was said about the maintenance of a good "working culture," but most employees were exposed to a frightening lack thereof.

In comparison to workers in the FRG and other European countries, workers in East Germany had longer working days, weeks, years, and lifetimes. Table 1 compares average numbers of working hours in 1989 in East and West Germany (data compiled by Winkler 1990, 103).

Income
Employee dissatisfaction with income in the GDR increased particularly due to persisting feelings of non-performance-oriented pay and the inability to

---

1. The figures for the FRG were taken from the *Statistical Yearbook* 1991, 686.

TABLE 1.   Average Number of Working Hours in
the GDR and the FRG, 1989

Workload	GDR	FRG
Working day	8.75 hours	8 hours
Working week	43.75 hours	40 hours
Working year	235 days	221 days
Work in lifetime	46.5 years	44 years
Vacation per year	21 days	31 days

Source: Data compiled by Winkler 1990, 103.

earn more than needed for everyday consumption. The wage policies in the
GDR were determined by arbitrary administrative decisions. The labor union
FDGB (Freier Deutscher Gewerkschaftsbund) was required to simply approve
these decisions. Particularly disturbing was the permanent wage leveling of
skilled and unskilled labor as well as of employees with and without leadership positions. This situation hampered the introduction principle that wages
depend on achievements. A few years prior to the GDR's fall, the government
attempted to stimulate work performance by initiating performance-related
pay incentives, yet they amounted to a net pay increase of only 150 marks on
the average and were further dependent on political criteria.

In the 1980s nominal net pay of the GDR population did not grow above
4 percent. In 1989, net income increased by 3 percent in comparison to 1988.
Despite all official statements to the contrary, the income of female employees
was generally lower than that of their male counterparts.

The average monthly household income in 1989 was 2,115 marks. The
small income improvements in the years prior were counteracted by the simul-
taneous price increase for consumer goods and services. The price index for a
four-person household with a middle-class income rose from 107.1 in 1985 to
112.3 in 1989. Although real income statistics are not available, it is obvious
that life in the GDR became increasingly expensive.

Transportation and Communication
Dissatisfaction was also high in regard to the completely deteriorated infra-
structure. Western firms that took part in the Leipzig Trade Fair prior to the
GDR's fall experienced the communication problems that GDR citizens faced
firsthand. When after the GDR's fall tens of thousands of West Germans
flooded into the new provinces, they experienced that making a telephone
call, calling a taxi, reserving a hotel room, or simply eating in a restaurant
could become an adventure.

Taking a taxi is a good example of the transportation dilemma in the

GDR. In almost 20 years (between 1970 and 1989) the number of taxis increased by only about 260. The 5,956 taxis present in 1989 carried a total of 38.535 million passengers. Every GDR citizen thus could have taken a taxi on an average of 2.3 times a year. Trying to call a taxi in GDR times was next to impossible. The state of streets, highways and railways was catastrophic. There was no domestic air transportation. Late or canceled trains were the norm.

Hotels and restaurants operated according to mysterious business principles, and the personnel usually were happier to have no guests rather than a full house. The number of hotel and pension beds decreased over time. In 1985, there were 89,043 beds available for guests; this number had dropped to 76,818 in 1989. The number of hotels in the GDR decreased from 451 in 1985 to 397 in 1989. In 1988 there were 26,570 restaurants, with room for 1,432,717 guests. This makes one seat for every 20 GDR citizens and their guests. If one waited patiently and long enough in front of the door, one was lucky enough to be "seated" by the waiter.

Private telephone lines were another disaster. The waiting period of up to 20 years was the second longest waiting period, next to that for a Trabi—a car produced in East Germany. In 1989 only 17.2 percent of GDR households had a telephone line, notwithstanding the bad quality of the connection.

Forms and Extent of Dissatisfaction

In this section, we will first show how the dissatisfaction of the GDR citizens was embodied in popular jokes. We will then present some findings of our survey regarding dissatisfaction.

Jokes

Dissatisfaction with political and economic conditions took expression in the form of jokes. In his collection of GDR jokes, Arn Strohmeyer (1990, 4) commented on this phenomenon:[2]

> Political jokes have their good and bad times, although bad times inspire good jokes and vice versa. In other words, the political joke is a direct result of the political lie. There was therefore always a fresh batch of political jokes going around. Indeed, the jokes took on a function of actual opposition: With a fist (in his/her pocket) a person was able to express his/her anger (quietly) and the joke mercilessly revealed the contradictory web of deception between pretension and reality.

---

2. A large number of GDR jokes also can be found in de Wroblewsky 1990 and Damm 1990.

The humor was targeted at the old men of the Politburo, with Erich Honecker at the top, as well as at the desolate supply situation, the lacking work productivity, the socialist planned economy, the tasteless socialist memorials, the problematic relations with the Soviet Union, the mass exodus out of the GDR and, last but not least, the Trabi—the GDR's Volkswagen.

This is how the opening ceremony of the Politburo meetings was characterized: hauling in of the Politburo members, distribution of pacemakers, singing the song "We are the Young Guard." Or the question was asked, "What's the difference between a washing machine and the Politburo?" Answer: "A washing machine can be delimed."

The city of Wandlitz, where only the high-level politicians lived, was called Volvograd. The last national anthem went: "The sun laughs above Moscow, and the whole world at us!" The Palace of the Republic in Berlin (*Palace* in German reads *Palast*) was termed the "ballast" of the republic, which sounds in Saxon dialect like *Palast* but has the same meaning as the English word *ballast*. It was also said that Honecker put an ad in the paper which read: "Wanted: workers and farmers. Country is provided."

There were endless numbers of jokes about the GDR's economy. One joke asked: "How many economists does it take to milk a cow?" Answer: "Nine: four hold the udder, another four take a hold of each leg to move the cow up and down, and the ninth one holds the pail." Or the question was asked: "Why is work productivity higher in the West than in the East?" Answer: "Because the communists aren't allowed to work in the West."

There were as many jokes about the supply situation as there were about the planned economy and production. One joke described the difference between the capitalist and socialist hell. Both of them boiled sinners in big pots over a raging fire. Yet in socialist hell, this action could never be carried out because sometimes there were no matches, no wood, and no oil in the pot, and even when everything was there, the devil was always busy counting his cash.

In regard to GDR and Soviet relations after Gorbachev's rise to power, jokes were heard such as: "The motto used to be 'learning from the Soviet Union means learning to win,' but now it becomes 'We must learn how to learn from the Soviet Union.'"

The popularity of political jokes in the GDR played an important social psychological role: The jokes sensitized the population to the system's weak points and the laughter strengthened common rejection of people in power and programs. Sigmund Freud recognized this in his famous analysis of the joke in 1905 (1985, 93):

> By making the enemy small, low, detestable, and ridiculous, we bask in the delight of overcoming him. This joy is easily shared with the audience by means of their laughter.

The aggressive joke (and most political jokes are aggressive) replaces true aggression. A direct attack is not possible because the joke's object is protected by its powerful position. Freud described the *tendentious joke* (that is, a joke that serves political purposes) as a "psychological factor of power" (1985, 122):

> Due to its aggressiveness the tendentious joke turns the indifferent audience into fellow "haters" and "despisers" and creates an army of opposers, where there was first only one.

The political joke tends to focus on specific individuals. The many Honecker jokes destroyed the image of the "faultless representative of the people." One of those jokes went like this: Gorbachev gives Honecker a new car. Honecker looks under the hood and says, surprised: "But there's no motor in it." "You don't need one," replies Gorbachev, "Everything in the GDR is going downhill." Honecker responds: "But what if things start going uphill again?" Gorbachev replies: "Then you won't be in the driver's seat anymore."

Survey Findings

In our survey, we ascertained why and to what extent people were discontented (for details see the appendix). Figure 1 shows that dissatisfaction with the state of the environment has the highest arithmetic mean of 4.5. This is only slightly below the highest possible value of 5. The values for the other forms of dissatisfaction are high as well. Total political dissatisfaction—that is to say, the arithmetic mean of all specific forms of discontent—has a value of 4.3.

As to social dissatisfaction, a relatively high level of *satisfaction* was found regarding child care. This rating corresponds to the real conditions. There were enough kindergartens for children and they were very inexpensive. There were certainly some difficulties with child-care facilities for infants, yet on the whole the provision of child-care facilities was sufficient. This situation enabled many women to work.

We also ascertained *changes* in economic dissatisfaction for the year 1989. Our questionnaire included the question:

> Do you believe that the situation in the GDR between January 1989 and October 9, 1989, generally became better, worse, or didn't change?

Sixty-nine percent believed that the economic situation had worsened, 29 percent believed that nothing had changed, and only 2 percent believed that an improvement of the economic situation had taken place within this period of time.

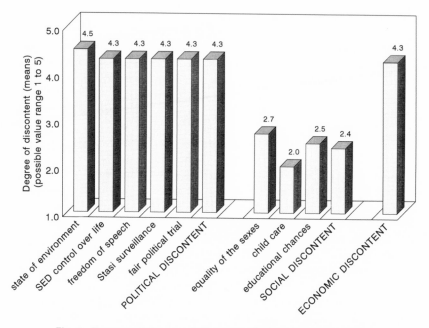

Fig. 1. Forms and degree of discontent before October 9, 1989

The extent of dissatisfaction also depends on the standard of comparison with other countries. We asked:

Did you compare the economic situation in the GDR with that of other socialist countries or with West Germany?

Although Czechoslovakia and Hungary usually had better-stocked stores than the GDR did, the other socialist countries, especially the Soviet Union, were definitely worse off. Yet only 37 percent made such comparisons. The majority (63 percent) compared their own situation with that of West Germany, which made things look pretty bleak in the GDR.

Similar comparisons were made in regard to the political situation. We asked the respondents the following question:

Consider the different *political* systems of the GDR and West Germany. To which system did you feel more close?

GDR citizens' identification with their country seems to have dropped rapidly. Fewer than one out of every two citizens (46 percent) said they identified more strongly with their own country.

The Goals of the Revolution

In this section we will address how opposition groups responded to these different forms of dissatisfaction in their political programs, as well as the extent to which these grievances were mentioned during the protests.[3]

Sources

The revolution in the GDR was documented with German thoroughness. The Leipzig Monday demonstrations were followed by loads of official and unofficial reporters, professional and hobby journalists, radio and TV teams, and photographers. Brochures and flyers were collected, slogans were noted, and even sociological surveys of the demonstrators were made (Förster and Roski 1990; Mühler and Wilsdorf 1991). The protesters laid down the protest signs they carried in front of the city hall before going home to see themselves on the TV news.

Christoph Kaufmann of the Historical Museum of the History of Leipzig remembers the situation:

> The banners, posters, signs etc. really had to be cleared from the streets. My colleagues and I knew from the beginning that these events were important and unique. The demonstration always ended in front of the new city hall, and in the beginning the people just dropped their banners etc. when it was over. Or they nailed the signs on the front of its entrance door. That was kind of a symbolic act of handing over to the city council because many demands were initially local, such as in the case of environmental protection. And I gathered as many of these banners etc. as I could carry and brought them into the museum. The city hall employees were also clever enough to collect the signs late at night or early in the morning, in order to save them for us. Of course, I also went up to demonstrators and asked them if I could have their banners etc., although their reactions varied. Yet many people did not want to give their banners etc. away, especially those that were graphically well designed. Unfortunately, private collectors very quickly kept us from getting some of the good ones.

In our account of the revolution's goals, we not only make use of official documents but also of documentations, of appeals, slogans, and political programs. We furthermore asked detailed questions about the goals of the

---

3. See particularly Hoppert 1990, Lindner 1990, Schüddekopf 1990, Tetzner 1990. This literature deals with political programs, slogans, and other contemporary material.

protest movement in our qualitative interviews. Finally, our questionnaire contained specific questions in this regard.

Slogans

The slogans are excellent reflections of the dynamics of the revolution. There was a noticeable change in goals expressed in the slogans that were used between September 1989 and December 1989 and again between January 1990 and the elections on March 18, 1990. In the beginning there were demands for freedom and democracy. Then came slogans calling for the dissolution of old power structures, then ecological and economic improvements were called for. Only in November 1989 could loud calls for German unity be heard for the first time. At the same time, aggressive and bitter demands to punish all those guilty of contributing to the misery in the GDR were made.

The following slogans were calls made by individuals speaking in unison. They were painted on banners, signs, sashes, arm bands, patches, and flyers. Some slogans were only used at a single demonstration, others, such as the phrase "No violence," were always present. An analysis of the content of the slogans yielded nine topic categories:

1. *Freedom in general, human rights:* "Freedom is always the freedom for those who think differently!" "Freedom, equality, and solidarity!" "For an open country of free people!"
2. *Freedom of movement, freedom of travel:* "Freedom without limits!" "Freedom of travel, not mass migration!" "Freedom of press, freedom of travel!" "We want out!" "Visa-free till Hawaii!" "Bike tour through Europe today without waiting till we're old and gray!"
3. *Opposition against the state:* "Stasi get out!" "Stasi workers, get real jobs!" "No violence!"
4. *Against the SED:* "With the SED and the FDJ you're always sitting in the back row!" "SED—no thank you!" "Where the SED works, it hurts!" "Many words, but nothing rhymes—central committee members resign!" "SED resign or emigration will climb!" "The SED should lead us—but all they do is cheat us!"
5. *Self-determination:* "We're staying here!" "We are the people!" "Leipzig—heroic city of the GDR!" "If the people weren't here, reforms would never appear!" "Protest is the foremost civil duty!"
6. *For more democracy:* "Legalize the Neues Forum!" "Democracy—now or never!" "Free elections!" "Protect rights, not the state!" "Neither ox nor donkey will hinder true democracy!" "Direct democracy, not polit-bureaucracy!"

7. *Environmental protection:* "Ecology, not economy!" "Don't make green trees a figment of yesterday, fight for environmental protection today!" "Stasi-money for the woods!" "Dead rivers, dead forests, and no money for them, this is all that remains—environmental protection must reign!" "Fighters for the Eco-front!" "Money is more needed for the environment than for the military!"

8. *Wealth and money:* "Tin coins are no assurance, we need real currency!" "Egon, hand over the real money!" "Egon, Erich, Eberhard, where did you bury the money?" "Stasi money for travel funds!" "Longer vacation and 40-hour weeks for everybody!" "Social Market Economy is needed—we'll do it on our own!" "Planned economy no, market economy yes!" "Hard currency for hard work!" "Minimum pension in freedom!"

9. *Reunification:* "Germany, unified homeland!" "Germany's reunification is our only hope!" "Only one German room in a European House!" "One German people, one homeland!" "No more experiments—reunification now!" "Let Germans sit at one table!"

Unfortunately, the English translation of the slogans often does not convey their rhyming and artistic quality.

The slogans and their usage express the political culture of the demonstrations. Almost all the slogans were spontaneously created. There were no mandatory slogans as under the SED. The high point of this development was the giant demonstration on November 4, 1989, in (East) Berlin, which had been called for by artists and writers in the GDR.

There are clear connections between the forms of dissatisfaction described earlier and the goals of the protests presented here. *Political dissatisfaction* refers to the extent to which the SED controlled everyday life, to Stasi surveillance, freedom of speech, to the assurance of a fair trial before October 9, and the state of the environment in the GDR. These were also the points expressed in the slogans. This applies to slogans regarding *economic dissatisfaction* (referring to wealth and real [Western] money) too.

Social dissatisfaction was the only exception to be found. This kind of dissatisfaction stemmed from such areas as equal treatment of men and women, child care, and educational opportunities. As this form of dissatisfaction was not as widespread (see fig. 1), demands referring to this type of dissatisfaction were not included on the banners and signs the demonstrators carried.

Political Programs

Autumn 1989 was not the first time that opposition groups had made political demands. Such demands first appeared at the beginning of the 1980s. At this time the first "autonomous" groups of pacifists, human rights supporters, environmental protectionists, Christians, and artists arose, inspired by the peace movement in the West. They wanted more political self-determination. Timid in the beginning, but then increasingly self-confident, alternative views of the world developed. The Church and some associations of artists were providing support. And, as expected, these first attempts at a new way of thinking were thoroughly suppressed by the "ideology guards" of the socialist system.

The breakthrough to the public only occurred at the time of the mass protests in autumn 1989. Starting in September 1989, opposition groups sprang up like wild flowers. By March 18, 1990, 57 parties, movements, and organizations had registered themselves in the GDR Volkskammer [people's chamber]. They ranged from new citizen initiatives such as the Neues Forum and the Initiative für Frieden und Menschenrechte [Peace and human rights initiative] to established parties such as the CDU (Christlich Demokratische Union [Christian Democrats]), SPD (Sozialdemokratische Partei Deutschlands [Social Democrats]), and political exotics such as the Deutsche Biertrinker Union [German beer drinkers' union].

We found twelve political areas mentioned continually between the time of the first flyers made by the Initiative für Frieden und Menschenrechte (1985) and the founding of the Deutsche Umweltschutzpartei [German Environmental Protection Party] on March 12, 1990 (just prior to the first people's chamber elections on March 18, 1990):

> Basic values, goals, and political stance; concepts of democracy and governmental stance; economic policies; social policies; environmental policies; health policies; educational policies; scientific policies; cultural policies; local policies; foreign and security policies; national policies.

When several dozen groups speak out on the same political topics, overlapping themes are inevitable, and clearly setting one position apart from another becomes difficult. There was also little time for the movements to develop political programs; most had less than half a year to prepare for the people's chamber elections on March 18, 1990. The protesting citizens and later the voters therefore focused on a few better-known groups and parties, such as the Neues Forum in the beginning and the CDU later.

Each group made statements about four topics: (1) concepts of a democratic government; (2) economic and social policies; (3) environmental protection; and (4) reunification of West and East Germany. The statements regarding concepts of democratic government ranged from direct democracy to representative democracy; regarding economic and social policies from ecological/social to liberal; regarding environmental protection from alternative lifestyles to nuclear energy, and regarding reunification of West and East

Germany from two states within a confederation to a united Germany. The traditional left-right scheme of political thought was thus reproduced in a short period of time, with the opposition movement leaning more toward the midleft.

The new opposition groups were not able to have discussions on basic issues and could not create committees on basic values or programs that worked over months. They had to deal with daily issues and react flexibly to the quickly changing political situation. Most of the programs therefore seemed incomplete and disorganized. Detailed designs for a new society and fundamental economic ideas were missing. Statements in regard to ecological policies were taken from the broad spectrum of Western alternative movements. The programs reflected a sense of being against rather than of being for certain issues.

Changes in Goals

Attempts to distinguish between different periods in the process of the GDR revolution vary according to theoretical intentions. Accordingly, we find quite different classifications (see Wuttke and Musiolek 1991, 13–16; Reißig 1991, 37–38). The most useful classification of the time periods within the GDR revolution is this:

Stage 1. Illegality: up until October 9, 1989;

Stage 2. Transition to legality: up until November 9, 1989;

Stage 3. Triumph over the old power apparatus: from November 10 to the end of 1989;

Stage 4. Election campaigns: from January 1990 to March 18, 1990.

The decisive turning points and simultaneously the starting points of each new stage were the first large nonviolent Monday demonstration in Leipzig on October 9, the opening of the borders to West Germany on November 9, the admission of the Neues Forum, and the various announcements of free elections at the turn of the year. The Staatsrat [state council] of the GDR finally announced the people's chamber elections to take place on March 18, 1990.

The announcement of the founding of the Neues Forum on September 10, 1989, is the major event of the first stage. The Neues Forum was founded by Bärbel Bohley, Rolf Henrich, Sebastian Pflugbeil, Jens Reich, and Hans-Jochen Tschiche. The announcement did not contain a complete reform program but, rather, merely articulated the general discomfort about the loss of communication with the government. It was a call for a democratic dialogue about problems in the GDR society. The decisive demands were justice, peace, democracy, and environmental protection. Essentially, all these rights were included already in the GDR constitution. Marianne Schulz (1991, 13 ff.) commented:

> On September 19, 1989, the members of the Neues Forum applied for recognition throughout the entire German Democratic Republic as a non-profit organization in accord with article 29 of the GDR constitution. In contrast to the other opposition groups, the Neues Forum had initiated its first genuine activity as a concrete demand to the government and dared to challenge it publicly. Because this demand for legality took place in the framework of existing formal constitutional rights, the government's reaction showed that its own politics were unconstitutional and it was therefore clear that any form of rule of law was absent.

The second stage was also closely connected with the political activities of the Neues Forum. Jochen Läßig, at that time speaker for the Neues Forum and currently speaker for the party Bündnis 90 [League 90] in Leipzig's city parliament, was asked in one of our qualitative interviews if the opposition movement in October 1989 had a certain political concept:

> Our conception was that we simply wanted to help create a more democratic system and we believed that we could do it. We believed in a sort of democratic socialism, but we hadn't thought through all the details at the time. We only had certain program points, such as freedom of the press, freedom of speech, freedom to convene, freedom of travel, pluralism, and so on. This can best be demonstrated by means of a speech held on October 30. It was the first public speech by the Neues Forum. It took place on Karl-Marx-Platz with a megaphone. A ten-point list was read. These were the points which we had always seen as important. It essentially had to do with the creation, or better said, *recreation* of civil freedoms. Those were the essential points. We believed that this could occur, let's say, not within the old system, but in a system other than that of the Federal Republic of Germany.

Yet the second stage did not only involve the legalization of the Neues Forum, but also the general legalization of all opposition groups, opposition movements, and parties. During this stage, calls were continually made during demonstrations for the provision of basic human rights and democratic reforms. The most common slogans were:

> "We're staying here!" "*We* are the people!" "No violence!" "Legalize the Neues Forum!" "Gorbi! Gorbi!" "Free elections! Freedom of the press

and travel!" "Where the SED works, it hurts!" "Stasi workers: get real jobs!" "Ecology before economy!" "Egon, tear the wall down!" "Put the Central Committee in a home for old people!" "Free elections for more democracy!" "Egon, reform or resign!"

Pastor Matthias Petzoldt, one of the partners in our qualitative interviews, who had been active in the group Demokratischer Aufbruch [Democratic upraising], said:

We weren't yet thinking about German unity in October. We were focusing mainly on protest against current conditions and for immediate changes, that is, for more freedom: freedom of the press, of elections, of travel. Those really seemed to be the basic freedoms we were focusing on. And then, here were the groups that needed support. You see, people were always calling for the Neues Forum—this was really all we had in mind at that time.

The basic political demand of the third stage was the call for an end to the SED's claim to sole political power. This call was accompanied by demands for free elections and a united Germany. The surprising fall of the Berlin Wall on November 9, 1989, created a completely different constellation for the opposition movement. "A turn in the turning point" occurred (Reißig 1991, 39). The endless discussion about German reunification was solved by these events, first in Berlin and then throughout Germany. The civil rights groups could not offer convincing plans for a reformed and democratic socialism. The majority of the people in the GDR completely rejected any new experiments with socialism. Typical slogans during this phase were:

"We don't need an SED power monopoly, just free elections!" "SED bye-bye!" "Citizens beware, the SED won't give up their power share!" "Egon resign—you're hurting us!" "Put Honecker on people's trial!" "The leaders should resign! Provisional government until the new elections!" "Egon, close the Stasi doors, only then the people will believe you!" "No experiments! SED and socialists have met their end!" "Germany, united fatherland! Referendum for unification!" "One German people, one fatherland!" "Nazis get out!"

These demands were made in an increasingly aggressive manner. The confident calmness of the second stage was replaced by angry impatience. Bernd Lindner (1990, 172) described the situation:

With the development of public opinion, the building of new groups, organizations and parties in the GDR, there was a tendency for slogans to be more differentiated and extreme. After the focus on demands for reforms in October, symbolized by the demand for legalization of the Neues Forum and democratic elections, the opening of the borders created a turning point. The step by step revealing of high functionaries' misuse of their positions also led to a continually heated demonstration atmosphere.

The fourth stage was shaped solely by the election campaign. Yet some critics from the left overestimated the true impact the parties had on the behavior of the voters. An entire people, which had just accomplished a victorious revolution, had not been misled. The majority realized that socialism had failed not only in the GDR, but also worldwide, and that further experiments in this direction would put personal life chances at risk. For another 40 years of the GDR, although perhaps better this time, only a few wanted to take the risk. Thus, they chose the only possible alternative from their point of view: the quick unification with the Federal Republic of Germany.

Survey Results

To what extent can the prior hypotheses be confirmed by our survey of the population of Leipzig? We asked those respondents who participated in one of the demonstrations *why* they personally demonstrated before (i.e., until) and after October 9. Figure 2 shows the percentage of respondents indicating they had demonstrated for one of the respective goals.

Before as well as after October 9, almost all participants—89 percent or more—demonstrated for more democracy, free elections, dissolution of the Stasi, legalization of opposition parties, and the SED government's resignation. Comparing those who demonstrated for those goals before and after October 9, we find only small differences.

The results for the other goals are less clear. It is striking that even *before* October 9, 68 percent of the respondents indicated they had demonstrated for a market economy; 58 percent for democratic socialism, 56 percent for unification with West Germany and 52 percent for the abolishment of socialism. We thus see that differences among GDR citizens were larger in regard to these goals than for the block of goals mentioned earlier.

It is understandable that demands for unification, a market economy, or abolishing socialism were not *expressed* in the initial phase of the protests. This would have been in line with the SED propaganda, which said that the demonstrators were enemies of socialism. Nevertheless, those goals *existed* and were supported by the majority of the population.

Comparing the percentage of respondents who had those goals *before and after* October 9 we found that, according to our previous considerations,

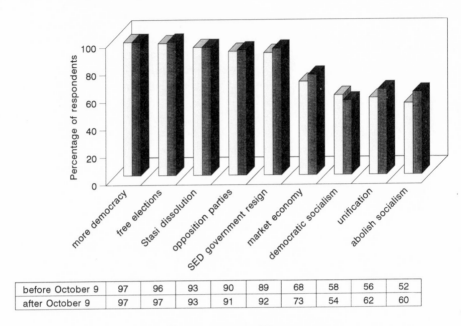

	more democracy	free elections	Stasi dissolution	opposition parties	SED government resign	market economy	democratic socialism	unification	abolish socialism
before October 9	97	96	93	90	89	68	58	56	52
after October 9	97	97	93	91	92	73	54	62	60

☐ before October 9 ▨ after October 9

Fig. 2. What participants demonstrated for before and after October 9, 1989

the demands for a market economy, unification, and abolishment of socialism increased, whereas fewer participants wanted democratic socialism. However, the differences before and after October 9 are less clear than we would expect by watching the demonstrations and the slogans shown during the demonstrations.

We were also interested in examining the extent to which participants changed their goals. We thus ascertained the percentage of those citizens whose goals were stable versus not stable before and after October 9. Figure 3 shows that the goals of the respondents were very stable. For example, 98 percent supported more democracy before and after October 9, and "only" 86 percent demonstrated for a market economy. Our data thus do not support the hypothesis that the demonstrators changed their goals.

We were also interested in the goals of those individuals who were members of opposition groups, and whether or not their goals differed from those of average respondents. For some goals, our data indicate that such differences exist: Members of opposition groups demonstrated *less* frequently than nonmembers did for the abolishment of socialism, for unification, and

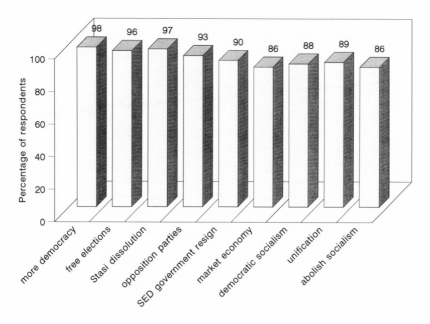

Fig. 3. Participants who demonstrated for the same goals before and after October 9, 1989

for adopting a market economy. This situation holds true for the demonstrations before as well as after October 9, thus confirming the assumption that many members of opposition groups believed long after October 9 that socialism could be reformed.

The same trend is evident if we compare the goals of nonmembers of opposition groups from the representative Leipzig survey and the goals of the opposition group members from the opposition group sample (see the introduction, chapter 10, and the appendix). Both before and after October 9, 1989, members of opposition groups were clearly against unification, a market economy, and the repeal of socialism, but in favor of a democratic socialism, including legalization of opposition parties.[4]

---

4. For the statistically informed reader: We compared three groups: (1) nonmembers of the opposition groups of the general population survey of Leipzig; (2) members of the opposition groups of the former survey; and (3) members of opposition groups of the opposition-group sample. We compared the percentage of respondents who accepted the various goals. For the goals mentioned in the text, the percentages of opposition group members of the population survey mostly lay between those of the other two samples. If we mention differences in the text, we always refer to differences that are statistically significant at the .01 level.

Summary

In the first part of this chapter, we focused on the causes of discontent in the GDR. The political and economic situation led to a high extent of dissatisfaction, which increased over time. Results of our survey also indicate that political and economic discontent was very high, whereas social discontent was relatively low. One way of expressing discontent was through jokes, which were illustrated with some examples.

In the second part of this chapter we dealt with the goals of the revolution. We analyzed slogans and political programs of various opposition groups. These analyses indicate that the goals changed over time—we distinguish four stages. These changes are confirmed by results of our survey but less strongly than expected. Almost all demonstration participants said they demonstrated both before and after October 9 for a Western-style democracy and the demise of the SED government. It was surprising that 68 percent of the respondents said they wanted a market economy and 56 percent demanded unification even before October 9, compared to 73 percent and 62 percent after October 9. There is thus a change of goals, yet this change is not as strong as the slogans would suggest. We assume that participants in the demonstrations did not dare to *express* particular goals—such as pleading for a market economy. Another result is that the *individual* participants' goals remained largely stable.

CHAPTER 4

The Dissatisfied Citizen: Why Should I Protest If I Can't Change Anything Anyway?

Karl-Dieter Opp

In this chapter we will return to some hypotheses from chapter 2, focusing on the role of dissatisfaction for the emergence of political protest. We will extend these hypotheses and examine their empirical validity by means of our survey.

Was Dissatisfaction a Cause of the Revolution in the GDR?

Is there a relationship between the extent of dissatisfaction and political protest? In chapter 3 we differentiated between *political dissatisfaction*, *social dissatisfaction*, and *economic dissatisfaction*. If the dissatisfaction hypothesis holds true, then the larger each of these forms of dissatisfaction is, the greater should be participation in political protest actions.

If the discontent proposition is correct, we will expect that individuals tended to take part in protests to a high degree when they believed that the *economic situation worsened in 1989 up until October 9*. Furthermore, citizens should have participated rather frequently when they *compared the political or economic situation in the GDR prior to October 9 with West Germany*. These citizens were probably "relatively" dissatisfied because the economic as well as the political situation of West Germany was better than that of the GDR.

If dissatisfaction leads to protest, then we would expect each of the mentioned forms of dissatisfaction to have approximately the same effect on both mentioned forms of protest:

Hypothesis 1: The greater each of the aforementioned kinds of people's dissatisfaction up until October 9, the greater their participation in general protests and the greater their frequency of participation in demonstrations. Each of the different forms of dissatisfaction displays the same effects.

Our statistical analyses show that this hypothesis does not hold true.[1] The forms of dissatisfaction mentioned had completely different effects on participation in general protest and demonstrations. Political dissatisfaction had the strongest effect on *general protests*. Those who were dissatisfied with public services (social discontent) also protested quite frequently, yet the effect on general protests was weaker. Economic dissatisfaction did not increase protest at all. In fact, there is no correlation between economic discontent and participation in general protests. The other forms of dissatisfaction also did not affect participation of the citizens.

Participation in *demonstrations* can *only* be explained on the basis of political dissatisfaction. All other forms of dissatisfaction had absolutely no effect on participation in demonstrations.[2]

These results may appear contradictory to some readers. Our data show on the one hand that the *amount* of our respondents' political and economic dissatisfaction up until October 9 was about the same and relatively high, while on the other hand, social dissatisfaction was clearly lower on the average (see chapter 3). How, then, is it possible that economic dissatisfaction played no role in participation in general protest, although it was as high as political dissatisfaction? And how is it possible that social dissatisfaction was relatively low yet nevertheless affected participation in general protests to a relatively high degree? The answer to these questions is that a factor (an independent variable) that is present to a high degree does not necessarily have to have a strong effect on a (dependent) variable. A factor (discontent) has a strong effect on a variable (protest) only if those individuals with high

---

1. For the statistically informed reader: The results of the statistical analyses are based on regression analyses in which the dependent variables "participation in general protests" and "participation in demonstrations" were regressed simultaneously on the mentioned forms of dissatisfaction.

2. For the statistically informed reader: The standardized regression coefficients for participation in general protests (dependent variable) and the mentioned forms of discontent (independent variables) up to October 9 have the following values: political dissatisfaction .30, social dissatisfaction .12, economic dissatisfaction $-.14$, worsening of the economic situation 1989 .02, comparison of the economic situation in the GDR with that of the FRG .03, comparison of the political system in the GDR with that of the FRG .07. The first three coefficients were significant at the .01 level; the coefficient .07 is significant at the .05 level. The adjusted explained variance is .14. It is interesting to note the negative sign of the coefficient for economic dissatisfaction, which is due to the zero correlation between economic dissatisfaction and protest and to (weak) intercorrelations of the discontent variables. For participation in demonstrations (dependent variable), only political dissatisfaction is statistically significant: beta is .21, significant at the 0.01 level.

(low) values in the factor (discontent) also have high (low) values in the dependent variable (protest). However, such an association need not exist. To illustrate, assume GDR citizens had on the average a relatively high preference for the color red and protested frequently. This does not imply that there is also a correlation between both factors in the sense that those with a high preference for red also protest frequently.

Why did political dissatisfaction affect political participation against the SED regime more than social and economic dissatisfaction? We presume that at that time, the GDR citizens believed it more promising to change the political circumstances rather than the economic or social conditions. Freedom of travel, the power of the Stasi, or freedom of speech could be introduced immediately by changing the laws. Yet changes in the economic order, such as increasing efficiency and simultaneously maintaining socialist ideals, were much more difficult to initiate. It is therefore no coincidence that political circumstances were the main motors behind the demonstrations.

**Citizens' Influence on Politics:
Perception, Reality, and Effects**

In this section we will examine the extent to which GDR citizens considered themselves influential, how successful they believed collective protest to be, and the degree to which they accepted the unity principle.

How Citizens Saw Their Political Influence

A widespread hypothesis maintains that the individual citizen actually has no influence on the politics of his or her country and that dissatisfaction therefore cannot be a cause of protest. After all, citizens will not attempt to reach their goals by taking to the streets if they know very well that their protest will not contribute to the attainment of their political goals. To what degree did GDR citizens really believe that they had no political influence up to October 9? We will examine the following hypotheses:

> *Hypothesis 2*: GDR citizens believed themselves to be politically influential.
> *Hypothesis 3*: GDR citizens believed protest to be effective.
> *Hypothesis 4*: GDR citizens accepted the unity principle.

If hypothesis 2 is correct, then our respondents should have checked the answers "likely" and "highly likely" in answering the four questions measuring perceived influence. Figure 1 shows that this is indeed the case. Thirty-three percent of the interviewees believed they were "highly likely" or

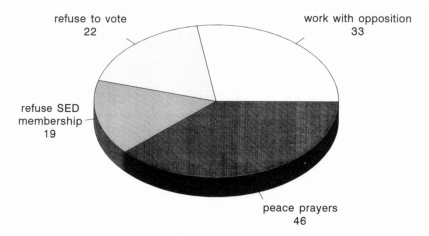

refuse to vote
22

work with opposition
33

refuse SED
membership
19

peace prayers
46

**Fig. 1. Perceived political influence of four actions before October 9,
1989 (percentages refer to responses "likely" and "highly likely")**

"likely" to bring about changes by working in or founding an opposition
group. Even 46 percent believed that participation in peace prayers or other
church activities would be politically influential. Refusing to participate in
elections or to become an SED member, in contrast, was considered less
effective: only 22 percent and 19 percent respectively, answered "likely" or
"highly likely." Thus, it cannot be maintained that the interviewees generally
believed protest to be ineffective.

How effective did respondents consider participation in demonstrations
before October 9? We determined this by two questions. Regarding the emigration wave, we presented the interviewees with this statement:

I thought: If I take part in demonstrations and similar activities now, I
personally can make a difference.

A total of 53 percent of the 1,282 respondents who responded to this statement said that it either "holds true" or "holds completely true." Only 29
percent said that the statement "does not" or "does not at all" hold true. The
same statement was presented referring to the liberalization in Hungary and
Poland (e.g., legalization of labor union Solidarity). In this case, 47 percent
of 1,283 interviewees with a valid answer responded that this statement held
true or definitely held true, while 33 percent of the interviewees responded
that this statement did not or did not at all hold true. These results show that
the emigration wave caused the GDR citizens to believe to a greater degree

than the emigration wave that their personal influence to achieve reforms by means of political activity had grown.

Let us turn to hypothesis 3. The degree to which interviewees believed in the effectiveness of protests in general (not their personal influence) before October 9 is measured by the following item, which refers to the emigration wave:

> It was clear to me that there was now a definite opportunity to make a difference if the population as a whole participates more often in protest activities.

A total of 68 percent of the 1,288 respondents who gave a valid answer agreed to this item. Collective protest was therefore viewed to be effective.

Hypothesis 4 was examined by this item:

> Every single member is necessary for the success of a political group, regardless of the size of the group.

Of the 1,273 respondents with a valid answer, 81 percent agreed. Thus, the unity principle was accepted to a large degree.

Why Did Perceived Political Influence Increase in 1989?

Some of the survey results we presented in the preceding section provide an answer to this question. It appears that because of the emigration wave and the liberalization in Eastern Europe, interviewees believed that their own political activity would be effective. It is therefore correct to maintain that the liberalization in Eastern Europe and the emigration wave contributed to the revolution in the GDR—as is claimed in macrolevel explanations (see chapter 2). We now see *why* this is the case: Those events changed the motivation to protest because they led, among other things, to an increase in perceived political influence. And as we will see, this in turn increased participation in protest actions.

Political Influence and Protest

Even if political and, to a lesser extent, social discontent affect political participation, their effects may be different under certain conditions. These conditions were addressed in chapter 2 and we will summarize them:

> *Hypothesis 5*: The more that people believe they are able to effect changes by means of political action; the more that people believe

collective protest is effective; and the more that people believe only joint action will be successful (belief in the unity principle), the more they will participate in general protests and the more frequently they will take part in demonstrations.

Our statistical analyses[3] indicate that the first statement of hypothesis 5 is well confirmed. It is indeed true that a high perceived personal influence to effect changes by participation in general protests or demonstrations led to increased political protest.

It seems plausible that those individuals protest often who believe that because of the emigration wave, "a definite opportunity exists to effect changes if the population as a whole participated more in political protest activities." Yet this was the case only in regard to participation in general protests. There was thus no relationship between participation in demonstrations and perceived effectiveness of collective protests. This is probably due to our wording of the survey question. Interviewees were asked if they supported the statement that said the emigration wave created a genuine opportunity to create change, "*if* the population as a whole participated more in political protest activities." If prior to October 9, respondents had not expected the population to become more active, supporting the statement would not lead to greater activity. We should have asked, in addition, how *likely* respondents believed it was that a large part of the population would participate.

Do those individuals who believe in the unity principle protest frequently? Our statistical analyses show that an acceptance of the unity principle affects participation neither in general protests nor in demonstrations. Therefore, the last statement of hypothesis 5 cannot be confirmed.[4]

Political Influence, Dissatisfaction, and Protest: Joint Effects

So far have we analyzed the effects of dissatisfaction and influence on political protest separately. These results are certainly interesting, yet the rational actor

---

3. For the statistically informed reader: We ran regression analyses with "participation in general protests" and "participation in demonstrations" up until October 9 as dependent variables. The following influence measures were included as independent additive variables in the equation for general protests: "personal influence by general protests up until October 9," "acceptance of the unity principle," and "perceived effectiveness of collective protests." For the dependent variable regarding demonstrations, we used the scale "personal influence by participation in demonstrations" instead of the scale "personal influence by general protests," as well as the variables "acceptance of the unity principle" and "perceived effectiveness of collective protests," which were also included in the analyses for participation in general protests.

4. It is possible that this is due to the skewed distribution of the variables. The number of respondents for the five answer categories (1 for "does not hold true at all," 5 for "holds completely true") are 30, 60, 147, 298, and 730.

theory implies that there is an interaction effect of discontent and influence on protest (see chapter 2). In other words, the effects of dissatisfaction depend on the extent to which individuals consider themselves influential and vice versa. For example, if a citizen believes herself or himself to be uninfluential (influence is zero), then discontent will not have an effect on participation.

The hypothesis of the joint effect of dissatisfaction and our influence measures (perceived political influence, expected effectiveness of collective protests, and acceptance of the unity principle) is only partially confirmed. In regard to participation in general protests before October 9, we found that the effects of political and social dissatisfaction depend on personal political influence and the expected effectiveness of collective protests. The analyses show that the effect of social dissatisfaction is relatively low in comparison to political dissatisfaction. Furthermore, among the influence measures, the effect of perceived personal influence is relatively strong. In other words, participation in general protests was due in particular to political dissatisfaction and perceived personal political influence.

For participation in demonstrations, we found that only political dissatisfaction and not social dissatisfaction had an effect. And, as with the general protests, the effect of political dissatisfaction depends on personal political influence. All other influence measures are irrelevant. Compared to participation in general protests, the effect of personal influence had a particularly strong effect.[5]

---

5. For the statistically informed reader: We tested the hypotheses mentioned in the following manner. We claimed that the variables "dissatisfaction," "personal influence by participation in general protests/demonstrations," "perceived effectiveness of collective protests" and "acceptance of the unity principle" have a multiplicative effect on "participation in general protests" and "participation in demonstrations." Dissatisfaction was constructed by adding political and social dissatisfaction and then dividing the sum by two. Thus, two equations result, with participation in general protests and participation in the demonstrations as dependent variables and a complex interaction term (the compound dissatisfaction scale multiplied with each influence measure) as independent variable in each equation.

Such equations can best be evaluated by taking the logarithm of all dependent and independent variables and including the independent logged variables additively in the regression equations with logged dependent variables (for details, see Finkel, Muller, and Opp 1989). This procedure results in two models in which the logged independent variables are additive terms of the regression equations. If we refer to "effects" of the mentioned independent variables in the text, this means that the coefficients of the corresponding logged scales in the regression analyses proved statistically significant on the .01 level.

The analyses show that the adjusted explained variance for general protests (dependent variable, logged) and political/social dissatisfaction (independent variable, logged) is .12. When the scales personal influence, belief in the unity principle, and effectiveness of collective protests are included in the analyses, the explained variance increases to .19. In this equation only dissatisfaction (beta = .29), personal influence (beta = .22), and effectiveness of collective protests (beta = .12) are statistically significant on the 0.01 level. Performing the same analyses using this time only *political* disstisfaction instead of the compound measure decreases the explained variance only by .02.

These findings are of immense importance in understanding the revolution in the GDR. Dissatisfaction, especially political dissatisfaction, influenced the protests of the citizens. Yet if the GDR citizens had believed that political action was completely ineffective, the protests would have probably never occurred. Our findings help explain why dissatisfaction didn't give rise to protests for so many years. It was the external political changes in Eastern Europe and the Soviet Union that led citizens to see a chance for change by personal participation in protest actions.

Summary

We began by addressing the effects of political, economic, and social dissatisfaction on the protests in the German Democratic Republic. We found that (1) up to October 9, political dissatisfaction in particular and social dissatisfaction to some extent caused participation in general protests, whereas economic dissatisfaction played no role; (2) only political dissatisfaction was a cause for participation in demonstrations. Thus, economic dissatisfaction had an effect neither on participation in general protests nor on participation in demonstrations.

Our survey further shows that citizens considered themselves to be politically influential, considered joint protest to be highly effective, and accepted the unity principle. Furthermore, perceived political influence increased because of the emigration wave and the liberalization in Eastern Europe. The emigration wave in particular increased citizens" personal perceived influence.

How do the aforementioned factors affect participation in general protests and demonstrations? Our main hypothesis in this chapter was that the effect of dissatisfaction depends on personal political influence, perceived effectiveness of collective protests, and acceptance of the unity principle. This hypothesis could be confirmed only partially. The following holds true for general protests as well as for demonstrations: Political dissatisfaction and perceived personal influence to effect changes through participation determined participation decisively. It is important to note that dissatisfaction alone did not lead to protest against the SED regime. Rather, the effect of dissatisfaction depended on the degree to which citizens believed they could

---

The explained variance for demonstrations is .05, including only political and social dissatisfaction. When we include the other influence measures, the explained variance increases to .17. In this equation only dissatisfaction (beta = .12) and personal influence (beta = .36) are statistically significant (.01 level). Performing the same analyses using this time only *political* dissatisfaction instead of the compound measure doesn't change the explained variance. The standardized regression coefficient for political dissatisfaction even increases by .02, compared to the compound measure.

achieve their political goals by means of political action. Thus, if GDR citizens had believed that their protests would not have brought about reforms, a high level of dissatisfaction would not have led to protest. This was the situation that existed in the GDR for so many years. Only the changes in Eastern Europe and the emigration wave caused citizens to believe that reforms could be achieved by means of personal participation. This was the decisive factor for the citizens' political action.

CHAPTER 5

Moral Incentives and Political Protest

Karl-Dieter Opp

Sociologists say that a norm is "internalized" when obeying the norm becomes a motivation for an action (see chapter 2). Nonadherence to internalized norms is associated with costs: a person has a bad conscience, is ashamed, or the like. The more an individual has internalized a norm, the greater the costs of acting against it. Following norms is associated with benefits (in the sense of our general explanatory model): one has a good conscience, has done one's duty, and this provides feelings of joy and satisfaction.

Yet the fact that breaking norms is associated with costs does not mean that norms are always followed. We disregard quite a number of norms daily—that is, we often take actions that we believe are actually morally false. However, if a specific action does not collide with a given norm, this action would be carried out even more frequently.

In regard to the explanation of the protests, it is important to know whether protest norms existed in the German Democratic Republic and, if so, in which situations the citizens considered them applicable. We also ask in this chapter what effects protest norms had on general protests and participation in demonstrations.

The Obligation to Participate:
Conversations with Citizens of Leipzig

In our qualitative interviews with 19 citizens of Leipzig, we inquired about the role moral considerations played in their political action. Christian Scheibler responded when asked why he became politically active:

> For years I've felt compelled to change things. Yet there was never an opportunity to motivate others in the same direction.

Thus, he felt a moral obligation to take action against the regime. In the face of mass exodus and the liberalization, especially in the Soviet Union, Bernd-Lutz Lange commented:

My inner conviction was: We can't give in now. We're at the point where our demands can be fulfilled, where we can finally have democracy. All we really wanted was to build a democratic system after 57 years of dictatorship.

Petra Lux told us:

A friend of mine said to me, "What will you do when your children ask in 10 years why you didn't do anything? You can't say, you felt paralyzed . . ." and so I got up and did something. An acquaintance of mine had the address of a contact person of the Neues Forum here in Leipzig . . .

Christian Müller felt similarly: "Well, I didn't just hang around so that no one could accuse me of not doing anything, but also to not reproach myself."

Yet it would nevertheless be false to assume that *all* GDR citizens who took action against the SED regime acted out of moral obligation. When asked whether he felt morally obligated to take part in the demonstrations prior to October 9, Detlef Pollack responded:

No, I didn't. I didn't think that I had to participate. I talked with some who said the same. I could have stayed at home. I was actually just curious because I thought it was great that people came together and said, "We're not going to take this lying down anymore . . ."

Peter Kind commented similarly:

I was just curious to see how the police would react and how I would react. It was more curiosity and interest in being there if something important happened.

Thus, our conversations with citizens of Leipzig indicate that sometimes moral obligations played a role in the activity against the SED regime. They further suggest that the extent to which citizens internalized protest norms and the situation in which they saw an obligation to participate differed. Otherwise some respondents would not only have felt an obligation to act in 1989 and not before.

When Is There a Duty to Become Politically Active?

Our conversations with Leipzig citizens leave important questions unanswered, for example: How many citizens were prompted to participate in protests on account of moral considerations? Under what conditions do citizens feel an obligation to protest? Which moral norms have which effects on protest participation? We will turn to our survey to answer these questions.

Is There a Duty to Protest If One Is Politically Dissatisfied?

A citizen may consider it his or her obligation to participate in protests if he or she is highly dissatisfied. We asked the respondents to indicate their level of agreement (five categories, from 1 to 5) to the following statement:

> If a citizen is very dissatisfied with the government's policies, he/she should do something against it, such as demonstrate.

As figure 1 shows, the average agreement with this statement was at a level of 3.9.

We asked respondents if they felt an obligation to become politically active in order to contribute to changes in the GDR in the face of the emigration wave and the liberalization in Eastern Europe. The means (see fig. 1) were also high: 3.3 and 3.2, respectively (on a scale from 1 to 5).

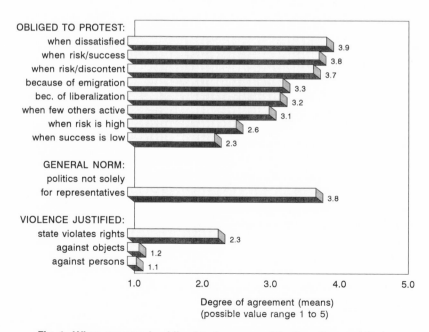

Fig. 1. When are people obliged to become politically active, and is violence justified?

Because the emigration wave intensified the situation of the citizens who stayed and the liberalization in Eastern Europe made the political situation in the GDR even more unbearable, we interpret the strong support for the related statements as suggesting that moral obligations to protest existed especially in situations of high dissatisfaction. However, the emigration wave also led respondents to view themselves as more influential. The statements might therefore measure protest norms in the face of dissatisfaction as well as the norm to protest if one's own or collective protest is considered to be effective.

We can therefore conclude that *the high level of dissatisfaction in the GDR had a double effect*. First, there is a direct effect of dissatisfaction in conjunction with the high level of perceived political influence on protest. Second, there is an indirect effect as the high dissatisfaction in 1989 created a situation in which protest norms became effective.

Is There a Duty to Protest Even If One Believes That It Won't Change Anything?

There were more respondents who disagreed with this statement than agreed. The mean value is 2.27, and thus lower than the middle value of 3.

Is There a Duty to Protest Even If One Has to Take High Risks?

Respondents were asked if one should take part in a political activity even if one could be put in jail for it. Most of the respondents answered no. The mean value was again below 3 (2.6) as we see in figure 1.

Yet there are conditions under which one must take high risks into account, such as in the case of one being "convinced that demonstrations contribute to change." The mean value of this statement (3.8) is relatively high. High risks, or as we put it in our question, "personal disadvantages," must also be taken into account if citizens are highly dissatisfied. The mean value of this statement is also high (3.7).

A protest norm thus exists despite high risks or personal disadvantages if dissatisfaction is high or if a protest is expected to be successful. *Increasing dissatisfaction and increasing political influence therefore led indirectly to growing protests in that they "blunted" the weapons of the Stasi and the police.*

Is There a Duty to Protest Even If There Are Not Enough Others Willing to Join In?

Approximately half the respondents answered no and half yes. The mean value is 3.1.

Should Politics Be Left to the Elected Representatives?

The results up to this point show that GDR citizens considered political action an obligation under a number of circumstances. We can expect accordingly that the large majority of the citizens do not generally reject protest and do not believe that the elected representatives should be the only ones for making political decisions. The mean value referring to the statement that politics should not simply "be left to the elected representatives" was 3.8. The high value is probably due to the fact that the "elected representatives" were not freely elected but, rather, selected by SED cadre politics. The same item was presented to 714 respondents in a representative survey in West Germany conducted in late 1987 and early 1988. The mean value in that study was 3.1.[1]

Is Violence Morally Justifiable?

We have not yet specified the *type* of political action that respondents believe should be taken. We presented three statements specifically on the subject of violence:

> Violence against objects (such as setting a car on fire) can be morally justified; violence against persons can be morally justified; if a government suppresses civil rights, the use of violence by citizens can be justified.[2]

Figure 1 shows that almost all respondents rejected the first two statements: The means are only 1.2 and 1.1. Support for the third statement was greater but also relatively low at 2.3, and thus clearly below our scale's middle value of 3.

These results illustrate that norms are often worded in general terms although their applicability is restricted to certain circumstances. This is the case in regard to the general rejection of violence against objects and persons. Respondents spontaneously rejected the general statements concerning violence against objects and persons. Then a particular situation is specified: a government suppresses civil rights by use of force. In this case, violence is viewed to be justifiable to a greater extent.

It is interesting to make a comparison with the Federal Republic of Germany. The study already mentioned (see note 1) also included the statements referring to violence against objects and persons. The mean value for the item regarding violence against objects in the FRG was 1.8 (GDR: 1.2)

---

1. The research was financed by the Volkswagen foundation. Finkel, Muller, and Opp 1989 and Opp 1992a provide details on this study.

2. For the exact wording of the statements, see the appendix.

and the mean value for the statement referring to violence against persons was 1.4 (GDR: 1.1). Thus, West Germans view violence against persons and objects at political protests as more morally justified than do former East Germans.

The Moral Causes of the Revolution

We first distinguish between different kinds of norms. If a respondent believes that one should take action if one is very dissatisfied with government policies (refer to the first statement addressed to the respondents in the previous section) he or she has a *discontent orientation*. If expected success of a collective protest is not a condition under which one must become active, we speak of *success neutrality*.

If a respondent believes that one should take part in protests despite any risks; that a risk should be accepted if discontent is high; or that a risk should be accepted if one's action could make a difference, we will say that a person has a *risk orientation*. In other words, participating in protest actions is regarded as a duty even if one perceives high risks.

We found that a minority of our respondents believed violence to be justified and thus displayed a certain amount of *violence orientation*. The more a person believes that violence against people and objects in the case of governmental suppression is justified, the greater that person's violence orientation. If respondents think that politics should not be left only to elected people's representatives, we say that there is a *general protest orientation*. Finally, if people feel obliged to protest due to the emigration wave and the liberalization in Eastern Europe, then they have a *protest orientation due to external events* (as other countries played a role in bringing about these events).[3]

We will now examine the extent to which these various types of norms (or orientations, including success neutrality) influenced the participation in protests. Regarding *participation in general protests*, we found that each type of orientation had a statistically significant effect. Discontent orientation and general protest orientation had the strongest effects.[4]

---

3. For the statistically informed reader: In order to measure those forms of orientation, for each respondent the values of the respective items were added and then divided by the number of items. The types of orientation we distinguished are thus scales that in part include several items. For details, see the appendix.

4. For the statistically informed reader: We ran a regression analysis with "participation in general protests" as dependent and the mentioned types of orientation as independent variables. The adjusted explained variance was .11. The standardized regression coefficients are: general protest orientation .12, discontent orientation .18, violence orientation .08, success neutrality .07, protest orientation due to external events .09, risk orientation .09. The coefficients are

Participation in demonstrations was also influenced by protest norms. Discontent orientation, as with general protests, had an impact, and in addition risk orientation.[5]

A further finding is significant. A positive attitude toward the use of violence did not correlate with political participation. An explanation of this finding will be provided in the next chapter.

Let us look at the various protest norms once again. Dissatisfaction with political decisions is certainly a necessary prerequisite for the application of a protest norm. One will usually not protest against political decisions if one is satisfied with them. The other protest norms describe other conditions by which protest is seen as an obligation. For those protest orientations, our findings confirm the following proposition:

The more *extensive* the protest norms citizens accept, the greater the likelihood of protest.

By the *extent of protest norms*, we mean the number of conditions under which a norm is considered applicable. If, for example, people believe that it is not important that others participate, that risks should not be considered, and that the success of a political action is not important for the existence of a duty to protest, then the extent of protest norms is relatively large—that is, there are many situations in which protest is considered an obligation. On the other hand, for those who feel that a duty to participate only exists if the risks are low and if there is a chance for success the extent of protest norms is low.[6]

Dissatisfaction, Morals, and the Free-Rider Problem

The unity principle (chapter 2) claims that every person is important for the success of a group. Often a moral claim is accepted: If a person *can* contribute to the success of a group by protesting, then this person *should* do so. Such an obligation is often accepted only under the condition that one is dissatisfied.

---

statistically significant at the .01 level, except the coefficient for success neutrality that is significant at the .05 level.

5. For the statistically informed reader: We ran a regression analysis with "participation in demonstrations" as dependent and the mentioned norm variables as independent variables. The adjusted explained variance was .07. The standardized regression coefficients were: general protest orientation .05, discontent orientation .15, violence orientation .05, success neutrality −.02, protest orientation due to external events .09, risk orientation .14. The coefficients for general protest orientation, violence orientation, and success neutrality were not statistically significant.

6. For the statistically informed reader: The correlation of the protest norms scale—see the appendix—with participation in general protests is .30, with participation in demonstrations .24. Both coefficients are significant at the .01 level.

One must additionally believe in the success of the group. These hypotheses were well confirmed for participation in general protests, yet only weakly for participation in demonstrations.[7] Thus we see again that moral beliefs were a cause of the protests in the GDR before the ninth of October.

Summary

In this chapter we first dealt with the question regarding the extent to which there were protest norms in the GDR prior to October 9. Our survey indicates that the following protest norms existed in the GDR prior to October 9:

If one is dissatisfied with a government's policies, one should engage in political action.

One should protest only if one believes one will make a difference.

One need not protest if the accompanying risks are high.

If one believes that one can achieve something by means of protest, one should take the risks and act.

If dissatisfaction is high, one should take action despite personal disadvantages.

There is no clear norm that says one should take action only if others are willing to join in.

Politics is not solely a subject for elected people's representatives.

There is no justification for political violence.

In regard to the participation in general protests, we found that all mentioned forms of protest norms have a statistically significant effect. The acceptance of a general protest norm ("Politics is not solely a subject for elected people's representatives!") and a high discontent orientation ("One should take action if one is dissatisfied with government policies!") had particularly strong effects on participation in general protests. As in the case of the general protests, discontent orientation had an impact on participation in demonstrations. Those respondents with a high risk orientation also took part in the demonstrations rather frequently. Another finding is important in this regard: those who had a positive attitude toward violence were not particularly active.

Our findings lead us to an important conclusion on the effects of political

---

7. For the statistically informed reader: In order to test these hypotheses, we proceeded in the following manner: We used "discontent orientation" as an indicator for "duty." An almost identical indicator was used in Finkel, Muller, and Opp 1989. The hypothesis was tested by taking the logarithm of the duty variable and including it in the equations mentioned in note 5 of chapter 4. In the regression equation for general protests, the standardized regression coefficient was .12, and in the equation for participation in the demonstrations, it was .06. The first coefficient is significant on the .01 level, and the second is just under the .05 level of significance ($t = 1,894$).

dissatisfaction. We noted earlier that dissatisfaction had a direct effect on protest, given that individuals regarded themselves as influential. We saw in this chapter that dissatisfaction also had an *indirect* effect on protest: participation in protests was viewed as obligation due to the high level of dissatisfaction in the GDR. The relatively high perceived political influence before October 9 also had such an effect: There is a norm that says dissatisfied citizens should take action if there is a high chance for success of protest. Finally, high dissatisfaction partially neutralized the expected governmental repression: a norm obtained saying that personal disadvantages should be accepted if one is highly dissatisfied and if the expectation of success is high. Thus, our findings show that the dissatisfaction in the GDR had multiple effects on participation in general protests and demonstrations.

CHAPTER 6

Why Were the Protests Peaceful?

Peter Voss

The participants in the East German revolution did not use violence—neither against objects nor against persons—the exceptions being the confrontations on October 4 and 5, 1989, surrounding the trains filled with the Prague refugees in Dresden, and with the police on October 7 and 8, 1989, in Leipzig and Berlin. We consider these events to have occurred prior to the revolution that began on October 9.

The storming of the notorious Stasi headquarters in Berlin's Norman-nenstraße in January 1990 was also no spontaneous outburst of "the people's outrage," as portrayed in the media. It is now well known that the forces stormed their own headquarters to hide dangerous reports about politicians (see the *Leipziger Volkszeitung,* August 5, 1991, p. 2; *Junge Welt,* February 3, 1992, p. 10).

Nonviolence is currently viewed as *the* characteristic of the revolution "made in GDR." Yet such a peaceful proceeding had not been foreseen. The Stalinist-style communist systems never hesitated to crush citizens' revolts. Remember June 17, 1953, in the GDR; the events in Hungary in 1956; the crushing of the Prague Spring in 1968; the events in China and Romania in 1989; and the brutal backlash of Serbian communists against the 1990s independence movements in former Yugoslavia. The use of violence against a country's own people was always justified by the false claim that the class enemy started the counterrevolution.

What was behind the nonviolent nature of the mass protests in the GDR? Let us begin by looking at some incomplete explanations. We will then—on the basis of our explanatory model—develop a number of hypotheses on the causes of nonviolence and, inasmuch as possible, test them with our survey data.

The question regarding the causes of the nonviolent character of the revolution will be divided into two partial questions: (1) Why did the citizens remain nonviolent? and (2) Why didn't the regime use violence? We will deal with question 2 in detail in chapter 11.

Eyewitness Opinions on the Causes of Nonviolence

Johannes Richter, pastor in the Thomas Church in Leipzig, says that "Saxon mentality" is responsible for the peaceful nature of the protests (1989, 184):

> One does his duty as a citizen, one expresses oneself more calmly. We just don't act aggressively and that is why this moderate form of demonstration developed, which perhaps can be considered a Saxon trademark, as a result of our mentality.

Hans-Joachim Maaz, medical doctor and psychotherapist, sees the situation similarly (1990). He attributes the nonviolence to an "aggressive inhibition," an inability of GDR citizens to deal with aggressive feelings since their childhood. This "inhibited character" is a grave character deformation of most GDR citizens due to a repressive method of upbringing. Maaz sees the highly praised nonviolence as a mere "revolt of the neurosis": "I do not see the celebrated 'non-violence' as the result of mature political action but rather mainly as an expression of our neurotic inhibitions" (168).

One argument against these kinds of "explanations" is that it is hardly possible to test them empirically. How can we determine whether or not GDR citizens had an "aggressive inhibition" or if a "revolt of neurosis" took place? We have a different explanation for the nonviolence and will offer data to support it.

Many people believe the reasons for the success of nonviolence lay with those who were in power. The SED leadership could no longer rely on the Breshnev doctrine of limited sovereignty for the socialist countries and the military support from the Soviet Union that once accompanied it. Gorbachev had announced distinctly to all: "Life punishes those who come late!" There were furthermore high dissatisfaction and reform efforts, even within the SED itself, which had to be considered. Rolf Reißig (1991, 34) writes in his analysis of the confrontations within the SED:

> Regardless of how one judges the strength and influence of the reform wing and the minor opposition within it—and a truly detailed analysis of this is only in the beginning stages . . . : Without this movement in the SED the upheaval—that was not initiated by this wing—would not have been so peaceful, without great resistance from the SED and the power and security apparati it controlled.

This analysis concurs with that of the designer of the unification treaty, Wolfgang Schäuble, who was certainly not an adherent of the SED. He even views the reform efforts within the SED as a "revolution!" (Schäuble 1991, 15 ff.)

This clearly stands in opposition to those who accuse the SED of having consciously risked bloodshed in suppressing the people's uprising and who were only stopped by Soviet military officers. In truth, the Soviet military had stopped having any influence on internal SED decision making long before (see Schabowski 1990, 80).

Nonviolence as an Individual Decision

The rational actor model that we use in this book implies that a citizen's decision to choose violent or nonviolent forms of protest depends on the resulting advantages and disadvantages. Figure 1 summarizes those advantages or disadvantages that we believe influenced the individual decisions of the demonstrators against the use of violence. Figure 1 further shows the extent to which these factors were present. In what follows, we will first explain the various components in figure 1 and then examine the extent to which these hypotheses are confirmed by our data.

Justifications of Violence

In chapter 5 we argued that internalized norms increase the costs of behavior that deviates from these norms. This argument implies that if citizens view only nonviolent forms of protest as morally justified or acceptable, then one can expect nonviolent activity to a greater extent than if violence were ac-

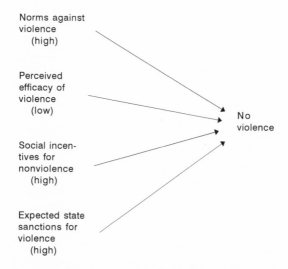

Fig. 1. Determinants of individuals' decision against violence

cepted as a legitimate form of political action. Our survey results show, as pointed out in chapter 5, that GDR citizens rejected violence to a high degree. However, the acceptance of violence norms does not mean that violence is in fact used as a means to realize political demands. Even those who accepted violence to a relatively high degree did not participate in violent actions. The extent to which violence is chosen depends on other factors that are discussed in the following sections.

Efficacy of Violence

Individual decisions for or against violent protest activities also depend on the extent to which people believe that their own activity and that of the group will be successful if they carry out violent activities. Thus, the *perceived efficacy of violence* is important. In our questionnaire we ascertained the extent to which respondents believed violence to be an effective means to achieving their goals. We asked respondents to appraise their "personal influence to change the political and economic situation in the GDR, regardless of actual participation in this action," for various actions. One of the actions was "violent activities, e.g. during demonstrations." The overwhelming majority did not believe that they could change anything by using violent activities: 73 percent answered "very unlikely," 21 percent "unlikely." Thus 94 percent believed that they couldn't change matters by using violence. The mean value for this item is 1.4 on a scale from 1 to 4.

In this case, rejection of justifications for violence and the low perceived efficacy of violence correspond. Yet this is not necessarily always the case. For instance, if violence is morally accepted as a means of achieving political goals, it might not be put to use if its perceived efficacy is low.

Social Incentives for Nonviolence

Various research findings on protest behavior indicate that an individual's actions depend to a large degree on incentives from the social environment. These social incentives may be positive or negative (chapters 2 and 4). As the GDR population overwhelmingly rejected the use of violence during the mass protests, the few supporters of violence had to reckon with negative sanctions from their social environment. Strong social incentives for nonviolence were indeed effective both before and during the demonstrations. During the prayers for peace in churches, calls were made for nonviolence, and representatives of the citizens' movement wore sashes with the logo "No Violence." Even "enemies" (especially members of the Stasi) were protected from possible attacks by courageous demonstrators who created a cordon sanitaire between the demonstrators and the representatives of the state.

In the qualitative interviews, we asked about the reasons for non-violence. The respondents always mentioned the importance of social incentives for nonviolence. Some respondents described the applied techniques in detail. Theologist Matthias Petzoldt told us:

One must assume that the church contributed a great deal to the non-violent nature of the events. We thought that things would get critical after the end of the celebrations on October 7. We were terribly afraid of a Chinese solution. Then during the prayers for peace in all of the four churches, flyers were distributed, essentially saying: *nonviolence!* This was for both the citizens expected to join the demonstration as well the police and security forces. And I saw how this led to an enormous discipline among the demonstrators, despite the seriousness of the situation. I experienced firsthand that some of the demonstrators were somewhat intoxicated; these people are normally attracted to mass gatherings. When a person became rowdy she or he was quieted by the crowd. This is just an example which shows how people were very careful to keep things peaceful.

Another interviewee, Pastor Harald Wagner, told us how clear instructions were announced in the churches for the behavior at demonstrations. The demonstrators should get to know each other, ask the name of the next person, grasp hands, and look for eye contact—even with the "enemy." Their gestures and facial expressions should express confidence, not fear, but without being provoking. In case the police line moved in, demonstrators were instructed not to resist but, rather, to sit down and hold onto each other.

Peter Zimmermann emphasized the calming effect of the appeal of the group in which conductor Kurt Masur was a member. The call urging people to keep calm was repeatedly broadcast in the streets on October 9, 1989, at 6 P.M. over Leipzig City Radio.

Jochen Läßig of the Neues Forum pointed out another effect of social incentives for nonviolence. The church and the various opposition groups naturally could not reach hundreds of thousands of people with their message of nonviolence. Thus, there must have been a *spontaneous nonviolence* in the masses. Läßig said: "This is surely due to the character of the GDR population. There was an incredible discipline present. If someone wanted to become violent, she or he was talked to or put back in the second row."

We thus see that social incentives against violence came from political entrepreneurs. They expressed their rejection of violence without exception. Political entrepreneurs in a narrow sense were mainly the representatives of the various opposition groups and civil movements. Most of them became active in the process of the revolution and therefore had not had any influence in the beginning phase of the protests as the question of violence was raised. Exceptions are church groups, such as the Initiative für Frieden und Menschenrechte [Initiative for peace and human rights] and the Neues Forum. The representatives of these groups were convinced that nonviolence was the most effective strategy to achieve their political goals. They wanted to prevent the criminalization of the protests by the GDR government at any cost, and for that purpose nonviolence was an absolute necessity.

The first, at that time illegal, announcement by the Neues Forum on October 4, 1989, was short and precise (Neues Forum 1990, 61):

> The Neues Forum calls urgently on all those who sympathize with it: Violence is not a means of political dispute! Do not let yourselves be provoked! We have nothing to do with right-wing radical and anti-communist tendencies! We want a sensible dialogue, serious thoughts about our future, no hazardous actions. In face of the current critical situation, we call on all people in the GDR to act and think responsibly and in solidarity.

Later, when things were still uncertain despite the demonstration in Leipzig on October 9, the Neues Forum again appealed for nonviolence. On October 16, a call was passed on to the state press agency ADN (Allgemeiner Deutscher Nachrichtendienst) that read: "We again make the urgent appeal to all parties to use nonviolence. We also demand that the demonstrators and those with different opinions not be termed criminals as this provokes violence" (Neues Forum 1990). The Neues Forum was given a voice in a GDR newspaper for the first time when this call was repeated in the *Union* on October 17, 1989.

Expected Repression for Violence

It is plausible that people also considered possible state reactions when deciding for or against the use of violence. If it is expected that violence is in turn answered by massive counterviolence, then norms to refrain from the use of violence will spread more easily, the perceived influence by violence will diminish, social incentives for nonviolence will rise, and political entrepreneurs will support nonviolence in order to not endanger their objectives. This is what happened in the fall of 1989.

The costs of being a victim of violent state action would have been very high. They included not only lawsuits and arrests, but also a threat to people's health and life. The events in Dresden before October 7 as well as in Leipzig and Berlin surrounding the celebrations of the 40th anniversary, when the security forces took to violent action, had made clear what the risks were.

This goes for the other side as well, because the police, the combat groups, and the state security people were not prepared to take massive action against their own people.

Nonviolence as an Interplay between Citizens and the Regime

The security forces did not use violence on October 9 nor after this date. We consider this an important condition for the revolution to remain nonviolent in the decisive phase. One can only speculate what would have happened if brutal police actions would have occurred on, for instance, October 9. Would the previously mentioned incentives for nonviolence have been strong enough to prevent bloodshed or a civil war? Wouldn't many demonstrators have lost control if the security forces had started using physical force? We know from reports that there were people among the demonstrators who were willing to act violently and who were stopped by others. This fact suggests that once security forces' violence would have broken out, there would have been violence on the side of the demonstrators as well. We thus believe that one reason for the nonviolent nature of the revolution was the nonviolent behavior of the regime.

Summary

Nonviolence of both the demonstrators and the regime was the distinctive feature of the GDR revolution. Each side had its own reasons for refraining from violence. Norms of nonviolence were widespread among the population, and there also existed strong social incentives for acting nonviolently. The majority of the citizens we interviewed did not believe that violent actions could have effected any political or economic changes in the GDR (94 percent). On the contrary, people expected severe negative state reactions in case of violent behavior, which created an additional incentive to refrain from violent action. We believe that although one side refrained from violence, this was not sufficient in preventing bloodshed. The conditions in autumn 1989 were favorable because the majority of the protesters didn't want violence and the rulers were no longer in the position to use it. Had the regime resorted to violence, the demonstrators probably would have done the same.

CHAPTER 7

The Social Causes of the Revolution

Karl-Dieter Opp and Christiane Gern

Various empirical studies have shown that social factors play an important role in the emergence of protests.[1] These social factors include membership in social groups (such as parties, labor unions, and leisure groups), but also the citizens' immediate social environment (including friends, acquaintances, family members, and fellow employees). In general, any relations between citizens are termed *social networks*. In this chapter we will investigate the role that social groups and the close social environment played in the emergence of the GDR revolution.

We would like to emphasize that we make no moral judgment about opposition group activities. Rather, our goal is a factual analysis. If it turns out that the opposition groups had no significant influence on the emergence of the revolution, this does not question the personal courage of these groups' members, who, in spite of extensive personal risks, strove for a change in the GDR.

The Role of Social Groups

We begin by determining the extent to which societal groups could have influenced the revolution in the GDR and proceed by examining the extent to which our hypotheses are confirmed by our data.

How Could the Groups Have Influenced the Revolution?

The social groups in the GDR were faced with a different situation than the groups in the FRG. In the GDR there was no right to join or form any kind of

---

1. See Klandermans 1984; Mitchell 1979; Muller and Opp 1986; Opp 1986, 1989; Opp et al. 1984; Opp and Roehl 1990a; Tillock and Morrison 1979; Useem 1980; Walsh and Warland 1983. The role of social groups in the development of protests and social movements is particularly emphasized by the resource mobilization perspective. See, for example, Gamson 1975; Jenkins 1983; McAdam 1982; McCarthy and Zald 1977; Oberschall 1973; Piven and Cloward 1991.

association that was not criminal. All associations in the GDR were supervised by the SED. Furthermore, the SED leadership created a number of mass organizations such as the Free Federation of German Trade Unions, the Free German Youth, the German Gymnastic and Sports Union, the German-Soviet Friendship Society, and so forth. Block parties (political parties other than the SED, which were approved by the SED and thus supported SED policies) and mass organizations were joined in a National Front. These organizations were an instrument through which the SED carried out its policies.

Church-based opposition groups and, in particular since August 1989, nonchurch opposition groups were formed. The church groups included in particular peace and human rights groups. Nonchurch groups include the Neues Forum, Demokratie Jetzt [Democracy now], the Initiative für Frieden und Menschenrechte, Demokratischer Aufbruch [Democratic awakening], and the SDP (Social Democratic Party), which was founded in October 1989.[2]

Of course, there were also basically nonpolitical groups, such as sports groups. They mostly existed as sections of the DTSB (Deutscher Turn- und Sportbund [German gymnastics and sports federation]) or as workplace-based sports groups.

What influence could these groups have had on the development of the revolution? In regard to opposition groups, our theoretical model (see chapter 2) suggests that actions of opposition groups could have changed either the incentives to participate or the reactions of the regime. Therefore, we focus on three questions:

Did the opposition groups change the incentives for protest?
Did the opposition groups coordinate the protests?
Did the opposition groups bring the regime to make concessions?

In what follows we will first discuss some hypotheses to answer these questions. To begin with the last question, the following proposition might hold true:

Hypothesis 1: The opposition groups could have caused the SED regime to introduce reforms.

First, the groups or members thereof could have negotiated with the regime. Second, it is possible that the regime or even the groups rejected negotiations but that the regime was afraid that the groups would mobilize

---

    2. On the role of social groups in the GDR revolution see in particular Grabner, Heinze, and Pollack 1990; Hanisch et al. 1990; Müller-Enbergs, Schulz, and Wielgohs 1991; Musiolek and Wuttke 1991; Opp and Gern 1993; Rein 1989; Pollack 1990.

large parts of the population. To prevent a loss of power as a result, the regime could have made concessions.

> *Hypothesis 2*: The activities of the opposition groups could have increased the incentives for protest.

For example, members of opposition groups could have distributed flyers or spoken to people directly in their workplace or in public. At this occasion, they could have appealed to moral obligations to protest. In this way, representatives of opposition groups could have increased the incentives directly to protest through mobilization attempts. Let us call this hypothesis the *mobilization hypothesis*. The influence of groups on the GDR revolution will be relatively large if the groups were able to increase the incentives for protest for many citizens.

Second, the opposition groups could have influenced the protests indirectly. Many GDR citizens were aware of the existence of opposition groups and the basic goals they supported. Information about these groups came from detailed reports by the Western media and was passed by word of mouth. The citizens could have sympathized and identified with the opposition groups. This would have led to additional incentives for protest. We call this hypothesis the *identification hypothesis*. The influence of opposition groups is considered relatively large if a large number of citizens identified with the groups.

The two hypotheses are not mutually exclusive because groups could have mobilized the citizens directly and citizens could have identified with the groups at the same time.

> *Hypothesis 3*: The opposition groups could have organized the protests.

We differentiated between four coordinating mechanisms of collective action (see chapter 2): the organization model, the micromobilization model, the threshold model, and the spontaneous cooperation model. If the opposition groups played a role in the coordination of the protests, either the organization or the micromobilization model must be valid.

> *Hypothesis 4*: The opposition groups could have increased their members' incentives to protest.

While the mobilization and identification hypotheses refer to citizens who were *not* members of opposition groups, hypothesis 4 refers to the group members. It is possible that high incentives for political action result from contacts with like-minded people in the groups themselves. If one is a member of an opposition group, one receives a high degree of recognition and prestige if one takes part in the political activities of the group, thus social control takes place. We call this hypothesis the *control hypothesis*.

We can expect members of opposition groups to become socialized over a period of time. In other words, the groups could have contributed to the development of the protests in the GDR by changing the attitudes and opinions of the members (such as the internalization of protest norms), resulting in a higher probability to participate. We call this the *socialization hypothesis*.

> *Hypothesis 5a*: All social groups could have promoted the emergence of the revolution.

At first glance, it seems completely implausible that the SED or other mass organizations contributed to the emergence of the revolution. However, group membership may have in general a positive effect on participation in protests because group members have contact with many others so that at least the opportunity exists to instigate other politically dissatisfied citizens to participate. If this reasoning holds true, the kind of group of which a person is a member would be irrelevant for participation in protests.

> *Hypothesis 5b*: Only the opposition groups could have promoted the emergence of the revolution.

We presume that especially in opposition groups, and not in other groups such as the SED, positive incentives for protest existed. We therefore expect that, in particular, members of opposition groups protested against the SED regime.

The Opposition Groups and the SED Regime

Is hypothesis 1 accurate? The groups were not in the position to force the SED regime to introduce reforms. There were no negotiations between the groups and the representatives of the regime. The existence of the groups also had no indirect effect on the decisions of the SED leadership. The groups were observed and suppressed by security forces, as were all other forms of opposition. Günter Schabowski, former member of the Politburo, described how the Politburo assessed the opposition groups (1990, 57):

> The security officials were the only ones who dealt with the opposition groups. We knew, of course, that they existed but the party members and leaders simply viewed them as peripheral political groupings, which affected the population but in our view not decisively. They bothered us but we did not perceive them as a threat to our existence.

The SED therefore did not view the opposition groups as negotiation partners nor consider their goals when they made political decisions.

To What Extent Did the Activities of the Opposition Groups Increase the Citizens' Incentives for Protest?

To examine the validity of the mobilization hypothesis, it is first important to know how many members each opposition group had. Each member could approach only a certain number of citizens directly. Opposition group membership was low prior to October 1989. Elvers and Findeis (1990), who surveyed 31 "former leading group representatives in Leipzig and Berlin" at the beginning of 1990, found that the average membership of a group prior to October 1989 was 15. Information from the former Ministry of State Security confirms this figure. A report from June 1, 1989, is entitled, "Aspects of current effectiveness of domestic enemy, opposition, and other negative forces in personal associations" (Mitter and Wolle 1990, 46–71). The report says that approximately 160 associations meeting the mentioned description existed in the GDR. The report then lists the groups and their membership. Membership ranged from 3 to 39. It is estimated that the "entire potential of these associations" including "peripheral forces which usually simply take part in activities but don't do much on their own initiative" (47) was approximately 2,500 people. Pollack (1990, 18) estimates GDR opposition group membership at 10,000 to 15,000. According to another estimate (Poppe 1990, 68), approximately 325 opposition groups existed in the GDR as of 1988. Whatever the estimates, only a minor portion of the GDR population belonged to an opposition group. The opportunity for direct contacts with the population was therefore rare simply on account of low group membership.

Even if membership had been greater, contacts with the population could not have taken place because public events critical of the regime were immediately terminated by police and Stasi units. Christian Müller, whom we interviewed, vividly describes the conditions under which the groups had to work:

These were people who could be contacted. Their addresses were known only to a few. I actually saw the addresses only in the Nikolai Church at the beginning of September. They were also known in other parishes and in peace group circles, but could not be made public. Statements could also only be made in the churches. Sometimes a statement was posted on the outside of the church, but it never stayed there for more than a few hours.

Detlef Pollack, who also participated in our qualitative interviews, gives another reason why the opposition groups did not come out in public:

> The organization which members wanted to build would have been crushed the very moment it tried to support this illegal protest movement. Members were interested in the legitimacy and legitimization of their own little opposition grouping, formally registering it and the like. They wanted to make changes within the boundaries of the constitution and were therefore actually not prepared to do what the masses did. But that is understandable. The masses were anonymous and they could have acted illegally because one could immediately retreat from the streets back into one's house. And I had the impression that most of them were willing to disband again immediately if they were threatened with the use of force.

The groups also had few material resources at their disposal: telephones, paper, copiers or printers, and so forth were difficult to come by. Furthermore, there were differing opinions within the groups about the forms of activity (see Grabner, Heinze, and Pollack 1990, 89, 100, 107). This might have led opposition group members not to take part in mobilization activities. Our data show that only 13 percent of the respondents who were members in opposition groups that encouraged protest took part in the planning of political activities.

Important opposition groups were founded or became active fairly late. The call to found the Neues Forum was first made on September 10, 1989. The Neues Forum opened its first office in Leipzig on October 18, 1989. The groups Demokratischer Aufbruch and Demokratie Jetzt were not founded until the beginning of October 1989. There was also almost no contact between the groups, which could have led to joint activities against the regime (see Grabner, Heinze, and Pollack 1990, 107–8).

Jochen Läßig describes the mobilization difficulties in one of our qualitative interviews:

> Even at the high point of the development in October '89, I was skeptical because I knew how strong our organization really was and I had also experienced people's willingness to really do something. The willingness was very low. People came to me and wanted to become members of the Neues Forum. But I could get very few of these people to really embark on political work. People came and signed up as members and were willing to take part in some evening activities, but nobody really wanted to take a personal risk by saying, "Yes, we will invest our energy. We'll forget our professions for a while and invest time in a new organization

for a new country and new politics." This willingness just wasn't there and so it was sad that it was just an "after hours" revolution.

The data show on the whole that opposition groups were only able to mobilize a minor portion of the population for protests. Thus, the mobilization hypothesis is hardly accurate.

How does the identification hypothesis correspond to the facts? It seems that the opposition groups in general were no reference groups for the population. Heinze and Pollack (1990, 85) describe this situation, although only in regard to the time prior to May 1989:

> Most of the GDR citizens looked on the groups which demanded social reforms as unrealistic dreamers and political chaotics who didn't count. Yet some people secretly admired them for their strong stance against the government.

It seems that the extent of identification with the opposition groups changed after the opening of the Austrian-Hungarian border and the increase in emigration in May 1989. Nevertheless, even at this time not too many details about the groups were known. Petra Lux, another interviewee, said: "Somehow the term *Neues Forum* kept coming up in the Western media but nobody really knew what it was."

Thus it seems that the groups neither could directly mobilize the population nor were reference groups that contributed to the development of protest simply by means of their existence.

Did the Opposition Groups Organize the Protests?

The organization model does not hold true for the demonstrations in the GDR prior to October 9, 1989. The announcement of the time and place of a demonstration alone would have been prevented by state institutions. According to the micromobilization model, the demonstrations could have come about by a form of snowball system. Yet this model does not describe the GDR protests, either. As we mentioned earlier, there was no group that initiated the demonstrations in the GDR.

Were Members of Social Groups More Active than Other Citizens?

While we have focused almost solely on the opposition groups so far, we will now address the role of membership in the SED and related groups as well (see also chapter 10).

*To Which Groups Did the Citizens Belong
prior to October 9?*
Figure 1 shows the percentage of respondents who were members of the most important groups. The number of members is printed directly behind the group's name. For example, 20.2 percent of the respondents were members of the SED (thus 79.8 percent were not SED members). Respondents could be members of a number of groups. The most widespread type of membership was in a sports group: just over one quarter of the respondents declared membership in such a group. One out of every five said he or she was a member of the SED before October 9, 1989. SED membership in the GDR totaled 2.3 million. The mass organizations were the FDGB labor union, the FDJ youth group, and the Kulturbund [Culture Federation]. As can be seen in figure 1, the FDGB dominated. Many organizations summarized under the "other" category were also related to the SED, such as the DBD (Demokratische Bauernpartei Deutschlands [Democratic farmers association of Germany]).

We can see clearly from figure 1 that only 5 percent of the respondents belonged to groups that we call opposition groups: the Neues Forum and church groups such as peace, environmental, or women groups. Membership

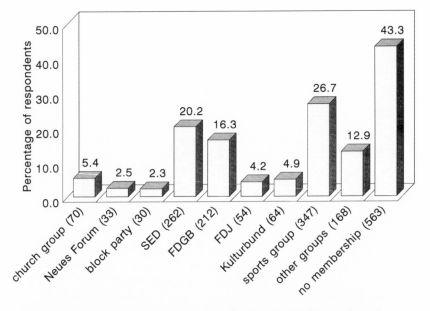

Fig. 1. Memberships in groups before October 9, 1989 (by number of members)

in opposition groups was not clearly defined because there was no such thing as formal membership. We presume that those who called themselves members attended the group meetings regularly.

A quarter of the respondents belonged to more than one group and 31 percent belonged to only one group, while 43 percent reported no membership. Thus, the opportunity to motivate other citizens for protest was present to a high degree.

To What Extent Did the Members of the Groups Participate in the Demonstrations?

Did political participation depend on the kind of group of which a person was a member? In order to answer this question, we first compared how many members of the various groups took part in the *demonstrations* up until October 9. We will first look at those respondents who were *solely members of one group*—that is, only in an opposition group, only in the SED, only in one of its related organizations (such as the FDGB or the FDJ), or only in a sports group. We will then look at those respondents who were members of *more than one group simultaneously*—that is, in the SED and a sports group, in an SED-related group and a sports group, or in any other combination. Other more specific membership combinations could not be analyzed because of low membership numbers.

Why do we differentiate between single and multiple memberships? In this way, we can better separate the effects of memberships in different groups on protest than if we did not consider that many people were members of more than one group. For example, if we ascertain participation in demonstrations by SED members, this group encompasses people belonging to other groups as well.

We expect members of the opposition groups to have taken part more often in demonstrations because protest-promoting incentives were probably present to a high degree within these groups. Vice versa, we assume that members of the SED and related groups demonstrated the least because we assume that within these organizations more negative incentives for protest were present. Those people who were members of sports groups would therefore have demonstrated to a "medium" extent because there were probably no protest-promoting incentives present in these groups. We also expect an average extent of participation for people with no membership at all.

Let us first look at those respondents who held one membership only, either in an opposition group, the SED, an SED-related group, or in a sports group. It indeed holds true—see figure 2—that the members of the SED or its related organizations took part less frequently in demonstrations than all other group members. It also holds true that the members of opposition groups took part in demonstrations more often than did members of the SED or its related

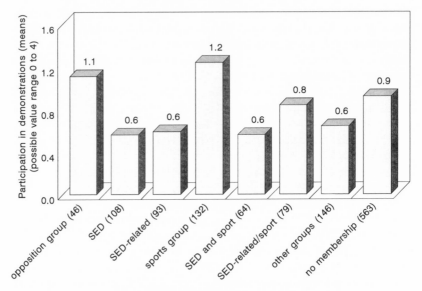

Type of group (exclusive memberships)

**Fig. 2. Group memberships and participation in demonstrations be-
fore October 9, 1989. Figures after group names refer to number of
members. Group membership includes only respondents who are excusively members of the respective groups.**

groups. Yet the hypothesis that the members of the opposition groups were the
most active could not be confirmed: surprisingly, members of sports groups on
the average took part more often in demonstrations than opposition group
members. We will address this point later. Additionally, the differences between nonorganized individuals (far right bar in fig. 2) and members of
opposition groups are small.

Let us turn now to those who were members of two groups simultaneously. Average participation of "members of sports groups and SED
members" (0.6) was the same as that of respondents who were members of
only the SED (0.6), but different from participation of respondents who were
members of only sports groups (1.2). The pattern is similar for members of
SED-related groups and sports groups, although not as strong. It appears that
in the SED, particularly strong negative incentives for protest were effective.
We will address this point later.

The differences between the average participation rates are comparatively small.[3] This is especially true when the average participation of group

---

3. For the statistically informed reader: The eta-coefficient for the means shown in figure
2 is .16, significant at the .01 level.

members and nonmembers is compared: the nonmembers' average participation is .9 (see fig. 2). The values for those who were members of the mentioned groups are only slightly different (see again fig. 2). This becomes even clearer if we investigate the relationship between frequency of demonstration and group membership using the statistical technique of regression analysis. When analyzing the effects of the various types of group membership on participation in demonstrations simultaneously, we found that membership in an opposition group had no effect on the frequency of demonstration, compared with being no member in any group. Furthermore, the membership in an SED-related and a sports group had no effect on the participation in demonstrations, either.[4] The effect of any group membership on participation in demonstrations is thus negligible.

To What Extent Did Group Members Take Part in the General Protests?

If we compare the differences between the groups in figure 3 with those in figure 2, we see that the differences between the various groups are larger for general protests than for demonstrations. Members of opposition groups were the most active, while members of the SED and individuals who were members of the SED and sports groups were the least active.[5]

The hypothesis that group membership in general, regardless of the type of group, promoted political action does not hold true for the GDR. This conclusion is also supported by the finding that people with many memberships protested to a similar degree as those with few memberships.[6]

Why Did Political Protest Differ among Members of Different Groups?

Our explanatory model leads us to expect that if the members of a particular group protest relatively often, they are faced with *protest-promoting incen-*

---

4. For the statistically informed reader: A regression analysis was run with "participation in demonstrations" as dependent variable and the group membership variables as dummies, using "nonmembership" as the reference category. The adjusted explained variance was only .02. The standardized regression coefficients ranged between $-.08$ and $+.08$. The regression coefficient for membership in an opposition group was .03.

5. For the statistically informed reader: The regression analysis with "participation in general protests" as dependent variable and the membership variables as dummies (whereby "nonmembership" is the reference category) shows better results than for "participation in demonstrations": the adjusted explained variance is .13. The four highest beta coefficients were obtained for membership in opposition groups (.23), in sports groups (.16), in the SED ($-.17$), and in the SED and sports groups ($-.12$).

6. For the statistically informed reader: The bivariate correlations between "number of group memberships" on the one hand and "participation in general protests" and in "participation in demonstrations" on the other hand were $-.05$ and $-.07$, respectively.

It could be suspected that "membership in opposition groups" is confounded with the

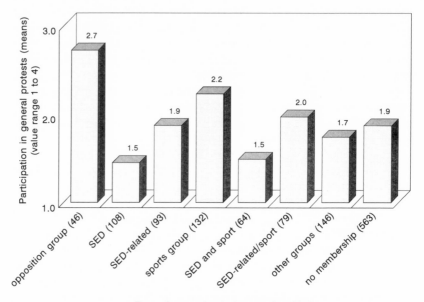

Type of group (exclusive memberships)

Fig. 3. Group memberships and participation in general protests before October 9, 1989. Figures after group names refer to number of members. Group membership includes only respondents who are excusively members of the respective groups.

tives for political activity to a high degree. To what extent is this expectation accurate?

We saw that members of sports and opposition groups were the most active. For these group members, the protest-promoting incentives in fact

---

dependent variable—that is, the first and last form of protest (work in an opposition group and participation in peace prayers; see the appendix) may measure similar phenomena as the mentioned dummy variable "membership in opposition groups." However, *membership* in an opposition group on the one hand and *work* in an opposition group or *participation* in peace prayers on the other are different, although a correlation is *empirically* plausible. Especially in the GDR, where the costs of membership were high, it is to be expected that members also work for the group. Yet this connection was not as extensive as we expected. The bivariate correlations between membership in opposition groups on the one hand and work or participation in peace prayers on the other were both .24.

How can this result be explained? Some of the church group members could not have considered themselves members of opposition groups and thus did not report having *worked* in an opposition group. The church groups were indeed very heterogeneous. For example, a woman who belonged to a women's church group would normally not consider herself a member of an opposition group. Only 17 percent of church group members responded that they had worked in an opposition group.

show the highest arithmetic means: their political dissatisfaction is very high and so is their perceived political influence; their reference persons (see also the section Personal Networks in the GDR in this chapter) value political activity positively; finally, those members feel a strong ethical obligation to take action. Another protest-promoting incentive is the extent to which protest is directly encouraged within a group. A total of 122 of our 1,300 respondents said they were encouraged by (at least) one group in which they were a member. As expected, it was in particular members of opposition groups who said they received support from their groups.

We saw that the members of the SED and those who were both members of the SED and sports groups were the least active. As expected, the protest-promoting incentives of the members of these groups were low, at least notably lower than those of the members of opposition and sports groups.[7]

The fact that sports group members took part in the protests rather frequently could also be explained in the following manner: nonmembership in the SED and the opportunity to meet, talk, and mutually support each other regularly in a sports group contributed to the relatively high participation in protests.

We noted that our data are compatible with the socialization and control hypotheses. However, a relationship between group membership and political participation is also consistent with another hypothesis. Let us assume that those who are politically dissatisfied and who view themselves as influential form an opposition group. Again, we would find that members would take action quite frequently. Yet this would not be due to the effect of group membership but, rather, to the recruiting of members—this explanation could be termed the *recruitment hypothesis*. Does the group form the attitudes of its members (socialization and control hypotheses) or do people with certain attitudes form groups (recruitment hypothesis)?

It appears plausible that only those people who had similar political ideas as a group's members joined that group. Certainly only those people who viewed the SED regime critically became members of the Neues Forum. On the other hand, contacts among the members furthered the development of positive incentives to protest and also influenced the political ideas of those members. However, we cannot determine the *extent* to which members changed their opinions during membership nor the extent to which recognition, prestige, and so forth, emerged during group interactions and influenced

---

7. For the statistically informed reader: The statements about the protest-promoting incentives for members of the different groups refer to arithmetic means: For the different groups, the means of each incentive were compared, and etas computed. The eta-coefficients were as follows: political dissatisfaction .33, personal influence by general protests .20, personal influence by demonstrations .18, protest norms .10, expectations of reference persons .19, group encouragement .42, fear of sanctions .09, probability of sanctions .10. Each coefficient larger than .10 is significant on the .01 level.

participation in protests. For relatively new groups such as the Neues Forum (founded in September 1989), similarities between members are probably mostly due to a recruitment effect. However, members of church-based opposition groups have certainly undergone socialization processes. We generally assume that the groups' different levels of political activity can be accounted for by both the interaction of members (socialization and control hypotheses) and the preexisting similarities of their members (recruitment hypothesis).

The Influence of Personal Networks

Social rewards for protesting come not only from social groups, but also from friends, family members, or fellow employees—from personal networks. Thus, individuals in protest-supporting social environments will take part in protest frequently. Was it at all possible for a person to freely criticize the SED regime in the presence of friends or acquaintances in the GDR? After all, one had to reckon with Stasi agents among friends and acquaintances who would report critical statements.

There is no information available about the extent to which there exist personal networks in repressive societies or the extent to which existing networks promote protests. The SED regime limited personal communication. For example, only about 17 percent of the households had telephones. In comparison to the FRG, the number of restaurants and bars was very low. Cars were also scarce. Since the threat of betrayal and repression was always present, individuals might have decided not to talk politics in personal conversations. In this case, personal contacts would have provided only minor opportunities to win others for protest.

However, personal networks of politically like-minded individuals might have originated even under authoritarian regimes. How might they develop? There are many signals in everyday conversation that indicate a person's political beliefs, yet are not explicit enough to lead to repression. Inferences about political attitudes can also be made on the basis of social activities such as actively working for the SED. Personal networks of politically like-minded people can thus also develop under highly repressive regimes (see Goldfarb 1978, 1982, 1992). Trust will grow in such a network so that communication including political topics will be relatively free.

We believe that such networks do not emerge in extremely repressive societies. The Soviet Union in the 1930s is a case in point: merely being suspected of holding an opposing opinion could have led to the death penalty. Since the expected repression in the GDR was not that extreme, we believe that personal networks promoting the development of protests did originate in the GDR.

We further believe that friends and coworkers were the most important networks in which protest could be promoted. If a person has relatively close relations to fellow employees and if a relatively large number of fellow employees or friends are critical of the regime or took part in protests, then a person will be active to a high degree, too.

The social environment also includes *reference persons*—that is, family members or other people, such as supervisors, whose opinion is important to an individual. If such reference persons support participation in protests, then a person will also be politically active. To what extent do these considerations hold true?

Personal Networks in the GDR

Let us begin with *relations with fellow employees.* Our questionnaire included items to answer the following questions, referring to the time prior to October 9:

1. How close were relations with fellow employees?
2. How many fellow employees expressed criticism of the conditions in the GDR?
3. How many fellow employees participated in peace prayers, demonstrations, and similar activities?

Seventy-nine percent of the 1,112 respondents who gave a valid answer said that their relations with fellow employees were "very close" or "rather close," while 21 percent found their relations with colleagues to be "rather distant" or "very distant." It may be that at work people didn't discuss politics. Yet this was apparently not the case, as we see in figure 4. Only 1 percent of the respondents said that *no one* expressed criticism concerning the conditions in the GDR. For coworkers to know that the overwhelming majority of their fellow workers were critical of the SED regime, politics must have been a conversation topic. This supposition is further confirmed by the fact that only 3 percent of the respondents answered "don't know" when asked about how many of their fellow employees were critical of the conditions in the GDR.

We see in figure 4 that 45 percent said that "almost all" their fellow employees criticized the conditions in the GDR. A total of 72 percent said that "many" or "almost all" coworkers were critical. Even 24 percent said "some" coworkers were critical. A mere 1 percent claimed "no one" among their coworkers was critical. It seems that respondents were better informed about the political *opinions* of colleagues than about their political *activities*. In response to the question about critical opinions of fellow employees, only 3 percent said that they were not well informed ("don't know"). When asked

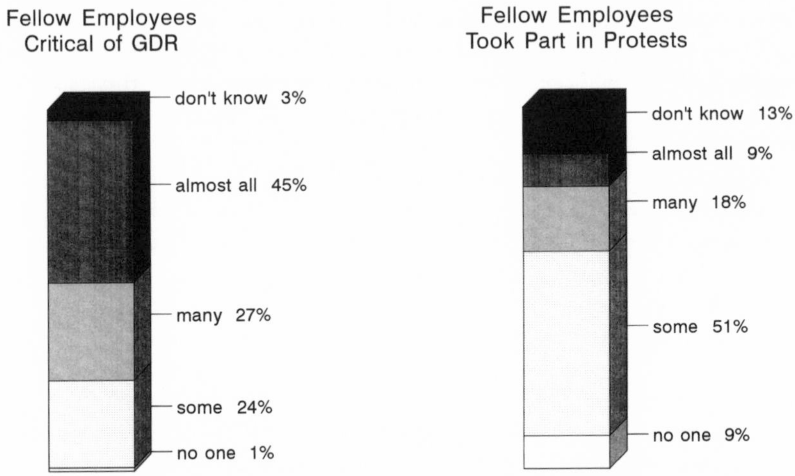

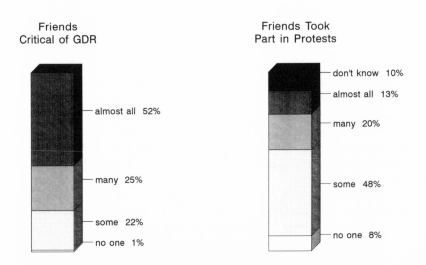

Fellow Employees
Critical of GDR

don't know 3%

almost all 45%

many 27%

some 24%

no one 1%

Fellow Employees
Took Part in Protests

don't know 13%

almost all 9%

many 18%

some 51%

no one 9%

Fig. 4. Critical and politically active fellow employees before October 9, 1989. Example: 45 percent of respondents reported that "almost all" coworkers were critical of the conditions in the GDR.

Friends
Critical of GDR

almost all 52%

many 25%

some 22%

no one 1%

Friends Took
Part in Protests

don't know 10%

almost all 13%

many 20%

some 48%

no one 8%

Fig. 5. Critically and politically active friends before October 9, 1989. Example: 52 percent of respondents reported that "almost all" of their friends were critical of the conditions in the GDR.

about the political activity of fellow employees against the SED, 13 percent said they didn't know (fig. 4). A total of 27 percent of the respondents said that "many" or "almost all" fellow employees were active, and 51 percent said that "some" colleagues took part in protests. Only 9 percent said "no one" among their coworkers had protested.

Thus, our data show on the whole that close relations existed among coworkers and that many fellow employees were critical of the SED regime. Apparently, political topics were discussed in daily workplace conversations. Thus, repression in the GDR did not lead to the suppression of critical political communication in the workplace.

Let us now turn to *relationships with friends*. We asked the same questions as before with the exception of the first question regarding the closeness in the relationships. The results are similar to those regarding fellow employees, as can be seen by comparing figures 4 and 5. Yet even more friends than colleagues proved to be critical of the conditions in the GDR.

The *overlapping* of personal networks is relevant for the emergence of protests. For example, if there are many cliques in a society that are isolated from each other, information or political opinions will spread less than if there is contact between the different groups. If the colleagues of a person are identical with his or her friends, the connectedness of the personal network is relatively low. In contrast, if only some friends of a person are also fellow workers, information and opinions could spread rather easily. In this case, one would have relatively separate circles of friends and fellow employees, although contact would exist between the two circles. Fellow workers would in turn have other friends, who have contacts with other fellow employees. To what extent do the social circles of fellow workers and friends overlap?

We asked respondents to state how many of their friends were also work colleagues. Again, answer categories were "no one," "some," "many," or "almost all." The majority of respondents, 88 percent of 1,186 with a valid answer, said that "no one" (40 percent) or "some" friends (48 percent) were also fellow employees. Eight percent said that "many" and only 4 percent reported that "almost all" colleagues were also friends. Because the networks of friends and colleagues overlap only to a limited extent, the spread of information should have been no problem.

To find out how the respondents' closest friends or relatives valued protest against the SED regime, we asked respondents how their reference persons (people "whose opinion is important to you") would have viewed the respondent's taking part in a political activity such as a demonstration in order to stand up for personal political goals. In total, 66 percent of the 1,275 respondents with a valid answer said that this activity would have been viewed positively or very positively, while 24 percent answered "partly positively, and partly negatively."

Did Personal Networks Promote Political Protest?

The results reported in the preceding section show that prior to October 9, conditions in the personal networks were such that information referring to political action could spread, critical opinions could be exchanged, and protest activity could be encouraged. If many fellow workers express criticism of the conditions in the GDR, one could also expect one's fellow workers to support one's participation in a protest. The closer the relationship, the greater the chance that one will protest because the expected rewards will be particularly high. If a person also knows that a large number of colleagues participate in protests, this person will expect to receive social rewards to a high extent by also taking part.

The same reasoning applies to friends. If many friends criticize the conditions in the GDR and take part in the protests frequently, then one can expect to receive recognition and other positive reactions from friends for participating as well. Furthermore, if a person's reference persons value protest participation positively, a person will be motivated to take political action also.

Are these hypotheses correct? Let us first examine whether the social environment influences participation in the general protests. Did close contacts with fellow employees who criticized the regime promote participation in general protests? Our data show that this was *not* the case. If a person had close relations to fellow employees who were critical of SED policies and who protested frequently, this did not lead to greater participation. However, if individuals had critical and politically active friends, and if reference persons valued participation in protests positively, then they participated in protests frequently.

We found similar effects regarding participation in demonstrations. Contacts with critical fellow employees again have no effect on participation. Yet those individuals who had critical and politically active friends participated quite frequently in the demonstrations. Also, as expected, the more positively reference persons viewed protest, the more respondents took part in the demonstrations.[8]

---

8. For the statistically informed reader: The bivariate correlations of "number of critical co-workers" with "participation in general protests" was .03, and with "participation in demonstrations" was .04. The corresponding correlations for "number of critical friends" were .34 and .28 for general protests and demonstrations, respectively. The correlations of "expectations of reference persons to protest" were .27 (general protests) and .21 (demonstrations). "Number of critical co-workers" remains insignificant in regression analyses with both protest variables as dependent and the network variables as independent variables, while the standardized regression coefficients of the other two variables remain highly significant.

Group Membership, Personal Networks, and Incentives for Protest

We have not yet dealt with the *joint* effects of group memberships and personal networks on participation in protest. It may be the case that memberships in certain groups influenced protest only because the members of these groups had many critical friends. Possibly only critical personal networks promote political activity.

Let us look at the statistical analyses we ran to determine the joint effects of group membership, personal networks, and the incentives discussed so far. We included the following independent variables in the regression analyses: group memberships, number of critical coworkers, number of critical friends, encouragement by reference persons, public goods motivation, protest norms, encouragement of reference persons, membership in protest-promoting groups, probability of and fear of repression, experience of repression, and, finally, membership in the Protestant or Catholic church. The repression variables are dealt with in detail in chapter 9 and in the appendix.

Let us first look at participation in general protests. We found that the factors that had significant effects in the separate analyses presented earlier (including previous chapters of this book) remained significant when other factors were included. Public goods motivation proved to have the strongest effect, followed by critical friends. Protest norms, membership in protest-supporting groups, and membership in the Protestant or Catholic church had somewhat weaker effects. SED membership lowered participation. The remaining factors, such as membership in sports groups, had relatively weak effects.[9] Only two factors had strong effects on participation in demonstrations: public goods motivation and number of critical friends. All other factors had only very weak effects.[10] Both forms of protest have in common that the important determinants were the public goods motivation and contacts with critical friends.

---

9. For the statistically informed reader: We ran regression analyses with "general protests" as dependent variable. Using the mentioned scales as independent variables, the adjusted explained variance was .35. The factors we termed as effective in the text had standardized regression coefficients of at least .10 and are accordingly significant on the .01 level. The mentioned beta-coefficients were .20 (public goods motivation), .16 (critical friends), .13 (member in protest-supporting groups), .13 (protest norms), .12 (membership in Protestant or Catholic church), −.12 (SED membership), and .11 (probability of sanctions).

10. For the statistically informed reader: The variables mentioned in the preceding note were included in the regression analyses. The standardized beta-coefficients were .14 for number of critical friends, .34 for public goods motivation. Only membership in the SED and other SED-related groups were otherwise significant (.05 level), yet only with the low beta of .07. The adjusted explained variance was .21.

Summary

Prior to October 9, the SED regime viewed the opposition groups as irrelevant interference factors, which were successfully controlled by the security forces. The groups' activities hardly increased the incentives for protest by means of direct contacts with the population (mobilization hypothesis). The low number of group members, the activities of the security organs, and barely existent resources (telephones, paper) made it impossible to mobilize the population to protest.

Because most of the GDR citizens were unaware of the exact goals and activities of the opposition groups, they could not identify with these groups, by which additional incentives could have been created (identification hypothesis). Furthermore, the opposition groups did not organize the protests; rather, the protests occurred spontaneously.

Members of the opposition groups nevertheless did contribute to the nonviolent nature of the protests. For example, members of the Neues Forum called out for "No violence!" during the demonstrations and prevented demonstrators from attacking objects such as Stasi buildings. Members of the opposition groups and sports groups participated relatively frequently in the general protests, while the members of the SED participated rarely. This finding can be explained by the fact that those group members who protested frequently were faced with strong protest-promoting incentives. In regard to the participation in demonstrations, there were only negligible differences between the groups.

Our respondents reported that a large percentage of their fellow workers and friends criticized the conditions in the GDR. Sixty-six percent of our respondents said that their reference persons viewed participation in protest positively. In regard to the effects of personal networks, our research shows that only critical friends, and not fellow workers, were important for both participation in general protests and demonstrations.

Regarding the joint effects of group memberships, personal networks, and incentives, we found that for general protests, the major determinants were public goods motivation, membership in protest-encouraging groups, and protest norms. For participation in demonstrations, only two factors had clear effects: public goods motivation and membership in personal networks. All other factors had only very weak effects. Thus, both forms of protest have something in common: the most important determinants were public goods motivation and contacts with critical friends.

CHAPTER 8

The Role of the Church

Peter Voss

Although we use the term *the church* in this chapter, we will focus only on the *Protestant* Church in the German Democratic Republic because the Catholic Church did not take on a comparable opposition role. Ehrhart Neubert, a profound expert on the subject of the church in the GDR, writes:

> The Catholic Church stayed away from both dialogue and critical discussions and remained strangely foreign in the GDR. Hardly any politically active groups were formed under its protection, and this caused some Catholics to consolidate with the Protestants. The Catholic Church did not offer its followers a church-supported substitute identity during the state of political deficiency, and this is why only a small number of [Catholic] Church functionaries took part in the GDR revolution at all. (1991, 24)

The overwhelming majority of religious citizens in the GDR belonged to the Protestant Church.[1] This affiliation is also reflected in our sample (see the appendix). The role of the church is one of the "social causes of the revolution," which we dealt with in chapter 7. Yet because the role of the church requires a relatively extensive discussion, we decided to dedicate an entire chapter to it.

Was It a "Protestant" Revolution?

Ehrhart Neubert and Gerhard Rein emphatically support the interpretation that the revolution in the GDR was a Protestant one. Rein believes that this began as early as late September 1987 with the synod of the Federation of Protestant Churches in Görlitz. At this synod the Bartholomäus parish from East Berlin made a proposal that caused a great uproar among the church leadership. The

---

1. According to church information sources, among the approximately 16 million GDR inhabitants, 21 percent belonged to the Protestant church and 3.6 percent to the Catholic Church.

"Rejection of the Practice and Principle of Separation" (see Rein 1990, 24–26) appealed to the documents of the Conference of Security and Cooperation in Europe and demanded the reestablishment of visa-free travel with Poland, the freedom of travel within the socialist countries of Europe, the guaranteed right of freedom of travel into Western countries, the lifting of politically founded immigration restrictions, and a public dialogue about the political and economic problems in the GDR. After a vehement discussion, the synod rejected the proposal. Those demands seemed too much to ask of the government. Yet this proposal was a public challenge to the SED and became the guideline for many politically alternative groups.

The "Protestant" revolution ended with the Volkskammer [people's chamber] elections on March 18, 1990. Many representatives of the church were elected, and five pastors were even named ministers in Lothar de Maiziere's government. It seemed as if the socialist GDR had become a "pastor republic" in which even the army was commanded by a pastor.

Yet this is not the reason why Neubert and Rein speak of a "Protestant revolution." Neubert writes (1991, 21; emphasis added):

> We view the GDR revolution as "Protestant," i.e., as a process of change whose essential factors stem from the *Protestant political culture*.

Yet Neubert neither specifies which features make up a Protestant political culture nor what evidence there is for their existence in the GDR.

Our survey provides us with some information about the extent to which a Protestant culture contributed to the emergence of the revolution. We will address this issue later in this chapter. Yet due to our previous arguments, we can say now that even if the Protestant culture influenced certain norms or goals that were relevant for the participation in the protests, this alone could certainly not explain the revolution. The fall of socialism in the GDR was as little a Protestant revolution as the change of power in Poland was Catholic, although it is true that the church accompanied and supported critical groups and therefore promoted the revolution. We would now like to look more closely at how the church contributed to the emergence of the peaceful revolution in the GDR.

"Church in Socialism": The Position of Church Leaders

On the one hand, there was the "state church" as an institution whose leadership tried to act loyal toward the SED and the state and appeased the opposition. On the other hand, there were the *pragmatists,* pastors who in their daily work accepted those who thought differently and supported their activities. In Leipzig, names such as Christian Führer, Harald Wagner, Hans-Jürgen Sievers, and Christoph Wonneberger stood for the selfless help from the church for all those persecuted by the SED state. Then there were the *theorists,* theologists such as Heino Falcke, Friedrich Schorlemmer, and Wolfgang Ullmann, who outlined a reformed socialism.

In 1971 the Bund der Evangelischen Kirchen in der DDR [Association of Protestant churches in the GDR] agreed to the phrasing "Church in Socialism." On March 6, 1978, this concept was approved by Erich Honecker and the churches were provided a certain amount of freedom. Church leaders made a continuous effort not to take advantage of the SED's "gesture of trust." On the thin line between assimilation and contradiction, the church was the only organization under GDR socialism that was able to preserve its autonomy—although at the price of a continually contested loyalty toward the state. The Protestant Church association is now criticized for allowing the "Church in Socialism," and it is maintained that the church's loyalty prolonged the SED's power.

In the second half of the 1980s, the "truce" between church and regime became increasingly difficult. Not only did the church use its provided freedoms for the work with groups such as handicapped, environmental protectionists, conscientious objectors, homosexuals, and so on, but it also organized large events (church days, blues fairs, peace workshops, art festivals) that reached thousands. The participants, mostly young people who were dissatisfied with the SED government, also saw offers for alternative lifestyles. This had to be a thorn in the party's side. The SED continually reminded the church leaders that they were not to play the role of the political opposition.

At the September 1987 synod in Görlitz, the question was how much opposition the church could burden the state with. Apparently the rubicon had already been crossed. Starting in November 1987, after SED officials searched the Umweltbibliothek [Environmental library] of the Berlin Zion parish and made arrests, relations became more critical. A detailed documentation of all confrontations between the church and the GDR government was made by Lorenz and Lorenz (1990). On February 19, 1988, Bishop Werner Leich was given a warning by the SED Politburo to refrain from "counterrevolutionary activities within the realm of the church."

There were also continuous differences in opinion between the "church below" and the "church above." When the church leadership criticized the counterdemonstration by opposition groups on January 17, 1988, in Berlin, the "church below" declared at once that church leaders should take part in the vigils for those who had been arrested.

The politically alternative groups were at the center of the confrontations. The groups found themselves caught between church and state. They wanted to change and renew society and knew that they could only achieve this within the latitude of the church. They therefore had to make compromises and respect the church's position. The church in turn was held responsible by the government for the actions of its groups and therefore had to check and regiment the groups in its own interest (see Poppe 1990). In this conflict of interests, the groups had to view the church's attitude as ambivalent.

The politically alternative groups became a factor of interference, not only in the orderly relations between church and state, but also within the parishes themselves. Representatives of the official church, as well as many pastors and many parish members, didn't know what to think of these "alien bodies" and were worried about their own religious mission (see "Open letter from Representatives of the Berlin-Brandenburg Church to Bishop Gottfried Forck" in Rein 1990, 68 ff.).

In February 1989 Leipzig pastors were interviewed on their relations to the politically alternative groups. Only one out of two supported the presence of these groups under the roof of the church. Most of those who were willing to offer the groups asylum demanded that the groups have "Christian motives" behind their sociopolitical activity (see Grabner, Heinze, and Pollack 1990, 47 ff.). This requirement led the alternative groups to pay lip service to these demands, which further encumbered relations. But many groups were thankful for the church's support of their work. Church leaders also had different opinions about the political mandate of the church and the treatment of opposition groups under the auspices of the church. These differing opinions are exemplified by the general superintendent Günter Krusche and Bishop Gottfried Forck. While Krusche demanded a clear demarcation from the groups (1990), Forck supported their integration.

The Church as a Catalyst for Protest: The Provision of Resources

The metaphor *catalyst,* which refers to a material that accelerates a chemical reaction without losing its original state, is a good description of the church's role in the GDR revolution. The church as an institution was not interested in publicly supporting or promoting protests against the state. The church itself did not organize any protest activities. It also did not directly encourage protest, such as by appealing to the duty of each citizen to take action. Thus, the church was no political entrepreneur. This situation caused conflicts with groups who by all means wanted to act as political entrepreneurs.

In accordance with Christian ideology, the church worked against injustice and oppression and gave sanctuary to their victims. Yet the church did not fight offensively against the political causes of injustice. Political changes were not and continue not to be the goal of church policies.

When the church groups saw the chance for political changes during the "boiling phase" of the revolution (August to November 1989), they hurriedly left the protection of the church, which had become a shackle for their opposition activities.

To what extent did the church provide resources for participation in protests? Resources include financial means, support from sympathizers, provision of meeting space, and opportunities for communication. Increasing resources decrease the costs for the behavior that is eased by the resources. If, for example, people who want to meet are provided a meeting place, they do not have to waste time looking for a place to plan their activities. The costs for meetings are reduced.

What exactly were the kinds of resources the church provided? First, resources were limited by the capacities of each parish. Groups were granted "sanctuary" in the rooms of the church, which required high levels of tolerance and solidarity for both parties. To some extent, groups were given access to church information channels. They were allowed to use church announcement boards and sometimes the church newspapers.

Yet the most important resource was the institution of peace prayers. In the course of 1989, a "politicization" of church activities took place step by step. Remarks on current political events, especially in the peace prayers, increased. Many people only attended the church events in order to receive current political information and opinions. We will address the role of the peace prayers in the revolution in chapter 12 (see also chapter 1). We would like to stress here only that the peace prayers were a necessary prerequisite for the emergence of spontaneous protests at that time. They also caused a wave of protests in almost every other area and therefore made a decisive contribution to the upheaval in the GDR.

Although the church provided resources, it did not do so to promote protest against the SED regime but, rather, to provide oppressed individuals a sanctuary. The Protestant church in the GDR did not want to be the "public house for opponents of the GDR society" (Rein 1990, 11) and was therefore accused of being hesitant and tactical. The principle of Christian brotherly love was always more important than the duty of resistance, which is why later the fallen Erich Honecker was able to find sanctuary from the people's hate only in the church (see Swoboda 1990, 289).

The political activities of the groups were not always promoted but, rather, hindered sometimes by the church because of conflicts with the official church and the parish heads. According to Heinze and Pollack (1990), the conflicts were not about goals but about *means*. Churches and groups agreed that socialism as such wasn't to be done away with,[2] but there were disagree-

---

2. This does not only apply to the Protestant church in the GDR. At the 1989 ecumenical meeting of Christians and churches in the GDR, 19 churches and church groups created a document in which the reorganization, not the repeal, of socialism in the GDR is demanded (*Gerechtigkeit* 1990).

ments about what should be done to improve it. The official church preferred a diplomatic manner in negotiations with the state, while the groups favored direct forms of action and demanded drastic reforms. The conflicts were about the necessary amount of pragmatism, with one side accusing the other of being the source of conflict.

The Church as an Agent of Socialization

This section centers around the question to what extent the church changed incentives for participation in protests. On the one hand, *nonmembers* of the church may have identified with the church and thus taken on certain protest-promoting attitudes (identification hypothesis, see chapter 7). On the other hand, the church could also or only have had an influence on *members* (socialization hypothesis, see also chapter 7). Both hypotheses will be discussed in the following sections.

The Identification Hypothesis

The identification hypothesis implies that those GDR citizens who had no direct connection to the church or to church groups, but who felt close to the church (identified with the church), could have taken on the perceived oppositional role of the church or the general Protestant political culture.

First, only a small percentage of the citizens (5 percent in our study) belonged to church groups. Yet even if we assume that an effective political socialization (changes in opinions, attitudes, and such) took place, this alone cannot explain the revolutionary behavior of tens of thousands of citizens, even if we take a certain "radiance effect" of the groups on the population into account.

Second, the church members (18 percent of our respondents) could have become reference persons for their friends and acquaintances because of their critical stance toward the SED regime and could have therefore influenced friends' and acquaintances' protest behavior indirectly. Our empirical material did not allow us to determine the extent to which this was the case.

Finally, the church leadership's position could have caused many citizens to identify with the church. Is it not possible that the church's relatively distanced position toward the SED regime encouraged those who were not members of the church or church groups to protest? There are two plausible answers. First, the population could have interpreted the limited independence of the church and the latitude granted by the regime that they believed they could express a certain amount of protest without being punished, which means that the expected state sanctions for protest would have decreased. Because the church helped in case of difficulties with the regime, the church's perceived position also could have decreased the fear of sanctions. Second, the church's continuous willingness for compromise might have strengthened the population's belief that resistance against the government was hopeless if even the church had to bow down to the constraints of the regime.

How well was the population informed about the church's position toward the SED? Word-of-mouth propaganda in the GDR functioned as well as in other dictatorial systems. Full employment provided beneficial opportunities for communication. A large portion of worktime was used for informal conversations, which were of an outspoken political nature shortly before the fall of the GDR. What went on in and around the church was followed with continually growing interest and open sympathy.

The public dialogue about the problems in the GDR society took place only in the arts and in the church. Because artists used an increasingly difficult language and symbolism to express their protest, they reached only a small circle of individuals. The church was all that remained. "The discussion in the churches reflected and contained all of the conflicts within the GDR society and it represented a claim beyond the private sphere and was therefore a ray of hope for democratization" (Neubert 1991, 24).

Many church documents contain "offers of identification" for the GDR citizens. We will mention only the "Twenty Points from Wittenberg for the Regeneration and Reorganization of the GDR" from June 1988; the documents about the ecumenical meeting "More Justice in the GDR—Our Responsibility, Our Expectations" from April 1989; and the results of the church association's synod "What Needs To Be Done in Order for People to Enjoy Living in Our Country" from September 1989 (see Rein 1989, 199–217).

The position of the church toward the communal elections on May 7, 1989, was also an offer for identification. The Saxony State Synod in Dresden called on Christians to vote "truthfully" and "responsibly" at the coming election. The synod also urged citizens to use the polling booths (which was already regarded as an oppositional act by GDR authorities) or to abstain from voting (which could also lead to difficulties) if they felt any inner conflict. Church groups took part in the public counting of the votes and brought attention to incorrect counting of "no" votes. Up until that time there had been no such thing at GDR elections.

The churches were filled with people who brought certain political expectations with them, and the pastors often had a difficult time striking a balance between their religious mission and the opposition role that had been thrust upon them. In a time of political disorientation, the people were hungry for information; they looked for outlasting values and concrete help in solving their everyday problems in the sermons of the pastors. The names of many church representatives were suddenly made public. The messages from their speeches were also spread outside of the church.

Thus, there is some evidence to support the identification hypothesis. A portion of the citizens probably identified with the church and thus took on a more critical position toward the regime. Thus, the church, as a source of identification, probably had an indirect influence on the participation in protests. Yet our data do not allow us to estimate how strong this effect was.

The Socialization Hypothesis

The socialization hypothesis focuses on the members of the church. It seems plausible that certain political attitudes were created through social interactions between members over a period of time, which promoted participation in protests. Let us look at the extent to which this hypothesis is accurate for the determinants of protest mentioned earlier.

We first examine whether or not being a member of the Protestant Church has an effect on participation in protests. If the Protestant church indeed created a form of protest culture, we would then expect the following hypotheses to hold true:

1. Church members participate more frequently in general protests and demonstrations than nonmembers.
2. Positive incentives for protest, such as political dissatisfaction or perceived political influence, are stronger for church members than for nonmembers.
3. The closer the affiliation with the church, the greater the participation in general protests and demonstrations and the greater the extent to which the positive incentives for protest occur.
4. Church members take part in general protests and demonstrations more often if they are members of opposition groups (church groups, Neues Forum) than if they are not members of those groups; the incentives for protest are greater for members of opposition groups than for nonmembers.

Church Membership
In order to test hypothesis 1, we will compare the extent of participation in general protests as well as demonstrations of church members and nonmembers. In our population survey, 18 percent of the sample (232 individuals) said that they were members of the Protestant Church. This is in contrast to 967 people who did not belong to a religious group. The rest of the respondents are not included in the following analyses—they either belonged to other churches or did not provide information for this question. Figure 1 shows that church members on a whole were more active than nonmembers. This applies to each kind of general protest and, thus, also for the composite measure. Yet the differences between the different forms of protest are minor with one

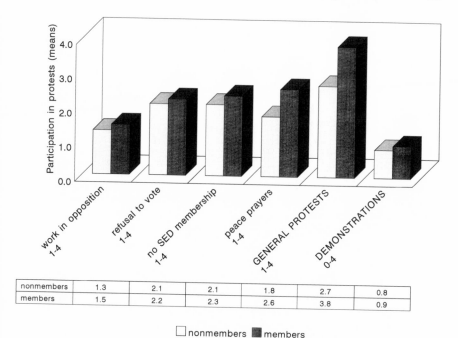

nonmembers	1.3	2.1	2.1	1.8	2.7	0.8
members	1.5	2.2	2.3	2.6	3.8	0.9

☐ nonmembers ■ members

Fig. 1. Membership in Protestant Church and political protest before October 9, 1989 (ranges in parentheses)

exception: church members took part relatively frequently in the peace prayers and church events. This is certainly not surprising. Furthermore, members of the Protestant Church worked in opposition groups, which includes church groups, somewhat more often than nonmembers did. Thus, for general protests, we found that church members were somewhat more active than nonmembers.[3] Church members participated almost to the same extent as nonmembers in the demonstrations before October 9, 1989 (fig. 1).[4]

Thus, hypothesis 1 is only partially accurate. Prior to the GDR's fall, many church members were in permanent opposition to the SED state, but during the decisive time of the mass protests, they behaved like all the other citizens. This behavior may be explained by similar incentives to which both members and nonmembers are exposed, which leads us to hypothesis 2.

---

3. For the statistically informed reader: Only the differences for "work in an opposition group," "participation in peace prayers," and "general protests" are statistically significant (.01 level). The values of the coefficient eta are .11, .29, and .19, respectively.

4. For the statistically informed reader: The value of the coefficient eta is only .04 and not statistically significant.

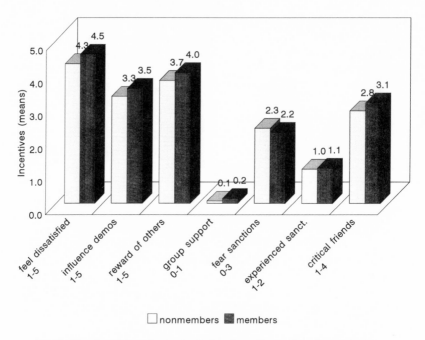

Fig. 2. Membership in Protestant church and incentives for protest before October 9, 1989 (ranges in parentheses)

Figure 2 shows the differences in the means of the incentives for church members and nonmembers. In figure 2 we only included those incentives that differed most strongly for church members and nonmembers.[5] Church members were more dissatisfied with the political conditions before October 9, 1989, than were nonmembers. They also believed more strongly that demonstrations could lead to change. Reference persons of church members were expected to value political action against the SED regime more positively than would reference persons of nonmembers. Church members were also more often members of groups which encouraged protest. Church members were less afraid of state sanctions and had faced sanctions more frequently than had nonmembers. Finally, church members had more critical friends than nonmembers did.

Church members and nonmembers did *not* differ in regard to the following incentives: members and nonmembers both expected the same amount of state repression in case of participation, and they did not differ according to the earlier mentioned moral incentives. This finding leads us to a number of

---

5. For the statistically informed reader: figure 2 contains only scales that are significant on at least the .05 level.

observations about the church's contribution to the nonviolent nature of the revolution. Opinions on this subject also differ widely. Our findings show that there are no statistically significant differences between church members and other respondents. Nonviolence as such was apparent, but it is doubtful whether the majority of demonstrators allowed themselves to be led by Christian ethics or, if not, whether the conditions we described in chapter 6 were the dominating factors for their behavior.

Hans-Joachim Maaz (1990) certainly overestimates the ability of the church to influence behavior in this regard. According to Maaz, the church's attempts at appeasement with radicals protracted the outbreak of the revolution and took away its impetus. He even accuses the church of collaboration with the SED (144). The church representatives we interviewed see the situation much differently. Pastors Hans-Jürgen Sievers and Christian Führer refer specifically to Martin Luther King and the ethics of nonviolent resistance he founded. The church-supported civil rights movement in the United States and the message from the Sermon on the Mount, they said, were always part of the churches' framework for resistance against the authoritarian regime. If these statements were true, church members and nonmembers should differ according to norms for nonviolence. Yet, as we have seen, this is not the case.

Affiliation with the Church

Perhaps church membership alone is not the only important factor behind activity. Maybe the degree of affiliation—that is, identification—with the church is important, as hypothesis 3 states. We asked church members: "How strong is your affiliation with your church?" The possible answers were "very strong," "strong," "not so strong," and "not at all." Thirty-five percent of the members answered "very strong" or "strong." One out of two (52 percent) had only a loose connection with their church, and 13 percent even felt no sense of affiliation to the church whatsoever. We divided the respondents into two groups. We term those members who felt little or no affiliation with their church *weakly affiliated,* and those who felt a "very strong" or "strong" affiliation with their church *strongly affiliated.* Thus we distinguish between three groups of individuals: nonmembers, weakly affiliated members and strongly affiliated members.

Let us begin by examining whether church members with strong and weak affiliations differ according to their protest behavior. Figure 3 shows that the church members who felt a strong affiliation were always more active than were weakly affiliated members.[6]

Let us now compare all three groups: nonmembers, members with weak

---

6. For the statistically informed reader: All differences are significant on the .01 level. The lowest eta-coefficients were obtained for "participation in demonstrations" (.16) and "refusal to vote" (.19).

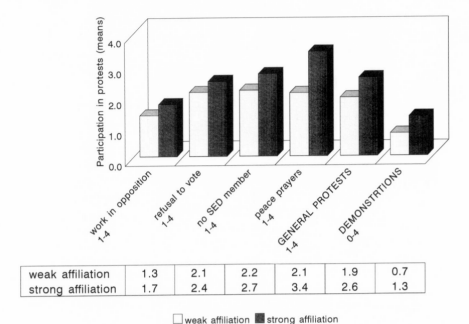

	work in opposition 1-4	refusal to vote 1-4	no SED member 1-4	peace prayers 1-4	GENERAL PROTESTS 1-4	DEMONSTRTIONS 0-4
weak affiliation	1.3	2.1	2.2	2.1	1.9	0.7
strong affiliation	1.7	2.4	2.7	3.4	2.6	1.3

☐ weak affiliation ■ strong affiliation

**Fig. 3. Degree of affiliation with Protestant church and political pro-
test before October 9, 1989 (ranges in parentheses)**

affiliation, and members with strong affiliation. The extent of political participation for nonmembers is shown in figure 1. If we compare the (mean) values
of the nonmembers (fig. 1), the members with weak and the members with
strong affiliation (fig. 3) for each kind of general protests, we find that the
extent of general protest for nonmembers and members with weak affiliation
is quite similar. More pronounced differences exist between these two groups
on the one hand and the strongly affiliated group on the other.[7]

If affiliation with the church has an influence on political activity, then
the strongly affiliated members should display high levels of incentives. Figure 4 contains only those incentives that differ relatively strongly.[8]

The following findings are particularly interesting. The strongly affiliated
church members were just about as dissatisfied as the weakly affiliated, but
the strongly affiliated perceived more influence by demonstrations. Strongly

---

7. For the statistically informed reader: If we compare the etas for the three groups and the
etas only for weakly and strongly affiliated members, we find that the latter etas are clearly larger.

8. For the statistically informed reader: All selected incentives are significant on the .01
level. The etas range from .21 (personal influence by demonstrations) to .32 (encouragement of
groups).

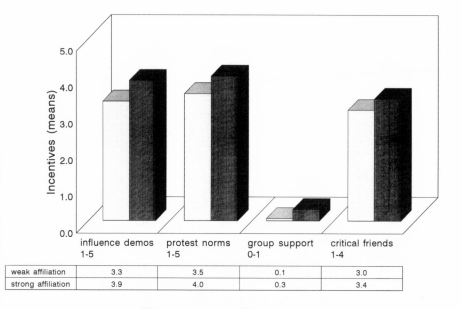

	influence demos 1-5	protest norms 1-5	group support 0-1	critical friends 1-4
weak affiliation	3.3	3.5	0.1	3.0
strong affiliation	3.9	4.0	0.3	3.4

☐ weak affiliation ■ strong affiliation

Fig. 4. Degree of affiliation with Protestant church and incentives for protest before October 9, 1989 (ranges in parentheses)

affiliated church members also felt a greater obligation to take action. Strongly and weakly affiliated members do not differ according to their acceptance of violence: violence is rejected to the same extent. The strongly affiliated church members are also more often members in protest-promoting groups and have more critical friends. The two groups do not differ according to their perceptions of sanctions.

Let us now compare the incentives for the nonmembers on the one hand and the strongly and weakly affiliated members on the other. We also found here, as for general protests, that nonmembers and weakly affiliated members show similar values for the incentives. The values for the strongly affiliated members are clearly higher. In regard to protest norms, we found that nonmembers accepted protest norms more than the weakly affiliated did. The acceptance of protest norms by the strongly affiliated is nevertheless clearly higher than by the other groups.

Church Groups as Opposition Groups
The term *church group* refers to groups that formed under the auspices of the church and tried to achieve political goals. Such groups include peace groups,

human rights groups, environmental groups, women's groups, and so forth. Since the beginning of the 1980s, a new quality of church groups could be observed that expressed a high level of ethical and democratic activity. The topics "peace," "preservation of the world," "bread for the world," and "social justice" especially attracted young people who wanted to become politically and socially active.[9] Beginning in 1985, critical citizens increasingly came together under the auspices of the church, and the GDR-typical interlinkage of Christian milieu, alternative lifestyle, and political opposition started. Uwe Funk (1990) estimates the number of these groups at 500 in February 1989. Ulrike Poppe (1990) mentions 325 registered groups.

Peace, ecology, and human rights groups, which strove for social changes based on the idea of basic democracy, soon found themselves in church and nonchurch conflicts where they had to learn to stand up for and protect themselves. Friedrich Schorlemmer describes them as "disturbance groups" for the church and indispensable for a lively work of the church (see Pollack 1990, 17–23).

Let us characterize the members of church groups in our sample more closely. For the time *prior* to October 9, 6 percent (70 respondents) of our sample said they were members of such a group. Yet more important than the number of members is the question regarding whether political socialization took place in these groups to the point where attitudes and behavior were changed in the direction of opposition activities. This seems to have been only somewhat the case because only one in two group members claimed to have been encouraged by the group to take part in demonstrations or other activities directed at changing the political conditions in the GDR.

An analysis of the *motives* for becoming a group member and for the activities of the group members within the group also shows that only some of the members strove for political goals. We show the reasons for membership in church groups as follows, ordered according to the size of their means. The values in parentheses are the mean values of a scale ranging from 1 ("does not hold true") to 5 ("holds completely true").

"I became a member because it was important for me to be in a group of people who shared my political views." (3.7)

"I became a member because I am convinced that each person is important for a group to be able to achieve its goals." (3.6)

"I became a member in order to better achieve my political goals." (2.2)

---

9. The total number of young people who worked in church groups was actually low compared to the number of young people living in the GDR. Estimates have been made at about 4 percent (Lemke 1991, 176), which corresponds to our own findings.

"I became a member so that I would have support if I was confronted with the security forces." (2.0)[10]

It is important to note that people only rarely became members of the groups in order to better achieve their political goals.

In regard to the individual *activities* within the groups, the mere participation in meetings of the groups was the most important action. Only one in five group members participated in the planning of political activities. About half the members were primarily concerned with their group's affairs such as finding new members, collecting money, or spreading information. The various group activities are listed according to their frequency as follows. The numbers in parentheses show the percentages of group members who carried out the particular activity:

Regular participation in the group's meetings (72 percent)
Spreading of information about the group's meetings (56 percent)
Recruiting new members (50 percent)
Collecting money or other resources relevant to the group's work (42 percent)
Planning political activities (20 percent)
Participating in the founding of the group (11 percent)

Thus, the planning of political activities was only rarely mentioned.

The aforementioned reasoning refers to group membership *prior* to October 9, 1989. We want to emphasize again that only a very small portion of the GDR population were active members of groups who were organized by or under the auspices of the church. The majority of group members primarily wanted the social contact with like-minded individuals; only a few group members formed the politically opposing nucleus of the groups.

Only 76 percent of the church group members were also members of the Protestant Church. Our survey also reflected a fact known through other sources: many nonreligious citizens joined the church groups because they looked for a favorable environment for their political activities. Pastor Heino Falcke from Erfurt denied most of the groups even a clear church identity (1990).

---

10. Pollack (1990, 129 f.) found similar motives in his empirical research. He calls the four motives "subjective perplexity," "assistance in how to conduct life," "striving for autonomy," and "curiosity." Pollack concluded: "Christian motives hardly played a role for the constitution of the groups" (145).

On the other hand, church members, in comparison to the rest of the population, were more often members in church (opposition) groups. We found that 18 percent of the church members were also members of various church groups, while the percentage of those who were not members of the church was scarcely 1 percent.

Let us turn to hypothesis 4. Testing its first part showed results similar to those found when we tested hypothesis 1. Church members who were also members of opposition groups[11] prior to October 9, 1989, participated more frequently in general protests than did church members who did not belong to such groups. This was particularly the case in regard to work in opposition groups and participation in church activities, which is not very surprising. Members of opposition groups were hardly more active in the other forms of protest than were nonmembers. No such relationship could be found for participation in demonstrations. Thus, on a whole, if a church member is also a member of an opposition group, participation in the general protests is only somewhat higher; for participation in demonstrations there is no difference at all.

To what extent were the incentives different for church members, who were or were not members of opposition groups? We found no statistically significant differences. A number of incentives for the members of opposition groups are present to a higher degree than for the nonmembers, but the differences are minor nonetheless.

From our testing of hypothesis 4, we can conclude that church members were hardly more active if they were also members of opposition groups. Thus, membership in opposition groups appears to have had almost no socializing effect on the church members. This does not mean that church groups had no influence on their members whatsoever. Pollack (1990, 145) writes about the church groups:

> Their contribution was the strengthening of the individual against the clutches of society in the offer of small support groups in which the individual could find recognition, strength, security, warmth, comfort, encouragement, and leeway for self-realization. Their contribution was the offering of an alternative "counter-culture." The individual is not connected to the existing society.

---

11. For testing hypothesis 4, aside from the members of the church opposition groups, we also included those six church members who also belonged to the Neues Forum. It is again the case that church members are significantly more often also members of the Neues Forum. In all, the test of hypothesis 4 is based on 47 respondents who were simultaneously church and church group or Neues Forum members.

Summary

In the years prior to the fall of the GDR and in the stormy days at the end of 1989, the church was the preferred place of sanctuary for those who had serious problems with existing socialism in the GDR. The peacefulness of the revolution is to a great deal due to the balancing work of many pastors. They mediated discussions between the representatives of the old power and the representatives of the growing civil democracy in a time of a political power vacuum and proved themselves successful moderators at the roundtable discussions.

For a short period of time, all social forces unconditionally recognized the moral authority of the church. This recognition enabled and simplified the way for many pastors and church representatives to enter politics. There they shared the floor with other representatives of the opposition movement. The message was: either bow down to the political constraints or say goodbye to the parliament and a government position.

But the church did not want, and thus did not make, the revolution—at least not in the form it developed. It always avoided labeling itself the political opposition, let alone acting like it. The socialist constitution of the GDR, along with the SED's claim to power, was not questioned as such. All demanded changes should have been made by or with the SED but not against it.

This is not to belittle its role. The way the church sees itself is different from the objective consequences its actions had. In retrospect, it appears that formation of the opposition in the GDR was only possible because of its way of acting. In this sense it can be maintained that the church not only stabilized the system, but also was a dynamic factor.

In this chapter, we have tried to analyze in detail the role of the church in the revolution. Let us summarize the most important findings of our analyses:

The Protestant Church provided resources (opportunities for political activity) and therefore promoted the emergence of the revolution. It provided in particular meeting space, protection for groups, and the peace prayers.

Many GDR citizens have probably identified with the goals of the Protestant Church because of its somewhat critical stance toward the SED regime. This identification promoted participation in the protests.

Members of the Protestant Church participated only somewhat more often in general protests than did nonmembers. There is no difference between members and nonmembers in regard to participation in the demonstrations.

Members and nonmembers differ only slightly in regard to their incentives for protest. There is no difference in regard to the acceptance of protest norms and the rejection of violence.

Individuals who were strongly affiliated with (that is, who strongly identified with) the Protestant Church clearly participated more often in the general protests and the demonstrations than did nonmembers and members who felt only weakly affiliated to their church.

Accordingly, the incentives for protest for the strongly affiliated members were generally strong. Yet they don't differ from all others in regard to the rejection of violence.

These findings support the assumption that socialization effects were present. However, this assumption applies more to those who felt strongly affiliated with their church, because the nonmembers and the weakly affiliated members differed from each other only to a minor extent.

These findings suggest that it is exaggerated to refer to a "Protestant political culture." If indeed the official Christian teachings of opposing injustice and suppression influenced the actions of the members, the differences in the acceptance of protest norms, rejection of violence, and political dissatisfaction should have been much larger.

Our findings also suggest that it doesn't make much sense to term the revolution in the GDR "Protestant." The policies of church leadership toward the SED and the opposition groups, as we described them throughout this chapter, the fact that the church did not organize the decisive protests, and the minor differences between members and nonmembers show that the Church in no way "made" the revolution. Our analyses show that many factors played a role in the emergence of protests and the upheaval in the GDR.

CHAPTER 9

The Blunt Weapons of the Stasi: Why Were the Security Forces Unable to Prevent the Revolution?

Karl-Dieter Opp

The protests by large numbers of GDR citizens before October 9, 1989, were unexpected for one reason in particular: They occurred despite extensive repression. The version of socialism propagated by the SED was almost a state religion. The GDR population was expected to support SED policies without question. Criticism or opposing opinions were not tolerated. The legal system of the GDR served the propagated ideology, and deviations from the ruling political opinion could be and were strictly punished. To enforce this legal system, an extensive apparatus was created based, above all, on the ministry of state security—the Stasi. The sanctions consisted not only of direct punishment, such as fines collected from the "culprits," but also of problems at the workplace and the curtailment of other possible benefits, such as the opportunity to study at a university. Furthermore, state sanctions were directed at immediate family members.[1] The educational system was aimed at permanently anchoring the regime's ideology in the population and its subsequent generations. The founding of or involvement in voluntary associations was also put under surveillance. The regime did not tolerate any associations that stood in opposition to the Sozialistische Einheitspartei Deutschlands, or SED [Socialist unity party of Germany] and its policies.

This system of repression appears to have been very successful in the past. Protests against the SED regime were almost absent. When smaller protests occurred, they were crushed immediately, and the protesters often had to face grave consequences. It seems that the extremely low degree of political action against the SED during the entire existence of the GDR (with the exception of dates such as June 17, 1953) is particularly due to the repression apparatus. How else could one explain that protests occurred much more often in all industrialized countries without systematic repression than in the GDR and in other authoritarian systems? Why did the repression apparatus

---

1. For details on the legal system of the GDR, see Lieser-Triebnigg 1985. For information specifically concerning the Stasi, see Gill and Schröter 1991 and Schell and Kalinka 1991.

suddenly stop functioning in autumn 1989? This question is the focus of this chapter.

How Fearful Were the Citizens of the Stasi?

In chapter 2 we saw that expected state sanctions frequently have a deterrence effect. Sanctions are personal disadvantages, or costs, and thus reduce the sanctioned behavior. The extent of deterrence is dependent on the certainty of expected sanctions—that is, the *subjective probability of sanctions*. The deterrence effect also depends on the *severity of sanctions*—that is, the extent to which people fear sanctions. Thus, if state repression is expected with a high probability in case of protest and if the people involved view the expected sanctions as very severe (strong fear of sanctions), there is a strong *deterrence effect*—that is, the sanctioned behavior will rarely be carried out.

The GDR citizens probably differ according to how likely they considered it that sanctions would take place and how much they fear sanctions. For instance, citizens who have been previously punished because of statements critical to the regime may view the probability of punishment for critical statements as higher than if they had not been punished.

To what extent did GDR citizens expect and fear repression? Our qualitative interviews give us some hints to answering this question. Peter Kind describes the situation prior to October 9 in the following manner:

> When everything started to take off, the people's mood was a bit strange, but more like a tingling. People weren't really afraid. Well, I mean, we found out afterwards that people had been arrested.

Other respondents shared this view. Many participants in the demonstrations were probably not very fearful because they first heard about the preparations for deploying the security forces on October 9 after the fact. Maybe these citizens also believed that the government would not turn against its own people. Thus, some citizens only expected minor state sanctions.

Other respondents viewed the situation completely differently. Mathias Petzoldt commented in one of our qualitative interviews:

> We expected them to really deal harshly with us on October 7 after the celebrations were over. We thought they would just hold back until the national holiday so that it wouldn't look so bad to the rest of the world. We even thought that they might use a Chinese solution and that really scared us stiff.

Another respondent, Harald Wagner, cofounder of Demokratischer Aufbruch [Democratic awakening], said: "We all reckoned with the very high probability of bloodshed on October 9."

Even those who did not expect state repression prior to a demonstration probably changed their minds after arriving at the demonstration site. One participant of the Monday demonstration of October 9 describes the situation as follows (Tetzner 1990, 17):

> There was a whole line of vehicles filled with security forces in the Goethestraße. A cultural organization employee grabbed my arm and warned me with the words: "They've been instructed to shoot!" The rumor was spreading around a university that skinheads would defend themselves against the forces with machine guns. Army soldiers, it is said, called their wives and girlfriends in Leipzig that morning and told them not to go to the city center under any circumstances that evening. The hospitals were preparing to treat hundreds of wounded citizens. . . . we decide to join the demonstration. Waterhoses, more security vehicles and an emergency police unit were stationed next to the west wing of the main train station . . . the officers were wearing guns . . . tanks armed with heavy and light machine guns stood ready for action. . . .

Thus, as we can see, sanctions were perceived completely differently: Some citizens expected severe sanctions with high probability and some did not. Some were very afraid of sanctions and some were not. How did the population *as a whole* assess the sanctions? In our survey of Leipzig citizens, we ascertained both probability and fear of sanctions for four kinds of sanctions (see the appendix for more details): arrest, injury by security forces at a demonstration, problems at the workplace, and problems for close family members. Figure 1 shows the percentage of respondents who expected each sanction to be "probable" or "highly probable" if one took part in a demonstration. At least 29 percent, or roughly one third of the respondents, viewed each of the four kinds of sanctions as "probable" in case of participation. About half the respondents viewed injury at a demonstration as probable. An even greater percentage of the respondents, between 35 percent and 53 percent, regarded each sanction as "highly probable." If we add the percentages of respondents who viewed each sanction as "probable" or "highly probable," we find that at least 69 percent of the respondents expected sanctions prior to October 9. Eighty-three percent of the respondents expected to be arrested and even 91 percent expected to be injured by security forces.

A person may view sanctions as highly probable but not be terribly concerned. If, for example, a person parks illegally and is certain that he or she will get a ticket for 20 marks, he or she won't be very concerned. Figure 2 shows that about one third of the respondents perceived each sanction as "severe." Even more respondents perceived each sanction as "very severe." A particularly large part, 69 percent, perceived sanctions that were directed at their immediate family as "very severe." If we group together the respondents

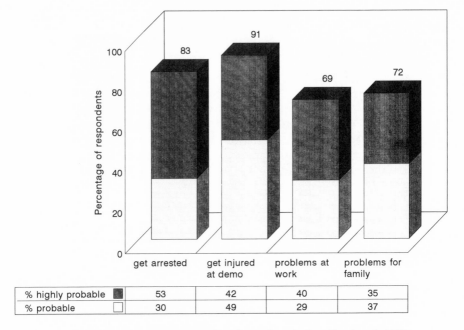

Fig. 1. Perceived probability of sanctions before October 9, 1989

	get arrested	get injured at demo	problems at work	problems for family
% highly probable ■	53	42	40	35
% probable ☐	30	49	29	37

who perceived a sanction as either "severe" or "very severe," we find that at least 74 percent of the respondents perceived each sanction as "severe" or "very severe."

We also ascertained the subjective probability of repression in another way. It is well known that the GDR government approved of the crushing of protests in China in early June 1989. It is plausible to assume that many GDR citizens therefore expected a "Chinese solution" if the protests were to increase. We asked the following question:

Recall the events at Tiananmen Square in Beijing in the summer of 1989. How did you react: Did you or did you not expect the security forces in the GDR to also take more harsher action against the demonstrators?

Sixty-nine percent of the respondents expected the security forces to take harsher action. Yet the majority of the respondents did *not* expect "Warsaw Pact troops to intervene if the upheaval in the GDR escalated" (wording of the survey question). Only 34 percent of the respondents expected this to happen.

Finally, we ascertained the extent to which respondents who had taken

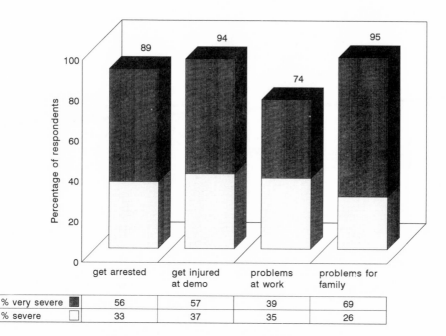

	get arrested	get injured at demo	problems at work	problems for family
% very severe ▣	56	57	39	69
% severe ☐	33	37	35	26

Fig. 2. Fear of sanctions before October 9, 1989

part in at least one demonstration before October 9 had feared sanctions in that particular situation. Respondents were asked to describe how they experienced their first demonstration before October 9. They were presented, among others, with two statements:

1. I was very afraid that the security forces would intervene.
2. I felt so secure with the many others around me that I thought nothing could happen.

Sixty percent of the respondents admitted to have been very afraid of security force intervention.[2] Only 37 percent of the respondents said they had felt relatively secure "with the many others" around them.[3]

On the whole, a clear majority of the respondents expected severe or very severe sanctions. Yet one third of the participants who had taken part before October 9 believed that "nothing could happen" at a demonstration.

2. This percentage is based on 390 respondents who had taken part in a demonstration prior to October 9 and gave a valid answer for the mentioned statement.
3. There were 378 respondents who gave a valid answer to this statement.

Did State Sanctions Have a Deterrence Effect?

Wouldn't we expect that only a few citizens took part in demonstrations under these circumstances? However, there were at least 70,000 present on October 9, 1989, in Leipzig. Maybe only those took part who believed that the security forces would not crush the protests or whose fear of sanctions was low. Our qualitative interviews show indeed that some of our respondents were deterred from protesting because they expected state repression. An example is cabaret performer Bernd-Lutz Lange, a partner in one of our qualitative interviews who responded to our question whether he was a member of an opposition group:

> No, I wasn't a member of such a group. I was a lone fighter. This was because my colleague, with whom I made the program, and I always said: "We have to try to continue with our cabaret work." If we had started working with those groups, it probably would have meant the end of our cabaret.

Lange said about participating in a demonstration during the ecumenical meeting in June 1989:

> I just didn't join in, because I thought to myself: "If you join in now, you'll have to wave your cabaret goodbye."

In a collection of eyewitness reports (Neues Forum Leipzig 1990, 48), a pupil talked about his experience on October 2, 1989:

> We met up and ran through the streets of Gohlis. We weren't sure if we should go or not. There were a lot of kids in our class who would have gone if they hadn't been so afraid.

Yet our qualitative interviews also show that citizens went to the demonstrations although they reckoned on the worst consequences. Mathias Petzoldt, who expected a Chinese solution after the celebrations on October 7, said:

> We went scared stiff to the demonstration on Monday. I went in an old coat and wore different glasses. My wife didn't come along on the first Monday, but she did on the second and the kids came along on the third. But our hearts were pounding with fear the entire time, I tell you. They stood there with their helmets and shields. It was a terrible situation and we couldn't believe our ears when they told us afterwards that the hospitals had made provisions for the expected wounded, that blood transfu-

sions had been prepared and that tanks had been ready and waiting outside of the city. We didn't know anything about that.

Thus, they expected the worst and participated in the Monday demonstrations anyway, even without knowing the real situation.

The quotes we just cited prove that there *were* citizens who knew that they would be taking high risks if they participated in the demonstrations and nevertheless did not let themselves be scared away. On the other hand, there were citizens who feared the regime's sanctions and did *not* participate in the protests. These isolated cases do not answer the question of how a high perceived probability of repression and a high fear of sanctions influenced political activity *in general*. In order to answer this question, we turn to our survey of the population in Leipzig.

Let us assume that the *deterrence hypothesis* is valid. In this case we would expect the following:

> The *more probable* citizens think the four kinds of sanctions are, the less often they will take part in general protests and demonstrations.
>
> The greater the citizens' *fear* of the four sanctions, the less often they will participate in general protests and demonstrations.

We assume for the time being that probability and fear of sanctions have additive effects. In other words, the effect of probability of repression on protests does not depend on the fear of sanctions and vice versa.

In order to test both hypotheses, we computed two overall measures for probability and fear of sanctions by adding the values of the separate sanction probabilities and by adding the values for the four items referring to fear of sanction (see the appendix for more details). Does probability of sanctions have a deterrence effect? Our analyses show the following:

> *Finding 1:* The higher the perceived probability of sanctions, the *more* likely participation is.

The effect of probability of sanctions on participation in general protests is clearly stronger than on participation in demonstrations. Finding 1 clearly disproves the deterrence hypothesis. On the contrary, increasing probability of repression has a *radicalizing effect*.[4]

This finding is supported by other results. If our respondents said that

---

4. For the statistically informed reader: Both overall measures of repression were included with "participation in general protests" and "participation in demonstrations" as dependent variables in regression analyses. For general protests there was a standardized regression coefficient of .20 and for demonstrations a coefficient of .09 of probability of sanctions (both coefficients are significant on the .01 level).

they "had contact with the police or security forces on political grounds," we asked: "Were you observed, interrogated, indoctrinated, arrested, or was an attempt made to win you over to the government side?" If the deterrence hypothesis is correct, the number of types of contact should correlate negatively with participation because those who had experiences with security forces would be more afraid of severe sanctions in case of not living up to the expectations of the regime.[5] The exact opposite is true. The more types of contact one had, the *more frequently* one took part in general protests and demonstrations.[6]

The following two findings also disprove the deterrence hypothesis for probability of sanctions. Those who said they were very afraid of security force intervention during *first* demonstration were particularly active. And those who thought that a Chinese solution or an intervention of Warsaw Pact troops would follow upheaval in the GDR also took part quite often.

How does fear of sanctions affect participation in protests? Our study shows:

Finding 2: The more severe one believes a sanction to be, the *less* one takes action.

This is true only for participation in general protests, but not for participation in demonstrations.[7] This finding therefore *confirms* the deterrence hypothesis only for participation in general protests.

Let us look more closely at the relationships between probability and fear of sanctions on the one hand and political protest on the other. We saw that probability of sanctions had a radicalization effect. Our data further indicate that if probability of sanctions (x-axis) is comparatively low, protest activity (y-axis) increases strongly—that is, there is a relatively strong radicalizing effect. The higher the sanction probability, the less strongly protest increases. That is to say, if probability of sanctions is very high, increasing probability leads only to a relatively low increase of political action. Thus, our analyses show that *the radicalizing effect decreases when probability of sanctions increases.*

We noted before that fear of sanctions has a deterrence effect. If fear of

---

5. Because *simple* contacts with the security authorities to win over the respondent to the government side do not have a sanctioning character, we did not include this item in the scale "experience of sanctions."

6. For the statistically informed reader: The bivariate Pearson correlation of experience of sanctions with "participation in general protests" is .18, the correlation with "participation in demonstrations" .13, both significant on the .01 level.

7. For the statistically informed reader: The standardized regression coefficient for general protests is $-.16$ (significant on the .01 level), and for demonstrations $-.04$ (not significant).

sanctions (x-axis) is low, political protest (y-axis) decreases strongly—that is, the deterrence effect is high. If fear further increases, then the decrease of participation becomes smaller—that is, the deterrence effect becomes weaker. Thus, severe sanctions do not deter as strongly as do light sanctions. Thus, our data are in line with a *decreasing deterrence effect for increasing fear of sanctions*.[8]

We have assumed thus far that expected repression influences participation in general protests as well as demonstrations. Yet is it not also possible that participation in general protests and demonstrations causes a person to fear sanctions as well as expect them more likely? However, experience of sanctions occurred before participation in demonstrations. Participation in demonstrations could therefore not have influenced the earlier experience of sanctions. We further ascertained the extent to which probability and fear of sanctions *before* October 9 influenced participation in general protests and demonstrations *after* October 9. These analyses by and large confirm the findings we reported earlier.

When Do Sanctions Have a Radicalization Effect?

Is there a situation in which the expected punishment becomes more severe, yet the behavior to be punished increases? Assume that for most pupils breaking school rules and the subsequent punishment is regarded as a test of their courage. "Passing" this test and withstanding the punishment are thus prestigious in the eyes of the other pupils. The harder the punishment one has to face, the higher the prestige one will enjoy. Pupils value it highly to enjoy prestige among their peers. Assume now that the principal increases the punishment for playing hooky. It may happen that being punished would increase one's prestige in class so much that one takes the risk of being punished severely. An increase in punishment would then cause an increase rather than a decrease in schoolchildren playing hooky.

In this situation, punishment is accompanied by positive incentives, such as prestige in a group, when the punished behavior is carried out. These positive incentives are so strong that the individual takes the risk of being punished. This in no way means that punishment is completely ineffective in the described situation. As we said earlier, punishment is a cost. If, for example, playing hooky would be punished with immediate dismissal and the

---

8. For the statistically informed reader: We tested the following equation: *Protest* = $a \times ProbSanc^b \times FearSanc^c$ (*ProbSanc* stands for "probability of sanctions" and *FearSanc* stands for "Fear of sanctions"). This equation was tested for general protests (*GenProt*) and for participation in demonstrations (*Dem*). These equations were logged and the coefficients computed. The analyses yielded the following coefficients: $GenProt = 1.479 \times ProbSanc^{.21} \times FearSanc^{-.13}$; $Dem = 1.23 \times ProbSanc^{.16} \times FearSanc^{-.06}$. For details see Opp 1994.

refusal of admission in any school in the country, there would be very few youths who would play hooky. The prestige one would gain is not so large that risking a high punishment will pay off.

How can we use this example to explain the radicalizing effect of sanctions in the GDR? Our example leads us to believe that:

The higher the probability and fear of sanctions, the higher the protest-promoting incentives.[9]

Political dissatisfaction is one of the protest-promoting incentives. Citizens probably view repression as an effect of the total political order in the GDR and not only as a questionable policy of the SED leadership. We believe therefore that high repression generally increases political dissatisfaction.

Repression may also lead to an increase in *perceived political influence*. Why? We saw that due to the liberalization in Eastern Europe and the emigration wave, most respondents believed that reforms were now also necessary in the GDR. Because citizens were highly dissatisfied with the surveillance by the Stasi, we can assume that a change in the use of repression was considered one of the reforms that needed to be introduced. The emigration wave and the liberalization in the East raised many respondents' feelings of personal political influence. It is plausible that the greater the repression practiced by the state, the greater the perceived personal influence.

High repression could also have been seen as a weakness of the regime, which respondents feel leads to greater dissatisfaction in the population, therefore increasing the chance of collective protest and thus the effect of personal political action.

Repression also raises *moral incentives*. Assume someone believes that one has to take action if dissatisfaction is high, and that she or he has to do so despite high risks. An individual who expects high repression in such a situation will be particularly indignant and will feel even more obligated to take part in protest. In other words, people with a high discontent orientation (see chapter 5) should protest to a high degree. Because repression increases political dissatisfaction, those individuals who feel obligated to take action *in general* if they are particularly dissatisfied with a government's policies will protest more frequently.

---

9. This hypothesis is also true for *experience* of sanctions. In Opp 1994, this variable was included in all analyses in conjunction with probability and fear of sanctions. The effects of experience of sanctions are very similar to those of probability of sanctions. In order not to complicate the argument unnecessarily, we do not want to further discuss this variable in this context. For details, see Opp 1994.

We also found in our qualitative interviews that state repression evokes a high level of moral indignation. Detlef Pollack commented in one of our qualitative interviews:

> Yes, I was afraid when I took part in a demonstration on May 7 in Leipzig, the election day . . . I saw how the police just grabbed people out of the crowds and threw them into trucks . . . and suddenly they grabbed the man who had been standing next to me, and that was really frightening. That's when I stopped playing the role of the observer. I became a participant to the extent that I became so furious I yelled along with the rest of the people.

Another respondent, Mathias Petzoldt, remarked:

> The thing which made us increasingly take part in the peace prayers, or simply to be present afterwards, was that the police reacted inappropriately. They started arresting people, and that made things escalate even more. The clashes escalated in a way that couldn't be taken any more. Above all, there was this inner protest against the idea that people were supposed to be intimidated by this massive police presence.

Repression also increases social incentives for protest. For example, if one is dissatisfied and indignant because of high repression, one will also encourage others to take action.

Let us turn again to the example of the schoolchildren. We said that punishment for playing hooky won't be risked any longer if the punishment becomes very severe. Our population survey confirms that this was also the case for the GDR. The relationship between repression and protest-promoting incentives corresponds to an inverted U-curve (see fig. 3). The following holds true for each of the three dimensions of repression (probability of, fear of, and experience of repression): If repression is relatively low—that is, it is in the ascending part of the curve—then an increase in repression leads to an increase in protest-promoting incentives, as pictured in figure 3. If repression exceeds a certain level—that is, it is in the sloping part of the curve—then positive incentives decrease. One will therefore no longer feel obligated to take action and will no longer encourage friends to do the same.[10]

---

10. See the analyses in Opp 1994, in which the findings of these analyses are presented in detail. The hypothesis that repression *also* has a multiplicative effect on incentives is confirmed: the integration in protest-promoting networks plays an important role in this regard.

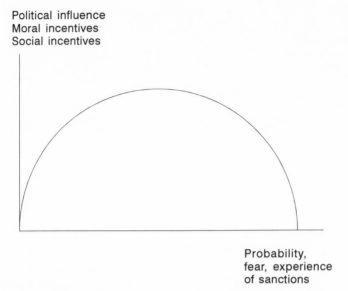

Political influence
Moral incentives
Social incentives

Probability,
fear, experience
of sanctions

Fig. 3. Repression and protest-promoting incentives: the inverted U-curve

Why Did Repression Become Ineffective Only in 1989?

We can more easily understand the answer to this question if we summarize our previous argument (fig. 4). We saw that repression either increases or decreases the protest-promoting incentives, depending on how high the values of the repression factors (probability and severity) are (see the inverted U-curve of fig. 3). Furthermore, repression as well as the protest-promoting incentives have direct effects on political participation.

Did Repression Decrease in 1989?

Why was repression in 1989 no longer effective? We believe that repression was still very high in early 1989 lying somewhere along the descending part of the curve in figure 3. The increase in general protests and demonstrations could be explained by the fact that repression decreased considerably. The positive incentives would then increase (fig. 3) and political activity along with it (fig. 4). Decreasing sanctions had an indirect effect in the sense that they raised positive incentives. However, sanctions also have direct effects on protest (fig. 4), yet these effects are low when compared to the effects of the positive incentives. An increase in the positive incentives is accompanied by a

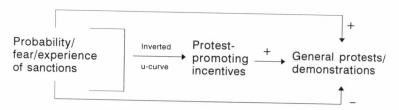

Fig. 4. Repression, protest-promoting incentives, and political protest

relatively strong increase in political activity, whereas a change in repression in this context has hardly any effect.[11]

In fact, it is maintained that the GDR citizens slowly lost their fear of repression during 1989. Cabaret performer Bernd-Lutz Lange describes the situation in one of our qualitative interviews: "I think that the fear in 1989 declined week by week. You could really see it." Many reports on the events in autumn 1989 show that criticism of the conditions in the GDR increased and came not only from opposition groups, but also from a growing number of citizens and even from members of the SED and FDJ. Increasing resistance included some citizens' refusal to provide private accommodations for the Whitsun meeting of the FDJ in Berlin May 14–16. Members of the FDJ symphony orchestra refused to play in the blue shirt, the official uniform of the FDJ. The decreasing effectivity of the sanction system can also be seen in the mass resignation of SED members. Such "insubordination" toward the regime was no more or to a decreasing extent sanctioned (see Schabowski 1991, 177–81). These facts relate to participation in general protests. We indeed believe that both expectations and fear of sanctions decreased for general protests. This would explain, or at least partially explain, as we will see, the increase in general protests.

Yet repression did *not* decrease for participation in demonstrations. Almost all collective activities prior to October 9 were dissolved violently. An example is the 70th anniversary of the murder of Rosa Luxemburg and Karl Liebknecht on January 15, 1989. As had occurred once before on January 17, 1988, a few hundred demonstrators demanded the right of freedom of expression, assembly, and press. Eighty people were arrested. This scenario—a demonstration takes place that is dissolved violently, and its participants are arrested—is typical for the time prior to October 9. Similarly dissolved demonstrations include the demonstrations against the forged communal election on May 7, 1989, and a demonstration on May 8 in which more than 500

---

11. See Opp 1994 for more details on this argument. See also the results of the regression analyses in notes 9 and 10 in chapter 7.

people in Leipzig demonstrated against the previous day's arrests and 16 people were arrested. Other such demonstrations include the Monday demonstrations in Leipzig and the demonstrations during the celebrations at the 40th anniversary of the founding of the GDR on October 6 and 7, 1989. Even a nonapproved music festival was dissolved on June 10, 1989, in Leipzig. Participants were arrested and punished. Other political activities that expressed criticism toward the GDR regime were stopped. On June 7, 1989, 120 civil rights supporters in East Berlin wanted to submit a petition against election forgery at the communal elections in May. They were all taken into custody.

Evidence of the willingness of the SED to use violence to crush mass protest is demonstrated by the fact that the *Neue Deutschland* [New Germany], the SED's press organ, defended the crushing of the democratic movement in China on June 5, 1989. A declaration by the Volkskammer [people's chamber], as usual unanimous, followed, which approved of the crushing of the democratic movement in China and described it as the "crushing of a counterrevolution." Many GDR citizens expected a "Chinese solution" accordingly. Sixty-nine percent of our respondents were afraid that "security forces in the GDR would now take more rigorous action," while 34 percent of the respondents even expected troops of the Warsaw Pact to intervene. Many citizens particularly expected a bloodbath on October 9 in Leipzig.

Our data also confirm that repression for the demonstrations did not decrease but, rather, increased. We asked our respondents how "afraid" they were the first time they demonstrated that "security forces would intervene" or how "secure" they felt "that nothing could happen with so many others around." The average agreement to these statements shows that the fear was greatest on October 9 and that participants also felt the least secure on this date.

One could contend that the following facts refute the hypothesis that says that repression for demonstrations increased. During 1989, it became easier for GDR citizens to leave East Germany. If a citizen came into trouble, there was always the chance to emigrate into the Federal Republic of Germany. One therefore no longer needed to fear repression. Bernd-Lutz Lange described the situation in one of our qualitative interviews:

At the demonstrations [in 1989] everyone could take the risk, thinking that if things don't change here, we'll just have to move to the West.

If we assume that the GDR citizens were principally willing to emigrate into the Federal Republic, this would not have protected them from getting arrested or injured while participating in a demonstration. But let us assume that the prospect of being able to emigrate into the FRG indeed decreased probability and fear of sanctions. If this was the case, we would have been able to ascertain this in the answers of the respondents. If, for example, a respondent answered the question about repression in the workplace and if she or he intended to emigrate if "problems" arose, then that person's answer to questions regarding probability or fear of sanctions would have been different if she or he had considered leaving the GDR. Thus, the opportunity to emigrate is expressed in the respondents' answers.

Let us thus assume that repression for participation in demonstrations increased in 1989. This decreased the positive incentives because, as we assume, the sanctions were very high (in the sloping part of the inverted U-curve). The radicalization effect of probability of sanction on participation in demonstrations was so low that this could not possibly explain the dramatic increase in the participation in demonstrations. How, then, can we explain the increase in demonstrations?

Did Protest Participation Become More "Rewarding" in 1989?

Our theoretical model implies that—given our previous argument—the increase in demonstrations can only be explained by the fact that positive incentives increased through external and internal political events. Such events include the emigration wave, Mikail Gorbachev's visit, and the liberalization in Eastern Europe. This is our central hypothesis. In chapter 12 we will show in detail which events led to changes in which incentives. Thus, our hypothesis is that certain political events increased the positive incentives for the participation in demonstrations to the point where repression became ineffective.

Political events also increased the positive incentives for participation in general protests. These protests therefore did not increase only because of a decrease in repression.

Summary

The presumption that state repression prevented citizens from participating in protests is not borne out by the data. We found that the more certain one was of state sanctions, the *more frequently* one took action. The perceived probability of sanctions therefore had a radicalizing effect. The radicalizing effect was stronger for participation in general protests than for participation in demonstrations. The expected deterrence effect was obtained for fear of sanctions, although only for general protests: the more severe the expected state sanctions were, the less often one took part in general protests.

With respect to the probability of sanctions, we also found that the radicalizing effect decreased when the sanction probability increased. Similarly, regarding fear of sanctions, the deterrence effect decreased with increasing fear of sanctions.

How can we explain that sanctions have a radicalizing effect? Our basic hypothesis says that the higher the repression, the higher the protest-promoting incentives. An inverted U-curve is valid here: Increasing repression (x-axis) initially increases the protest-promoting incentives (y-axis) to a certain point and then decreases them again.

This reasoning helps explain why repression was no longer effective in 1989. Figure 5 summarizes our argument. Let us first look at general protests (fig. 5a). We assumed that repression in the GDR was in the right-hand, downward sloping part of the inverted U-curve. Both probability and fear of sanctions for participation in general protests decreased in 1989. This increased the protest-promoting incentives (because of the inverted U-curve), which were further increased by political events. The decreasing fear of sanctions and the positive incentives increased participation in the general protests so much that the decreasing sanction probability hardly had a protest-

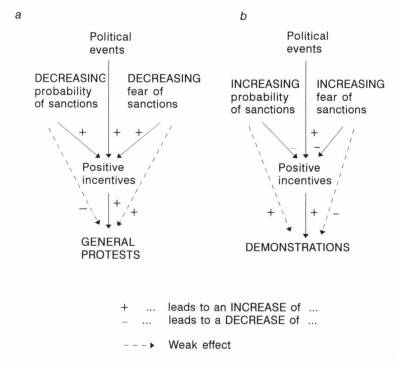

Fig. 5. Repression, political events, and protest

deterring effect (because of the decreasing radicalizing effect). Since the direct effects of fear of sanctions on participation in general protests were small, the increase of protest was largely due to the increasing positive incentives.

For participation in demonstrations, repression increased (fig. 5b), which led to a decrease in positive incentives. Demonstrations grew because the positive incentives were raised by political events and because the direct effects of the positive incentives on participation in the demonstrations were relatively strong.[12]

---

12. The direct effects of the repression variables are shown in table 3 in Opp 1994. In chapter 12 we will see that political events also influenced the SED regime's repression. In figure 4, therefore, there actually should be arrows pointing from "political events" to the repression factors. Yet because this relationship cannot be discussed here, we excluded it entirely so as not to unnecessarily complicate our discussion.

CHAPTER 10

"We Are the People!"
A Revolution without Revolutionaries?

Peter Voss and Karl-Dieter Opp

In the extensive literature about revolutions, *revolutionaries* are often defined as people or groups of people who played an exceptional role during revolutionary events. These include the Jacobins in the French Revolution and the Bolsheviks in the Russian Revolution. Where and who were the Robespierres, Liebknechts, and Lenins of the GDR revolution? We believe that the GDR revolution was a revolution without revolutionaries. The people, the anonymous masses, were on the streets. There were no charismatic leaders, no analytical thinkers, not even real fanatics. It was an after-hours revolution. Although there were no revolutionaries in the GDR, there were people or groups who were more active than others. Who are they?

The Actors of the Revolution

Which groups contributed most to the fall of the GDR? Rolf Reißig (1991) specifies four groups of actors: (1) the new political groups of the opposition movement, (2) parts of the Protestant church, (3) representatives of the critical intellectuals and cultural elites, and (4) the critical reformist sector of the SED. In regard to the first two groups, there is no difference between Reißig's opinion and our own. In earlier chapters we analyzed in detail the roles of the opposition groups and the Church for the GDR revolution. However, we only dealt with the critical intellectuals and the artists to the extent that they belonged to opposition groups or went public with certain forms of protest (see chapter 1). There were certainly many writers, songwriters, rock musicians, actors and cabaret performers, painters, and other artists who took part in various activities against the regime. Some natural or social scientists contributed toward "enlightenment" about the reality of socialism as it existed in the GDR, which can also be considered a form of oppositional behavior. Artists and critical intellectuals organized the demonstration in Berlin on November 4, 1989, which was probably the largest in recent German history.

Yet after the decisive demonstration in Leipzig on October 9, 1989, this was rather an isolated event.

However, in our opinion, the fourth group of actors does not belong to the bearers of the revolution. Our data show that only a small number of SED members worked in opposition groups and that SED members clearly protested less than nonmembers did (see chap. 7). Thus, if there were a critical current in the SED, it certainly had no relevance for the emergence of the protests.

Furthermore, there was a world of difference between the "reformers" in the SED and the representatives of the opposition movement. On the surface, both groups strove for democratic socialism, but their political origin as well as their choice of means and methods divided them like fire and water.

Were there other actors? The most important actor was the population. As we saw in particular in chapter 1, the revolution in the GDR was a spontaneous one.

Why Were the Dissidents Not Revolutionaries?

It was difficult for the opposition to admit their marginal position. On the evening prior to the 40th anniversary of the GDR (October 7, 1989) Bärbel Bohley spoke about the necessity of finally accepting the existence of an insignificant opposition in the GDR. That was a result of the extensive repression. Members of the opposition—for the sake of brevity, we call them dissidents—who took genuine political action were expelled. To permanently prevent their return, the GDR government also took away their GDR citizenship. This certainly contributed to the GDR opposition's weak presence: many of the political entrepreneurs were out of the country.

As long as the system was not generally questioned, limited protest was allowed. The boundaries of criticism allowed by the party sometimes appeared to be far drawn. Yet the SED was sure that the majority of citizens would respect these boundaries. If one wanted to cross the zone defined by the party and test the limits of the system, one had to reckon with great personal disadvantages, and most GDR citizens did not take the risk.

The dissidents were no exception in this regard. And because they did not truly want a revolution, they never demanded power. They wanted *reforms*, as we saw in chapter 3, and wanted to connect the ideas of civil democracy and socialism. That is why Christa Wolf rejected the phrase *turning point* and instead spoke of a "revolutionary renewal" (of socialism!) in her speech on Alexander-Platz and Christoph Hein also proclaimed that there is no alternative to "democratic socialism" (see Zanetti 1991, 202 ff.). Wolfgang Schneider clearly articulated the opposing, left-wing intellectuals' secret love of socialism (1990, 77). They didn't want to take over power but, rather, wanted to be the equal partners of a "chastened" SED in the reform process. This is why they agreed that the success of the peaceful revolution was administrated by Hans Modrow's transitional government. Yet this government finally chimed in with the chorus of "Germany, united fatherland."

During the revolution, the representatives of the opposition movement focused their entire political energy on defeating the Stasi. For them the Stasi was the root evil of GDR socialism. Yet they either did not perceive or did not react to the new tendencies turning up at the demonstrations. They neither expressed opinions on the question of unification, nor put their "third way" in concrete terms, nor did they provide any revolutionary program.

Two Types of Dissidents

Even if we cannot call any of the actors who "made" the GDR revolution "revolutionaries," our early analyses show nevertheless that members of opposition groups played a special role in the revolution in that they took part in general protests more than other citizens did. Dissidents further risked personal disadvantages as the result of their actions. It is therefore interesting to see the extent to which members of opposition groups differ from the average population.

One hundred and one of our respondents in the population survey were members of opposition groups (church groups, Neues Forum—see chapter 7 and the appendix). Because our population survey is representative, these members are also a representative selection of members of opposition groups.

Due to the low number of members in such groups in the GDR on the whole, we expected only a low number of members in our own sample. This expectation led us to survey an additional 209 individuals who claimed to be members of the opposition movement. Our opposition sample was not a random sample (see the introduction and the appendix for more details). Eighty of the 209 respondents said that they had been members of opposition groups, especially church groups and groups such as the Neues Forum, Demokratie Jetzt, and Demokratischer Aufbruch prior to October 9. We included these individuals in our analyses.

In this section we will use both the population and the opposition sample. In our population sample, we will analyze the opposition group members and nonmembers separately. Thus, we differentiate between three samples:

1. nonmembers of opposition groups of the population sample (1,199 people),
2. members of opposition groups of the population sample (101 people),
3. members of opposition groups of the opposition sample (80 people).

It might be appropriate to analyze the two types of dissidents (members of opposition groups) together, but this only makes sense if there are no statistically significant differences between them. In order to ascertain this, we first compared the three groups of respondents according to their political activity. Figure 1 shows the differences in participating in demonstrations. The mean values for both groups in the population sample (0.8 and 1.1) are similar. The dissidents of the opposition sample, however, clearly demonstrated more frequently than the other two groups did (mean value 2.2).[1] When it comes to participation in general protests, we find clear differences between the three groups.[2]

Do these differences indicate that our population survey is not representative? When cases are rare in a population, it may happen that they are not represented in a sample at all. Let us assume there is a school with 2,000 pupils, 5 of whom are (right- or left-wing) extremists. When 20 pupils out of 2,000 are randomly selected, it is highly probable that no extremist is included. If this happens, one can conclude that the number of extremists is very low or even nonexistent in that school. The same goes for our sample. Our sample of opposition groups showed that there were "extremists" among the population who were not included in the representative sample. Because the dissidents in the two samples differed so greatly with respect to their protest behavior, it is not appropriate to analyze them together. We will therefore deal with *three* groups of respondents.

Why are the dissidents in the opposition sample so extreme in regard to their political activity? The selection took place a year after the protests in autumn 1989. The interviewers approached people in the Haus der Demokratie [House of democracy] in Leipzig and asked them for an interview if they claimed to be members of the opposition movement. We believe that these were people who had such strong incentives for political activity before the collapse of the GDR that they also remained politically active after the revolution.

Let us first look only at the dissidents in the two samples: (1) Were there different motives to become a member? (2) Did the dissidents differ according to their activities in their groups? Those who said in the interviews that they were members in a group before October 9 and that they were encouraged to protest, were further asked why they became members. The respondents were provided with the following statements: "I became a member . . .

---

1. For the statistically informed reader: The eta-coefficient for the two groups in the population survey was only .06. If we include the members of the opposition sample, the eta-coefficient becomes .25.

2. For the statistically informed reader: The corresponding eta-coefficients are .25 for the two groups of the population survey. If we include the dissidents of the opposition sample, eta becomes .47.

Participation in Demonstrations
(means; value range 0-4)

Participation in General Protests
(means; value range 1-4)

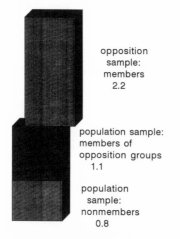
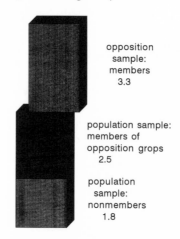

opposition
sample:
members
2.2

opposition
sample:
members
3.3

population sample:
members of
opposition groups
1.1

population sample:
members of
opposition grops
2.5

population
sample:
nonmembers
0.8

population
sample:
nonmembers
1.8

Fig. 1. Participation in demonstrations and general protests: population sample and opposition sample. Members or nonmembers refers to membership in opposition groups. Example: opposition group members of the opposition sample demonstrated on the average 2.2 times.

a. in order to better reach my political goals;
b. because it was important for me to be in a group with people who had similar political ideas as I;
c. to have support in case I would have to deal with the security forces;
d. because I am convinced that every individual is important for groups to be able to reach their goals."

On the average, the dissidents in the opposition sample agreed more with each of these items than did the dissidents in the population sample. Differences were especially great in regard to items a and d.[3]

Did the two groups of dissidents also differ according to the activity within the groups? In order to ascertain this, we asked whether they

a. participated regularly in the group's meetings,
b. took part in planning the meetings,

---

3. For the statistically informed reader: The eta-coefficients for the means of the four indicators, each for the two groups of dissidents, were .32; .11; .12; and .18, respectively. Because of the low N, only the first and last coefficient are significant (.01 and .05 level).

c. brought in new members,
d. were highly active in planning political activities,
e. collected money or other resources which were important for the group's work, or
f. participated in the founding of the group,

possible answers being "no" and "yes." We found that the dissidents in the opposition sample answered "yes" more frequently (with the exception of statement e) than did the dissidents of the population sample. The latter were somewhat more active in regard to e than the former. Yet the differences are low on the whole, except for d and f. In other words, the dissidents of the opposition sample were highly active in planning political activities and were more often founding members of their groups.[4]

Incentives to Protest and Demographic Differences: Dissidents and Other Citizens

Because the dissidents from the opposition sample were particularly active, we expect these individuals to also show high levels of the earlier mentioned incentives for protest. Our data confirm this. The dissidents from the opposition sample

> are politically and socially especially discontented, view themselves as politically very influential, accept protest norms to a particularly strong degree, perceive their groups as strongly encouraging protest, maintain they have been strongly encouraged by reference persons, and do not fear sanctions.

The nonmembers of opposition groups in the population survey have the lowest means in these variables. In regard to the probability of repression, the dissidents from the opposition sample hardly differ from the respondents in the population sample.

It is interesting to note that the dissidents of the opposition sample had fewer critical friends than the dissidents of the population sample did. Dissidents from both samples, on the other hand, had more critical friends than the nonmembers of opposition groups in the population sample did.

We saw that economic dissatisfaction was not relevant for protest activities. We could therefore expect the dissidents from the opposition sample to

---

4. For the statistically informed reader: The eta-coefficient for the indicators a to f were .03; .01; .15; .23; .08; and .19, respectively. Only the coefficients .23 and .19 were significant on the .05 level.

have particularly low values for economic dissatisfaction. This is indeed the case. The nonmembers from the population sample proved to have the highest economic dissatisfaction, followed by the dissidents from the population sample, and finally by the dissidents from the opposition sample.

The radicalization hypothesis discussed earlier is confirmed by the fact that dissidents of the opposition sample had had contact with the security authorities. Yet they were nevertheless more active than the other two groups' respondents.

How did the dissidents view violence? In the population sample, the dissidents rejected violence more than the nonmembers of opposition groups did, yet the differences were small and statistically not significant. It is interesting that the "genuine" dissidents of the opposition sample *accepted* violence to a greater extent than both groups of respondents in the population sample.[5]

We also found large differences in regard to a number of demographic characteristics. The dissidents of the opposition sample are younger (11 years on the average) than the dissidents of the population survey. They and the average citizens of the population sample differed only slightly in regard to age. The dissidents of the opposition sample (probably because of their youth) live more frequently with their children in the same household. On the whole, the dissidents of the opposition sample are also better educated than the dissidents in the representative sample. The two groups of the population sample hardly differed with respect to their schooling. There were no differences between the three groups in regard to the gender structure.

While the dissidents of the population sample were clearly more often members of the Protestant or Catholic church and identified with the church more than the nonmembers of the population sample did, the bonds of dissidents of the opposition sample with the church were *less* close than those of the dissidents in the population sample. Yet both types of dissidents have a clearly stronger bond to the church than do the nonmembers.[6]

Were the Members of Opposition Groups Political Entrepreneurs?

We defined *political entrepreneurs* as individuals with strong protest-promoting incentives (Opp 1991a; see also chap. 2). This definition implies that political entrepreneurs are politically very active. Both characteristics are true for both the dissidents of the opposition and the population sample.

---

5. For the statistically informed reader: The eta-coefficient is .15.
6. For the statistically informed reader: Eta for the two population sample groups is .37; for all three groups it is .41.

One can also lay down other criteria for the definition of a political entrepreneur, yet perhaps it is more appropriate to distinguish between different kinds of political entrepreneurs. The two groups of dissidents differ to the extent that they took part in the founding of the groups and mobilization activities (bringing in new members and so forth). In this regard, the dissidents of the opposition sample were more active than the dissidents of the population sample.

Another difference between political entrepreneurs is with respect to the success of their actions. Success may consist of getting others to protest or of providing incentives for protest. As we saw, the success of dissidents in general was, in this sense, very minor.

"Success" of political entrepreneurs can further be the extent to which their activity leads to the realization of their political goals. In this respect, dissidents in the GDR were no political entrepreneurs.

Demographic Characteristics and Protest

Participants in political protest activities in Western democracies are usually relatively young and members of the middle class. Is this picture also valid for the protests in the GDR? To answer this question we will use only the population sample.

Age is the only demographic characteristic that is relevant for both participation in general protests and in demonstrations. Our data show that the older the respondent, the less the participation. We ascertained the average participation in general protests as well as demonstrations for 13 different age groups. Regarding participation in the general protests, figure 2 shows that participation initially increases from 1.9 to 2.2. We then observe a downward trend, although with leaps. The means are relatively similar for the age span 21 to 40. For these age groups, the relationship between age and protest is statistically no longer significant.[7]

Regarding participation in demonstrations, we see that the participation rate of the 21 to 25 year olds is relatively low, while respondents aged over 25 and under 56 demonstrated more and with about the same frequency.[8]

Regarding *gender*, Förster and Roski (1990) and Mühler and Wilsdorf (1991) found that men demonstrated more often than women did. Although

---

7. For the statistically informed reader: Eta for the general protests and the grouped age variable is .28 for all age groups, the relationship being a negative one as seen in figure 2. The Pearson correlation coefficient for the ungrouped age variable has the value of $-.22$. For the mentioned respondents being older than 20 and up to 40 years of age, eta is .09 and not statistically significant.

8. For the statistically informed reader: The bivariate Pearson correlation between the ungrouped age variable and participation in demonstrations is $-.14$. The correlation for those between 25 and 52 years of age is .01.

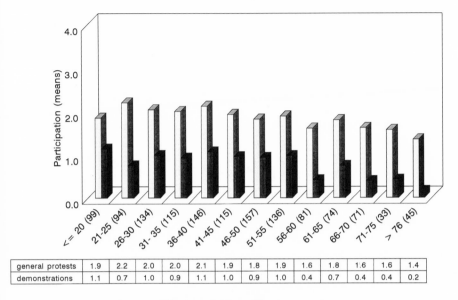

general protests	1.9	2.2	2.0	2.0	2.1	1.9	1.8	1.9	1.6	1.8	1.6	1.6	1.4
demonstrations	1.1	0.7	1.0	0.9	1.1	1.0	0.9	1.0	0.4	0.7	0.4	0.4	0.2

☐ general protests ■ demonstrations

Note the differing value ranges of general protests (1-4) and demonstrations (0-4).

**Fig. 2. Age and participation in general protests and demonstrations.
Figures after age categories represent number of respondents. Value
ranges are 1–4 for general protests and 0–4 for demonstrations.**

our data confirm this finding, the differences are not pronounced. As far as the
general protests are concerned, men and women took part to the same extent.[9]

Family status also had an effect on political activity. Single people participated the most in the general protests. There was no difference in the demonstrations. The number of children younger than 18 who live in a household is
also relevant for political activity, although only for participation in the demonstrations. The more children in a person's household, the less this person
demonstrated. Yet this effect is weak.[10]

Social class was measured, among other things, by education. This

---

9. For the statistically informed reader: Because the demographic variables correlate with
each other, we regressed participation in general protests and demonstrations on all demographic
variables mentioned in the text simultaneously. For participation in demonstrations, the standardized regression coefficient of age is −.16, for general protests −.18 (significance level for
each is .01). "Gender" has a standardized regression coefficient of −.10 (for demonstrations,
significant at the .01 level).

10. For the statistically informed reader: The standardized regression coefficient for "general protests" is −.08 (significant on the .01 level).

includes not having completed eighth grade, not having completed tenth grade, at least having completed tenth grade, Abitur (high school diploma). Values ranged from 1 to 4. There was a weak effect on participation in general protests: the higher the education, the more frequent participation.[11]

We also ascertained professional and vocational training: no vocational training (1), semi-skilled worker (2), and skilled worker (3), technical college degree (4), Meister (training as master) (5), and university degree (6). Our analyses show that professional education had almost no influence on participation in demonstrations. Interestingly, people holding a university degree on the average reported the lowest frequency of demonstration participation of the six groups described above. For the general protests, they do not come last but again were active to a fairly low extent: skilled workers, technical-college–trained respondents, and masters had a higher rate of participation.

Social class also is measured by professional position. We ascertained whether workers, employees, or self-employed citizens differed regarding their level of protest activity. We found no statistically significant differences, neither for participation in protests nor for demonstrations. Monthly net income also had no influence.

Students only played a guest role in the Monday demonstrations. Because they were especially selected, they could only hesitantly identify with the sudden loud demands on party and government for resignation and abolition of the entire socialist system. Professor Okun from the University of Leipzig commented in one of our interviews: "The students only started to react when the right-wing tendency at the demonstrations became larger. Then they tried to take countermeasures, very laudable but unsuccessful."

If one finds relationships between demographic factors and political action, one would like to know why such a relationship does or does not exist. According to our explanatory model, incentives are important for the emergence of protest, and therefore these incentives should be able to explain relationships between demographic factors and protest. For example, young people may protest quite frequently because they are faced with incentives for protest to a greater extent than older people are. Thus, if a relationship between a demographic factor and protest exists, this is because certain incentives for protest are also present.

Does this hypothesis hold true for the demographic factors we measured? Age has the strongest effect on both kinds of protest, and the effect is negative —that is, old age leads to low protest. We expect accordingly that for older people, positive incentives for protest are weak. This is indeed the case. Older people in particular hardly accept protest norms and are rarely members of

---

11. For the statistically informed reader: The standardized regression coefficient, significant on the .01 level, is .11.

protest-promoting groups. They also seldom believe that they can have any political influence by demonstrating. The only incentive showing a positive relationship to age is membership and association with the church. Older people are more frequently members of Protestant or Catholic churches and have stronger bonds with them.[12] Because the other demographic factors have only very weak correlations with protest, the relationships between these factors and incentives are also very weak. They are therefore not worth discussing.

Summary

There were no groups in the GDR that played an outstanding role in the revolution. There was no revolutionary class and no revolutionary party. There was also no charismatic personality who motivated the "masses" to revolutionary actions. One reason for this lack was that the members of opposition groups, who were particularly active in the protests, were also prisoners of the ruling socialist ideology and thus could not offer "the people" any basic alternatives.

To look more closely at the opposition groups, we used three subsamples: nonmembers of opposition groups of the population sample (1,199 people), members of opposition groups (dissidents) of the population sample (101 people), and members of opposition groups (dissidents) of the opposition sample (80 people). Our analyses show that the dissidents from the opposition sample were extreme in regard to activity as well as protest-promoting incentives. This is true in comparison to both the nonmembers and the dissidents of the population sample. The differences between the two groups of dissidents show that there were people in the GDR who were even more active than the randomly selected dissidents of our population sample.

Our hypothesis saying that economic dissatisfaction has no correlation with participation in protests was confirmed again. The nonmembers of opposition groups proved to have the highest economic dissatisfaction, followed by the dissidents of the population sample, and finally by the dissidents of the opposition sample.

Regarding acceptance of violence, the "genuine" dissidents of the opposition sample *accepted* violence to a greater extent than the respondents from the other two groups did.

---

12. For the statistically informed reader: The mentioned bivariate correlations are $-.16$ (protest norms), $-.11$ (membership in protest encouraging groups), and $-.18$ (personal influence by participation in demonstrations). The correlation between age on the one hand and membership and identification with the Church on the other is $.16$. All coefficients are significant on the .01 level.

While the dissidents from the population sample were clearly more often members of the Protestant or Catholic Church and identified more strongly with the church than did the nonmembers, the dissidents of the opposition sample had *weaker* bonds to the church than did the dissidents of the population sample. Yet both groups of dissidents had stronger ties to the church than did the nonmembers of opposition groups.

For the analyses of relationships between demographic characteristics and protest, we again used only our representative population sample. In regard to age, we found that older citizens generally took part less frequently than younger citizens did. Gender had no effect on participation in general protests. Women participated somewhat less in demonstrations than men did. Single people participated in general protests just as frequently as did those with another family status, although they did demonstrate somewhat more frequently. Our analyses also show that schooling had a weak influence on participation in general protests: the longer school has been attended, the higher participation. Professional position had no effect on political activity. It is noteworthy that university-educated people reported a very low level of activity. Monthly net income of all household members is irrelevant for participation.

According to our general explanatory model, correlations between a demographic factor and protest can be explained by correlations of the demographic factors with protest-promoting incentives. Our data confirm this hypothesis. Older people, for example, accepted protest norms only to a small degree, were rarely members of protest-promoting groups, and did not believe in exercising political influence through demonstrations.

CHAPTER 11

Like Hawks in a Trap: Why Wasn't the Protest Movement Crushed?

Karl-Dieter Opp

The SED regime's reactions to the protests in 1989 were astounding. Could it not have been expected that a regime backed up by an extensive repression apparatus would use its power to crush even the slightest protests in order to hinder future protests? The fact that the GDR leaders had approved of the measures by the Chinese government to crack down on the citizen protests in the summer of 1989 could also lead one to expect a "Chinese solution" in the GDR. Why, then, did the SED regime behave differently? This question is the focus of this chapter.

The SED Regime's Reactions to the Citizen Protests

Up until October 9, 1989, the day of the famous Monday demonstration in Leipzig, the regime had attempted to put down all protest by means of repressive measures. These measures have not been used again since October 9, 1989. The step-by-step dissolution of the Politburo began on October 18 with the official resignation of Erich Honecker. He was voted out of office during a Politburo meeting on October 17 by means of an initiative by Politburo members Egon Krenz and Günter Schabowski. After October 18, the power was first in the hands of the new general secretary, Krenz. He made the important decisions as Erich Honecker had done before. Krenz, along with the entire Politburo, resigned on December 3.

Krenz's leadership was characterized by replacements of several Politburo members. Party members protested for the first time against decisions of the Politburo, such as in regard to the calling-in of a party convention. The GDR's isolation from the rest of the world also increased. A policy of progressive concessions was practiced up to the opening of the Berlin Wall on November 9. It appears that these steps took place in a rather hectic and uncoordinated manner.

On November 13, Hans Modrow had been elected the new prime minister by the Volkskammer [people's chamber]. He led a transitional government that, after Egon Krenz's resignation, actually fulfilled government functions until the parliament elections were held on March 18, 1990.

The Goals of the SED Regime

It is often believed that politicians' major goal is promoting the welfare of a country's citizens. The New Political Economy disputes this assumption (McLean 1987, Mueller 1989). It claims that each individual, politicians included, is interested in having a high income, power, prestige, and other privileges. There can be no doubt that the members of the Politburo were concerned with their own personal privileges. This hypothesis is supported by reports about the luxury lifestyle of the SED leaders—luxury in comparison to the lifestyle of the GDR citizens—in the city of Wandlitz. On the other hand, the members of the Politburo were also interested in implementing an authoritarian Marxist ideology, which they believed led to the general welfare of the people and which was imposed on the citizens by force. The biographies of leading functionaries support this proposition: they either stem from communist families or supported the communist ideology at a time where they had to face grave disadvantages and could not have reckoned with achieving a privileged position through it (see the short biographies of Politburo members in Schabowski 1990). This hypothesis is further confirmed by an interview with Günter Schabowski (1990), who was a member of the Politburo.[1] He describes Honecker as a "devout communist" (18), and characterizes the members of the Politburo as having had a "profound conviction of the moral and political justification of the existence of the GDR. This was the basis for everything that occurred" (31). In the last sentence of this quotation, Schabowski refers to the way members of the Politburo justified repression and the command to shoot any refugees trying to cross the border to West Germany.

Whatever the concrete goals of politicians, and particularly of members of the SED regime, may be, they have one goal in common: staying in office. If they attain this aim other goals are achieved as well.

In this chapter we only assume that the primary aim of the SED regime was to stay in power. We will see that this assumption is largely sufficient for explaining the behavior of the regime. An additional assumption is that politicians, and other citizens as well, seek to avoid physical injuries and wish to keep a certain standard of living after their resignation.

---

1. Schabowski was unemployed at the time of the interview. His statements appear truthful because there seems to be no motive for him to make false statements in regard to the facts of interest in this chapter.

Tactics of Staying in Power

For a regime that seeks to secure its power, political organization and the actual power distribution are restrictions for political action. We will therefore first outline the political organization and distribution of power in the GDR as they were before the revolutionary events took place.

The Political Structure

Power in the GDR was concentrated among the members of the Politburo. They were elected by another SED committee: the Zentralkomitee [central committee]. This committee was in turn elected by the SED party convention. At the SED convention, the SED members were represented by SED delegates. The party convention was the highest organ of the SED. Yet it rarely met, usually once every four to five years. It seems that democracy was practiced within the party. Yet in truth there was always only one candidate, to be determined by the next higher party level. This candidate was usually elected without opposition. Furthermore, the SED worked closely with so-called mass organizations such as the FDGB labor union or the FDJ youth organization. Parties and mass organizations were united in the "national front."

The SED was so powerful because it received, together with the so-called block parties associated with the SED, almost all the votes at the elections. Participation in elections and voting behavior were under strict supervision. Nonvoters and those who cast an invalid vote (there was no opposition party to vote for) could be detected and punished. Therefore, the national parliament was actually controlled by the SED. According to the constitution, the national parliament was the highest organ of power. In reality, it was only an organ of consent for the decisions of party and government.[2] What possibilities existed for the Politburo to stay in office, given the political framework we have just described?

Tactic 1: Propaganda

Extensive resources were devoted to convince the citizens of the virtues of socialism (as the SED viewed it). Centrally controlled media, speeches at

---

2. In order to explain the reactions of the Politburo to the citizen protests, it is not necessary to present the political distribution of power in the GDR in great detail. See, for example, Dähn 1985. This book contains extensive material on the GDR constitution and its political reality. The first chapter addresses the question of how the SED developed its incredible power, a question not dealt with in this book. See also Glaeßner 1989.

many political events, and publications were used to present the same topics and claims again and again. The educational system was also part of the propaganda apparatus. The attempt to "educate" the GDR citizens, so that they would internalize the socialist ideology, began in baby cribs (Klier 1990; Maaz 1990, 25–31)

Yet it seems that the SED regime could not convince the larger part of the GDR population to accept the communist ideology. This is probably due to the fact that a great number of the communist leaders' contentions obviously did not hold true. An example of this was the contention regarding the "superiority of the GDR's economic system." Normative postulates such as freedom of speech, which were components of the SED party program and the constitution, were not realized. As a consequence, the citizens did not believe in the ideology nor did they accept those in power who represented it.

Most citizens did not express their grievances freely because they were afraid of the penalties. This *forced compliance* may have caused emotional stress; therefore, they might have accepted socialist ideology. The implausibility of this argument can be explained by the social-psychological theory of cognitive dissonance (Festinger 1957, also see Kuran 1989, 1991). Forced compliance will not lead to a change in opinion if the expression of a conviction opposite to one's own is primarily a result of force or threat of punishment (Festinger 1957, 85) and if the costs of expressing one's true opinion are very high. A discrepancy between true and expressed opinion also will endure if there is no social support for adaptation (Festinger 1957, chap. 8). Thus, if a person knows that many other citizens also don't believe what they say, this "schizophrenia" will be seen as normal and no social pressure will exist to match one's true opinion with the expressed opinion. These conditions were present in the GDR.

Tactic 2: Selection of Loyal Personnel

It was one of the SED's tactics to fill at least the most important positions with devout SED members. This was achieved by means of special SED-controlled selection procedures for political candidates.

Tactic 3: Distribution of Privileges According to Loyalty

Even if the filling of all important positions with devout party members is successful, one still cannot be certain that they will always act for the good of the party. Furthermore, it is often impossible to fill positions with loyal followers. To secure loyalty even in those cases, loyal behavior was rewarded, especially with material goods or special privileges.

Tactic 4: Repression

The SED was able to build up an extensive system of repression during its 40 years of existence. The police and the Ministerium für Staatssicherheit (MfS) [ministry of state security], also called Stasi, were responsible for the repression. The MfS operated an extensive private informer system of more than 100,000 citizens, in addition to its more than 85,000 full-time employees (Gill and Schröter 1991). The legal system and the courts were also used to support the ideology by punishing deviators.

Repression was extensive. Not only were those individuals punished who made critical statements, but oppositional parties were also forbidden and emigration was only possible with government approval. Repression took many forms, ranging from admonitions to prison sentences.

Tactic 5: Changes in Ideology

If a political program is only an instrument used to retain power, then a regime would consider changing the political program if it cannot be "sold" any longer. This may happen when central empirical propositions of a program are perceived as wrong. An example is the—wrong—assumption that a centralized planned economy is more efficient than a market economy. The Politburo could therefore have decided to extend private ownership of the means of production and introduce markets in order to instigate a higher amount of personal initiative of producers and consumers.

The Two Problems of a Dictatorship to Stay in Power

A political regime whose power is based largely on repression is faced with two problems. The *information problem* refers to the difficulty to determine the level of citizen support for the government. The *repression problem* means that repression cannot be increased at will without creating further problems endangering the regime's ability to stay in power.

The Information Problem

In order to develop effective strategies for staying in power, a regime will attempt to collect the most accurate information possible about the support it has. In democracies, opinion research is used for this purpose. In dictatorships, one cannot expect a respondent to make negative statements about the regime like in a democratic regime. Honest answers are more likely if survey questions are answered in written form and with full anonymity. Yet it is questionable whether the respondents would believe assurances of anonymity. This belief would depend on how the interviews were done. If a survey is organized so that no one can determine who filled out a questionnaire, one can reckon on honest answers to a high degree. Honest answers will also depend on how likely high negative sanctions for critical statements are expected and to what extent honest answers are considered a form of protest by the respondents. In the latter case, increasing incentives for protest would cause respondents to express criticism against the regime more often. In this situation, trends could be determined. For example, let's assume that 3 percent of the respondents criticized the supply situation at one point in time, and 10 percent at a later point in time. The percentage of dissatisfied citizens may in fact be 65 percent the first time and 89 percent the second time. Nevertheless, the results of the survey still would not reveal either the real percentage of discontented citizens or the real increase.

There were surveys in the GDR in which the political attitudes of the population, or parts thereof, were investigated. The Zentralinstitut für Jugendforschung [Central institute for youth research] in Leipzig carried out surveys among young people. Questionnaires were distributed in schools and were filled out and collected by the pupils. In a conversation Professor Walter Friedrich, the former head of this institute, said that the results of this research showed a high level of regime-critical attitudes among the respondents. These results were presented to the SED leaders. They argued that they knew what the population thinks and that the research findings must therefore be wrong. In the early 1980s, the opinion research institute of the central committee of the SED was closed because the reports passed on to the party leaders were too critical.

In this case, the problem was not that too little information about the extent of criticism against the regime existed, it was that the information was not put to use. The first reason for ignoring this information was probably that the party leaders were so convinced their program provided for the welfare of the citizens, they could not have imagined a large number of citizens rejecting it. The second reason may have been that the survey results contradicted other information that showed high levels of support by the citizens. The problems we have mentioned regarding the collection of dependable information in verbal interviews were increased if leading party functionaries ascertained opinions by having conversations with rank-and-file party members or firm employees. In such conversations, the probability of being punished if critical views were expressed was even greater than in answering survey questions.

Yet even if lower-level party functionaries had information about the problems of the population, there were incentives not to pass this information on to the higher party levels. Presenting information on such problems was seen as a sign of unsuccessful party work and presumably had negative consequences.

Finally, information on the extent of opposition could be provided by the employees of the MfS, yet the aforementioned problems were also common here. The security forces only partly uncovered regime-critical statements made by citizens. Such is also the case in regard to the existence of private informers of whom the citizens were aware. "Dangerous" opinions would be expressed only in the presence of close friends. Even if such friends were informers, they would often report only about people with whom they have no close relationship, or they would report "harmless" incidents.

Yet even if the MfS had dependable information about the true extent of opposition, there was still an incentive not to pass this information on to the regime, or to downplay the extent of opposition, because an increase in opposition could be looked on by the regime as the fault of the security authorities—for it is indeed their task to stop opposition and thus to secure the power of the regime. If opposition grows, this task has not been fulfilled. This situation would have negative consequences for the heads of the repression apparatus.

Furthermore, the SED regime itself arranged "applause" for its own policies. A large number of mass events, conferences, conventions, and the like were organized where various speakers praised the regime and the socialist ideology. An SED leader who experiences celebration and support on every possible occasion would hardly believe that only a small percentage of the supporters are loyal comrades.

The SED regime expended extensive resources for ideological work. If a regime exists for a long time, its functionaries will assume that these efforts have created loyalty to a high extent.

Some of the considerations we have described are supported by statements made by Erich Honecker in an interview (Andert and Herzberg 1991):

> I'd like to say that I read almost all the reports by the MfS . . . their reports . . . always seemed to be like a summary of the reports by the Western press about the GDR . . . I myself never really paid attention to them . . . MfS information was not all that dependable for the party and government leadership. (312)

> We provided ourselves with concrete information by traveling around the country and having various discussions. There was direct information, as bad as it might have been, from the basis organizations of the party. . . and we also continuously received information from the worker and farmer inspection. . . . It was a carefully selected collective, really in-

corruptible. . . . Despite all of the embellishment, and there was always embellishment wherever people were, there were also realistic reports. (313)

The important fact for our purposes is that the MfS's information was not considered dependable, apparently because the reports were still too negative. Honecker received his information from personal talks. Although he was skeptical, he largely believed what he was told because it corresponded to desired information. Nothing suggests that Honecker was fully aware of the incentive problems discussed earlier leading to a distortion of unwelcome facts.

The Repression Problem

Up till now, we have implicitly assumed that a dictatorship can increase the amount of repression at will. But this assumption is incorrect. A regime's repression apparatus consists of people faced with a regime's orders. Whether or not these orders are carried out depends on the benefits and costs of obeying them. If orders are not followed, costs consist of punishment while following orders leads to benefits such as professional promotion. But following orders may also create costs. If, for example, a police officer knows that he has relatives and friends among the demonstrators in front of him, he probably for moral reasons will not obey the order to shoot at peaceful demonstrators, even if he risks a prison sentence for disobeying orders.

The first problem of a regime increasing its repression is the *loyalty of the sanctioning apparatus*. The harder the sanctions demanded by the regime, the lower the loyalty of the members of the sanctioning apparatus—that is, the lesser the regime's chance of enforcing the desired sanctions. The loyalty of the sanctioning apparatus also decreases according to the degree to which the sanctioned behavior itself appears legitimate, morally justified, or even morally necessary.[3]

The decision to carry out orders referring to specific acts of repression is influenced by the contact to other members of the sanctioning apparatus as well. Instructions to increase punishment may be discussed among members of the sanctioning apparatus and considered morally questionable, and "informal" negative sanctions might be imposed if one follows orders. Similarly, the decision to carry through with repression activities may be influenced by other social contacts with friends and family members. These incentives not to follow orders of punishing others may lead in the extreme case to a situa-

---

3. These propositions hold for the GDR. We leave it open whether they are valid in all societal contexts.

tion where a government decides to increase repression and no member of the apparatus follows the pertinent instructions.

The second problem with which a regime is confronted when it wants to increase repression is a *solidarization effect*. An increase in repression often leads those who are being informed about others being punished to sympathize with the punished (see chapter 9). Repression in this case has a radicalization effect. An increase in repression could further lead to a *worsening of relations with other countries*. The greater a country's dependency on other countries, and the greater the chance that increasing repression could be sanctioned by them, the higher the costs of repression for a country. Finally, the leaders may have to take a *personal risk of ineffective repression* into account. The leading figures of a regime may expect protests that end in bloodshed to lead to severe punishment if they are not able to hold power.

Alternatives to Staying in Power in the GDR in 1989

In regard to why the SED regime reacted in a particular manner to the growing protests in 1989, the question arises why the discussed alternatives of staying in power were or were not chosen. In answering this question, we want to examine what role the previously discussed information and repression problems played for the reactions of the regime. We will not deal with the selection of loyal personnel and the distribution of privileges according to loyalty because both alternatives are *long-term* tactics of staying in power. If a regime is suddenly faced with increasing opposition, as was the case in the GDR, only the three other tactics will be considered: increasing propaganda, expanding repression, and changing the ideology.

Increasing Propaganda

The regime put this tactic into use. The government reacted to the protests with a great number of declarations and statements: socialism's triumphs were emphasized again and again in order to make the protests appear ludicrous and initiated by enemies of the working class. Demonstrators were stigmatized as troublemakers and rowdies and only a minority of the people.

Yet the propaganda was not successful. The main reason was that contradictions between the statements of the regime and reality were too obvious to the citizens. Couldn't the SED regime have predicted that propaganda wouldn't be effective? Taking the perspective of a Politburo member, it was at least not implausible to assume that intensifying the propaganda would bring the deviators, or at least a large number of them, to reason. After all, the propaganda machine seemed to have been effective for a long time. An increase in propaganda can also be explained by the fact that the SED highly underestimated the amount of opposition. If one believes that the majority of the population supports the regime, increasing propaganda may seem effective. Furthermore, because propaganda could be increased at little cost, it was at least worth a try. The minister of the MfS at that time, Erich Mielke, still seemed to believe in the success of propaganda on October 21, 1989 (Mitter and Wolle 1990, 230).

Apart from our theoretical argument, the following facts demonstrate that the government overestimated the loyalty and underestimated the disloyalty of its citizens. Günter Schabowski commented in an interview on the communal elections in the GDR on May 7, 1989 (1990, 54), that one could reckon on 5 percent to 7 percent of the population, distinctly more than before, standing in open opposition to the government. Schabowski also describes the perceived danger of the opposition groups to the members of the Politburo:

> The security forces were solely responsible for dealing with the opposition groups. We knew, of course, that they existed but the party members and leaders saw them as peripheral political groupings which had an impact on the population but not a decisive one. They bothered us but we did not perceive them as a threat to our existence. (57)

According to Schabowski, even after Erich Honecker's resignation on October 18, 1989, no one wanted "to believe that the prevailing concept of socialism had failed" (117). Only in mid-November did the extent of opposition toward the regime become clear (140–41).

The Politburo members' information was at least partially based on the information provided by the MfS. The nature of this information can be seen from the MfS orders and reports between January and November 1989, published in Mitter and Wolle 1990. This publication not only contains reports that were presented to the members of the Politburo, but also reports, minutes of meetings, and injunctions intended for MfS internal use. These materials prove, first, that the reports presented to the Politburo were drafted so that it appeared as if only a small number of people took part in the reported protest events. They prove, second, that these protest activities were always successfully stopped or controlled by state security forces. Therefore, the Politburo members must have had the impression that the opposition could not have threatened the SED's power. This notion is confirmed by Schabowski's remarks on how the Politburo evaluated the opposition.

The following report, which was presented to Politburo members on March 14, 1989, illustrates the points made in the latter paragraph (little opposition, successful actions of the Stasi). We quote the first two paragraphs of this report (Mitter and Wolle 1990, 28):

After the Monday peace prayer in the Nikolaikirche in Leipzig on March 13, 1989, was over (participation by approximately 650 people, among them a large number of emigration applicants as well as visitors of the trade fair; the "peace prayer" was of a religious nature) 300 people . . . gathered in front of the Nikolaikirche with the intention of forming a march towards the Thomaskirche (at the center of the city).

Approximately 850 members of the security forces, as well as other societal forces deployed according to a plan coordinated with the SED district head undermined this act of provocation.

However, in other reports that were not presented to the Politburo, the MfS did register the increase of dissatisfaction and protests. Yet even on August 31, 1989, these were not considered a threat to the SED functionaries. The following dialogue, which can be found in the minutes of a meeting on August 31, 1989, in the MfS, demonstrates this (Mitter and Wolle 1990, 125):

> *Comrade Minister:* How would you describe the situation?
> *Comrade Major Dangriess:* Comrade Minister, I would say, of course that the situation on the whole is stable. Yet there are tendencies that have to do with the problems in Hungary and those who stayed there. Things like this even make progressive forces ponder, especially about the consequences.
> *Comrade Minister:* Do you think that tomorrow an event will take place like on June 17th?
> *Comrade Major Dangriess:* No, it's not taking place tomorrow or at any other time and it's our job to make sure of that.

It seems that the situation was first assessed more realistically in an MfS internal report from September 11, 1989:

> According to information at hand, numerous party members . . . are deeply worried about the current general mood among a large percentage of the working population . . . with serious fears concerning the further political stability in the GDR. (Mitter and Wolle 1990, 148)

It is again striking that the critical situation in the GDR was described in reports that were not passed on to the Politburo. This fact confirms our theoretical assumption that the MfS made an effort to hold back information about the extent of opposition in the country. The Politburo received the first realistic report on October 9, 1989.

Increasing Repression

Why didn't the regime attempt to intensify repression, such as arresting all known members of opposition groups, violent prevention of the Monday prayers, and more brutal intervention at demonstrations? This did not take place because of the two repression problems. The loyalty problem was addressed in an internal MfS report from October 15, 1990 (Mitter and Wolle 1990, 221–22). It reports that some "collectives and fighters" had refused to be deployed for the "guarantee of public order and security" at the 40th anniversary on October 7, 1989, that resignations from the party and combat groups had been announced, and that orders were disobeyed. If there had been instructions in such a situation to strengthen repression, the loyalty problems among the members of the sanctioning apparatus would have been even greater.

The following facts also indicate that problems with carrying out repressive acts had increased particularly since September 1989. Members of the sanctioning apparatus were GDR citizens as much as those against whom the repression was directed, and they were therefore also increasingly faced with the mentioned protest incentives. Furthermore, the number of citizens participating in protest actions increased steadily. Therefore, assertions of the SED regime that described the opposition as made up of "rowdies," "criminals," and members of other marginal groups became incredulous. It became increasingly evident that it was indeed "the people" who stood in opposition to the regime. Members of the sanctioning apparatus therefore probably considered these protest activities to be morally justified. Furthermore, incentives to treat the opposition "harshly" were decreased because the mounting participation in protest activities probably made participation in repressive actions appear increasingly ineffective and dangerous due to expected counterreactions.

Security officials appear to have taken the "danger" of a solidarization effect into consideration. In an MfS report from June 1, 1989 (Mitter and Wolle 1990), which was presented to Honecker and other members of the Politburo, it reads (53):

> These [oppositional] forces continually attempt to create "martyrs". . . by provoking confrontation with the socialist government and attempting furthermore to receive international support for those people's and their own anti-socialist activities.

The report then continues (55) that

> varied, consistently appropriate sanctioning measures should be taken [against such organized forces]. It would be appropriate to support these actions by means of corresponding offensive political and ideological

measures in order to increase the intended disciplinary effect and prevent the possible reactions of other antagonistic, oppositional forces.

Thus, the use of armed force was indeed considered. Schabowski (1990, 75) writes in reference to the celebrations on October 7, 1989, for the 40th anniversary of the GDR's founding: "I knew that Mielke and Honecker had an agreement on the use of military force." The MfS's instructions and reports, which we already quoted, also show that Mielke considered the use of armed force. On October 9, 1989, he ordered that:

> Members [of security forces] who regularly carry arms are to have their weapons on them at all times according to the given requirements. (Mitter and Wolle 1990, 201)

Concluding a speech on as late as October 21, 1989 Mielke said (Mitter and Wolle 1990, 230): "We must be able to rely on the armed forces and the combat groups in every situation." We presume that this use of force was disconsidered because of the two problems mentioned previously.

A "Chinese solution" would have also worsened the GDR's relations with other socialist and nonsocialist countries. We do not know what role such considerations played in the decision not to attempt a Chinese solution. The internal problems we have described probably sufficed to make such a decision impossible. We can also not ascertain the extent to which the leaders were afraid of being held responsible in the case of a failed Chinese solution and how much this influenced their decision not to crush the protests.

The fact that the regime did not use force during the demonstration in Leipzig on October 9, 1989, is consistent with our theoretical argument. As we mentioned before, police units, combat groups, and MfS employees had gathered on Karl-Marx-Platz. Yet available materials do not show unequivocally who made the decision not to dissolve the demonstration and what motives lay behind this decision. Only one thing is certain: no order was made to shoot at the demonstration in Leipzig.[4]

Changing the Political Program

Why didn't the SED regime choose to take the reform course? The following explanation appears to be the most plausible one. One will not consider changing the party program if one believes the opposition to be so minor that

---

4. There are a number of reports on this topic in periodicals. See in particular *Der Stern*, issues 5 to 7, from January 1, 1991, to February 15, 1992. Also see *Der Spiegel* from November 27, 1989, and the series "Ich bin das Volk!" in issues 16 to 18, from April 16 to April 30, 1990. On the events in Leipzig, see Kuhn 1992.

other and more simple strategies will yield the desired effect of remaining in power. One will particularly not bear the costs of changing an ideology if one believes that propaganda is sufficient for this purpose. The fact that the Politburo first discussed reforms after it realized how extensive the opposition to the regime was is consistent with this explanation. In the Politburo, reforms were talked about only after Erich Honecker's resignation on October 18, 1989. Schabowski writes: "We completely underestimated the lack of a schedule to guide us. We thought we had a lot of time" (Mitter and Wolle 1990, 110). In other words, the regime did not believe the opposition to be so strong that a program change was necessary in order to remain in power.

The End of the Old Regime

How did the SED regime's fall occur? The GDR in fact had a democratic constitution, which was nullified by repressive practices. As these repressive practices became ineffective after October 9, 1989, democratic processes again came into effect. The dissolving of the SED regime occurred the same way governments are ousted in democratic systems: through elections.

Summary

In our explanation of the reactions of the Politburo (then the center of power in the GDR) to the citizen protests, we assume that the members of the Politburo were primarily interested in staying in power. Given the GDR's political order, power could be sustained by means of propaganda, selection of loyal personnel, distribution of privileges according to loyalty, repression, or changes in the ideology.

When a dictatorship attempts to use one of these strategies, it is confronted with two problems. The information problem consists of finding out how widespread opposition among the population is. If critical statements are punished, a regime will systematically overestimate public support. The repression problem refers to two barriers that are present when the amount of repression is to be increased. First, if the ordered sanctions extend beyond a certain limit, an increasing number of members of the repression apparatus will refuse to carry out ordered sanctions. Second, sanctions often create solidarity effects.

Which strategies did the SED regime believe to be most effective in the achievement of its goals? It chose to increase propaganda because it grossly overestimated the amount of public support. Intensifying propaganda therefore appeared effective. Increasing repression did not seem effective. Problems with the sanctioning apparatus members' loyalty arose and the "danger" of solidarization effects became evident with increasing repression. A change in the party program also did not occur because the SED regime underestimated the opposition and therefore believed propaganda would guarantee its staying in power.

Our explanation does not refer to *personality characteristics* of SED politicians, nor to their age. We believe that the situation of the GDR produced incentives that would have led to the same decisions irrespective of the personality characteristics or age of the leaders involved. Second, our explanation does not include the *economic problems* the GDR faced. It seems very implausible that an authoritarian regime resigns because the population's standard of living declines or because the adopted economic order yields highly inefficient outcomes. The regime may expect foreign aid—especially from the FRG. But even if the SED regime did not count on this, why should it not demand the population adapt to an even lower standard of living? A regime that puts its entire population in prison will not hesitate to aggravate the problems of the population by adding economic hardship.

CHAPTER 12

The Dynamics of the Revolution

Karl-Dieter Opp

We have not yet systematically analyzed why the revolution developed in the manner it did over time. In order to explain the increase in general protests and demonstrations in 1989, we must first show how the *incentives,* which were relevant for the development of these protests, changed over time. Second, we need to know *why* the incentives changed. We will show that both internal as well as external events played an important role in the growth of the protests. *External events* include decisions made in foreign countries, such as Hungary's decision to open the border to Austria, as well as the consequences of these decisions, such as protests of the population. *Internal events* refer to the decisions of the SED regime and their effects. For the sake of brevity, we will denote internal and external events as *political events.* Finally, in explaining the dynamics of the revolution, we will show how incentives and political events *mutually* influenced each other over time. These three questions are the subject of this chapter.

The Process of the Revolution: Some General Considerations

The citizens' protests were caused by certain incentives. These incentives were changed by political events (see fig. 1, arrows pointing from "SED regime" and "foreign countries" to "citizens"). The protests influenced both the reactions of the SED regime and reactions from foreign countries (arrows from "citizens" to "SED regime" and "foreign countries"). For example, the protests in the GDR might have influenced the decision of the Hungarian government to open the borders to Austria. Thus, there is a reciprocal influence between the protests on the one hand and the reactions of the SED regime and foreign countries on the other. Furthermore, reactions of foreign countries toward the protests in the GDR influenced the reactions of the SED toward the protests and vice versa (see arrow between "SED regime" and "foreign countries" in fig. 1). These processes will not be the subject of this

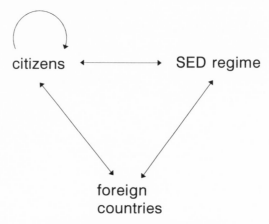

Fig. 1. The actors of the revolution

chapter. Finally, the growing protests encouraged other citizens to follow and thus increased the protest-promoting incentives (see the rounded arrow above "citizens").

The Situation at the Beginning of 1989

Several empirical studies indicate that *political dissatisfaction* was relatively high at the beginning of 1989 (Gensicke 1992, 16; see also chapter 3 of this book), whereas *perceived political influence* was low. In comparison to the years before, the situation in the GDR had not changed much at the beginning of 1989. The SED leadership continued to possess and use its absolute power. Any form of opposition was oppressed. Mikhail Gorbachev's new politics were rejected by the regime. Reforms in other Eastern European countries were not yet so advanced as to give GDR citizens any great hopes of making changes in their own country.

In regard to *protest norms*, we saw in chapter 5 that respondents believed protest norms to be applicable only under certain conditions: particularly if dissatisfaction is high, if the risk of participating is low, if the protests had a chance for success, and if a sufficient number of others were willing to join. At the beginning of 1989, dissatisfaction was high but the other mentioned conditions were hardly present.

Social incentives for participation in protests against the SED regime were relatively low at the beginning of 1989. Friends and acquaintances will not encourage participation in protests if expected repression is high and if the chance for success of the protests is low.

Repression was high at the beginning of 1989. As we saw in chapter 9, repression has a radicalization effect under certain conditions, but the deterring effect prevails when repression is very high.

Changes in Incentives from May 7 until October 9, 1989

We noted in chapter 1 that protests began to increase on May 7, 1989, when it turned out that the results of the local elections were forged. Protest-promoting incentives increased after that date. Political dissatisfaction notably increased in 1989. Köhler (1991, 120) reported on research in the GDR indicating that 47 percent of the respondents became politically more dissatisfied in May 1989. In August 1989, 68 percent were more dissatisfied.

The other protest-promoting incentives also increased after May 7, as we will see in the next section. Due to political events such as the emigration wave and the liberalization in Eastern Europe, perceived political influence increased and protest norms became applicable. This situation probably also led to an increase in the positive social incentives for participation in protest.

We noted in chapter 9 that expected repression for participation in demonstrations remained constant or even increased, while repression for general protests presumably decreased. We will address the changes in incentives again when dealing with the causes for their changes.

The Dynamics of the Revolution

In the following section we will first show that changes in certain incentives led to changes in other incentives. Why is it useful to know the relationships between incentives in explaining the revolution in the GDR? We noted that protest-promoting incentives often have a twofold effect: they influence political action directly as well as indirectly. If, for example, dissatisfaction increases, this causes an increase in social incentives, which in turn cause increased political activity. If we know the direct and indirect effects, we can better explain the effects of the changes in certain incentives. In the second part of this chapter we will examine which external and internal events caused the changes in incentives mentioned in the previous section.

The Dynamics of Incentives

If certain incentives change, does this cause other incentives to change as well? Figure 2 summarizes our hypotheses. We have already seen in chapter 9 that an increase in repression generally strengthens protest-promoting incen-

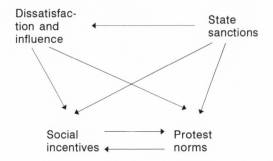

Fig. 2. The dynamics of the incentives for protest: hypotheses

tives unless repression is very high. State sanctions raise in particular public goods motivation (political dissatisfaction and influence), social incentives, and protest norms.

If public goods motivation increases, social incentives also increase as friends and acquaintances encourage protests. Protest norms become applicable. We noted particularly that increasing dissatisfaction increases a sense of duty to participate in protests.

There is a reciprocal relationship between social incentives and protest norms. On the one hand, if social incentives for protest are high, protest norms are applicable because in social networks where participation in protests is encouraged, there is also an appeal to protest norms. On the other hand, we assume that if one feels obligated to protest, one also will encourage others to take part.

Our population survey confirms the hypotheses summarized in figure 2, inasmuch as they can be tested with our data. We will briefly report on the results of our statistical analyses. We mentioned that *repression* and *positive incentives* encompass various factors. Repression consists of probability, fear, and experience of sanctions. Positive incentives are expectations of reference persons to protest, membership in protest-supporting groups, and critical friends. We tested the hypotheses in figure 2 for each of the separate factors— with one exception: the hypothesis that individuals who accept protest norms also encourage others to take part could not be tested. The reason is that our questionnaire did not include a question referring to the extent to which persons encourage others to protest. Figure 3 displays the results of our statistical analyses. An arrow means that a postulated relationship was confirmed.[1]

---

1. For the statistically informed reader: The factor "dissatisfaction and influence" was constructed in the following manner for the analyses in this section. We distinguished between two types of public goods motivation earlier. A first interaction term consisted of political

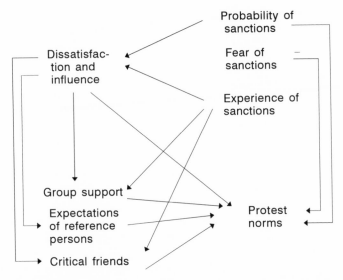

Fig. 3. The dynamics of the incentives for protest: results (all effects are positive unless marked otherwise)

Political Events and Incentives for Protest

Why did the incentives change in the way they did? In this section we will outline the most important internal and external events and how they influenced which incentives.[2]

---

dissatisfaction and influence by means of participation in general protests. The second interaction term included political dissatisfaction and influence by participation in demonstrations—see the appendix. For the analyses in this section, we transformed both interaction terms to the same value range, added the values for each respondent, and divided them by two. We did this because we wanted to test the effect of one type of public goods motivation not only on the incentives, but also on the entire collective good motivation.

In order to test the causal model of figure 2—with the exception of the effect of protest norms on positive incentives, as was noted before—we proceeded in the following manner. We carried out a regression analysis for each separate dependent variable in which all other independent, causally preceding variables (fig. 2) were included. For example, for each of the variables included in the factor "social incentives," a regression analysis was run, the dependent variables being "membership in protest-promoting groups," "expectations of reference persons," and "relations with critical friends." As independent variables we included "dissatisfaction and influence" as well as the three sanction variables.

Arrows in figure 3 denote regression coefficients that were statistically significant at least at the .05 level.

2. There is extensive literature on these events and generally on the history of the Eastern European revolutions. On the GDR, see in particular Weber 1991 and *Fischer Weltalmanach*

The Liberalization in the Soviet Union

Mikhail Gorbachev's rise to power in March 1985 and his reform politics are viewed by many scholars as one or the only cause of the upheaval in Eastern Europe and the revolution in the GDR. Brown (1991, 44) writes: "It couldn't have happened without Gorbachev." Gorbachev's reforms were not only an attempt to change the Soviet Union into a democratic state; they also caused a change in the Soviet Union's relations to the other communist countries. They were no longer considered satellites of the Soviet Union but, rather, countries that made their own politics. How did the SED leadership react to the reforms? Prior to 1985, according to the official SED ideology, the Soviet Union was the "big brother" whose policies were copied. This is illustrated by the slogan, "Learning from the Soviet Union means learning to win!" Yet the SED distanced itself from the Soviet reforms and strictly rejected their adoption. The SED didn't stop at verbal rejection of the reforms. It also attempted to suppress information about the reform process in the Soviet Union, for example, by banning the German edition of the Soviet magazine *Sputnik* in 1988 (see Weber 1991).

This is a typical example of the SED reactions to the events that occurred up until October 9: the party stuck to old policies although some SED functionaries became more open for discussion beginning in summer 1989. For the 40th anniversary of the founding of the GDR, Erich Honecker said in the SED-controlled newspaper *Einheit* [Unity] on September 5 that the GDR is a "state with a functioning, effective, socialist societal system which will, with its realized human rights, manage the challenges of the 90's" (Weber 1991, 343). What consequences did these reactions of the SED leadership have? Political dissatisfaction of the population as well as of the SED membership increased (Weber 1991, 178–79). First, information was filtered and distorted again. Second, there was dissatisfaction due to *unfulfilled expectations*. The GDR citizens were presented with a picture of the Soviet Union as a model state for decades. Suddenly, this model state introduced reforms. The citizens expected accordingly that reforms would also be introduced in the GDR. Unfulfilled expectations increase dissatisfaction. Finally, *relative dissatisfaction* became stronger. The Soviet "brother" introduced changes the GDR citizens also wanted, yet could not achieve.

Did personal political influence increase? That is, did the GDR citizens already believe in 1985 or 1986 that political action directed against the SED regime would speed up reforms? Did the GDR citizens already feel increas-

1990. On the events in the Soviet Union and Eastern Europe, see Banac 1992; Brown 1991; East 1992; Gwertzman and Kaufman 1990, 1991; Weiß 1990. The most informative account of the events in Eastern Europe in 1989 and before is East (1992). Brown (1991) contains an extensive chronology of those events.

ingly obligated to organize or take part in protests in 1985 or 1986 because of Gorbachev's policies? There is no information available on this subject. If our explanatory model is correct, we would indeed expect that because of increasing dissatisfaction, other protest-promoting incentives, namely protest norms and positive social incentives for participation in protest, increase. However, we suppose that only after the liberalization of other Eastern European countries did the mentioned incentives strongly increase. We will present data in the next section that confirm this claim.

Did Gorbachev's policies have an influence on the expected repression in the GDR? Before Gorbachev took power, GDR citizens probably believed that upheavals in the GDR would be crushed exactly like the protests on June 17, 1953. Shortly prior to October 9, 1989, most of the GDR citizens certainly no longer believed that the Soviet army would intervene. Sixty-six percent of the respondents did not believe prior to October 9, 1989, that Warsaw Pact troops would intervene in the case of large upheavals in the GDR. It is surprising that nevertheless, 34 percent of the respondents reckoned on intervention. We don't know how these expectations changed between 1985 and 1989. We presume that the citizens' fear of foreign troop intervention slowly declined with the continuing liberalization in the Soviet Union.

Would the revolution in the GDR have been impossible without Gorbachev's policies, as Brown maintains? In regard to the influence of the policies on the individual incentives for protest, we believe that Gorbachev's policies alone could not have been sufficient to cause the breakdown of the GDR. However, Gorbachev's policies may have indeed modified the individual incentives for protest *indirectly*. Before Gorbachev, Eastern bloc countries' efforts at autonomy were generally crushed. We will see later how the political changes in countries such as Poland and Hungary were important factors for the development of protests in the GDR. Gorbachev's policies were probably a necessary condition for these changes.

Furthermore, Gorbachev's policies influenced the SED regime's reactions to the protests. If the SED regime could have reckoned on the intervention of Soviet or Warsaw Pact troops, the regime's repression would probably have been harder. We thus believe that Gorbachev's policies decisively influenced the revolution in the GDR by creating internal and external events which then changed the individual incentives for protest.

Our previous argument illustrates an important point: the changes in the individual incentives to protest were not due to Gorbachev's policies alone, but additionally due to the reactions of the SED regime to these policies. If the SED regime had reacted differently—for example, by accepting Gorbachev's reforms—then the revolution might have proceeded differently or might not have happened at all. There is thus an *interaction effect*: the effects of Gorbachev's policies depended on the reactions of the SED regime and vice versa.

The Liberalization in Eastern Europe

Gorbachev's policies were a revolution "from above." This was different for Poland. The labor union Solidarity was founded already in 1980, although it was banned in December 1981. Extensive strikes in 1988 led to negotiations between Solidarity and the Jaruzelski administration. Solidarity was legalized in April 1989. The first free election in Eastern Europe in which noncommunists were also candidates took place on June 4, 1989. The communist party suffered a heavy defeat. On August 24, 1989, the first noncommunist, a candidate from the labor union Solidarity, was elected head of government: Tadeusz Mazowiecki. Poland was the only country in Eastern Europe in which a revolution resulted from worker strikes. The upheaval in Poland was neither prevented nor reversed by the Soviet Union or other Warsaw Pact countries.

The Hungarian case contrasts with the Polish one. There was a group of reform communists within the Communist party who took over the leadership of the party in 1988 and 1989. On January 11, 1989, the parliament passed a law that allowed independent political parties to be founded. In contrast to the GDR, the opposition movement in Hungary was relatively strong. Movement representatives organized protests and even entered into a dialogue with the regime. On June 14, 1989, negotiations between the regime and opposition movement representatives began at the roundtable. Symbolic events such as the state funeral of Imre Nagy on June 16, 1989, who was executed because of his role in the 1956 uprising, marked the departure from the authoritarian, communist regime in Hungary. Hungary's opening to the West began on May 2, 1989, when the border fortifications along the Austrian border were taken down. The borders to Austria were opened on August 4. On September 10, foreign minister Horn announced on national television that his government would allow all GDR citizens to enter Austria or Germany. Again, no Soviet or other Warsaw Pact troop intervention took place.

Yet there were communist dictatorships prior to October 9 under which only minor or no reforms were introduced. The political changes in Yugoslavia probably were not well-known in the GDR. On the whole, political changes in Yugoslavia were minor (Banac 1992, 186). Albania showed no sign of liberalization whatsoever prior to October 1989; changes first began at the end of 1990. In Bulgaria (see Todorova 1992) there was an opposition movement. The founding of the first independent labor union took place in February 1989 and the founding of the environmental protection association Eco-Glasnost in April 1989, yet the opposition had to face governmental repression prior to November 10, 1989. One form of liberalization was the provision of freedom of travel in the summer of 1989. In Romania changes first took place after the demonstrations between the 15th and 17th of December and the ousting and execution of Nicolae Ceausescu. There had been no opposition movement in Romania; repression was extensive. Although Czechoslovakia was one of the most repressive states of Eastern Europe, a relatively powerful opposition movement originated. The extensive student protests on November 17, 1989, led to liberalization measures and to the "velvet" revolution. The occasion for the protests were two anniversaries: the 50th anniversary of the murder of student Jan Opletal and the Hitler regime's closing of the Czechoslovakian universities.

Communist regimes did not exist solely in Eastern Europe. The democracy movement in China was crushed in June 1989 and the authoritarian regime remained in power. There has also been no liberalization in Cuba or North Korea whatsoever.

How could the described political events have affected the individual incentives of the GDR citizens to protest? Let us first look at those countries in which protests were successful. The liberalization in Eastern Europe has probably increased the GDR citizens' dissatisfaction with their political conditions as did the liberalization in the Soviet Union. *Relative* dissatisfaction increased in particular. If countries with similar political structures introduce political changes people want for their own country, dissatisfaction will increase.

Because protests in Poland and Hungary contributed decisively to the political changes there, GDR citizens may have come to three conclusions:

1. Communist dictatorships can be changed.
2. It is possible to make political changes by means of protest.
3. If protest leads to political changes, "sister states" troops will not intervene to reverse them.

Among other things, the reforms in Poland and Hungary will thus have increased the perceived chances for the success of extensive protests and the personal political influence of the individual citizen.

If dissatisfaction and perceived political influence are high, protest norms also become applicable, as we argued earlier (fig. 3). This in turn causes the social environment to encourage political activity more than before—that is, positive social incentives increase (fig. 3).

We tested the hypothesis that the liberalization in Eastern Europe led to an increase in perceived political influence and to the application of protest norms. The following two statements should measure how respondents felt about the political changes, especially in Hungary and Poland:

"I thought, if I took part in demonstrations and similar activities, I myself can change things."

"I thought, now I'm actually obligated to do something to contribute to changes in the GDR."

The first item measures personal influence. Forty-five percent of the respondents answering this question agreed to this statement, while 27 percent did not (28 percent partly agreed and partly disagreed). In regard to the second statement, referring to protest norms, 47 percent of the respondents agreed, while 33 percent did not (20 percent partly agreed and partly disagreed).

In Albania, Romania, Czechoslovakia, China, Cuba, and North Korea, no reforms took place in 1989. Did this cause GDR citizens to think that reforms could hardly be achieved by means of protest in communist countries? It is probable that many citizens thought exactly so. Yet it is also plausible that the "positive" examples of Poland and Hungary overshadowed the negative examples. The collapse of communist dictatorships due to the population's protest was so unusual in the relatively stable Eastern bloc countries that even a few successes of large-scale protests conveyed the impression that protest would also create changes in the GDR.

The Emigration Wave

In comparison to citizens of other countries, GDR citizens theoretically could emigrate to the FRG without having to face major difficulties with living in the FRG. The legal situation was such that, according to the law of the FRG, citizens of the GDR were FRG citizens and could therefore immigrate easily. The common language and special social provisions also eased integration.[3] In 1989, the number of emigrants increased dramatically. The emigration wave began with Hungary's tearing down its border fortifications to Austria on May 2, 1989. This action made leaving the GDR by way of Hungary easier, but the attempt remained risky. GDR refugees could have been seized by Hungarian border patrols and sent back to the GDR, where they would have had to face heavy punishment for "fleeing the republic." On September 11, Hungary opened the borders to Austria without consulting the GDR. Thus, GDR citizens could enter the FRG via Hungary and Austria with no problem, and many GDR citizens took advantage of the opportunity. According to official FRG statistics, approximately 17,000 GDR citizens entered the FRG via Hungary and Austria in September 1989.

---

3. See Table 1 in Hirschman 1993 on the development of the number of GDR emigrants since the country's founding. On the development of and motives behind emigration, see also Naimark 1992 with further references. A chronology of the emigration wave between August 4 and November 9 can be found in *Fischer Weltalmanach* 1990, 138–42.

Many citizens chose another route to leave their country. In July 1989, GDR citizens occupied the FRG embassies in Budapest, Prague, and Warsaw as well as the Ständige Vertretung [permanent mission] of the FRG in East Berlin. Most of the refugees were not sent back to the GDR.

There were various reactions to this emigration wave from the GDR authorities. First, Hungary and the FRG were heavily criticized for promoting or making possible the GDR citizens' emigration. Second, actions were taken to motivate the citizens to return to their homeland. For example, a camper was turned into a GDR citizen consultation office in Hungary. Third, the GDR negotiated, for example, with FRG Foreign Minister Hans-Dietrich Genscher and Czechoslovakian Foreign Minister Jaromir Johanes regarding the refugees in the German embassy in Prague. Finally, the SED leadership criticized the "refugees of the republic." As late as October 2, the SED-controlled newspaper *Neues Deutschland* [New Germany] still commented that the refugees had ousted themselves from society and that no one would cry for them.

How did these events affect the individual incentives for protest? First, the political dissatisfaction of the GDR citizens continued to increase. This is due on the one hand to the critical loss of manpower the emigration caused in the economic sphere and medical services. The negative portrayal of the emigrants, most of whom still had friends back at home, may also have increased dissatisfaction with the regime. Because of these events, we can also assume that the GDR citizens perceived greater chances of achieving changes by participating in joint protests. GDR citizens believed that the rapidly increasing number of emigrants and the inability of the regime to bring the emigration wave under control would cause problems for the regime: It would come under pressure to follow reforms of other countries in order to stop the exodus. The emigration wave and the SED regime's helplessness toward it may thus have increased perceived personal influence to put even more pressure on the government by protest actions and thereby contribute to political changes.

Both the prospect of being able to make changes by engaging in political action and the increasing dissatisfaction probably increased both protest norms and social incentives for protest. This is probably the reason why the calls for "We want out!" became "We're staying here!" after the peace prayers.

In our survey we ascertained the extent to which the emigration wave changed (1) the dissatisfaction, (2) the influence of collective protests, (3) personal political influence, and (4) protest norms. The results shown in table 1 confirm the preceding statements.

It may be argued that the emigration wave weakened the opposition movement. It seems, however, that most members of the opposition did not leave the GDR. Did the bothersome intellectuals expelled to the FRG include

TABLE 1.   Survey Responses to Emigration Wave

	Does not hold true (percent)	Holds true (percent)
Dissatisfaction		
I thought: Now things are going to get worse for us here.	41	41
Influence		
It was clear to me that there was now a definite chance to make a difference if the population as a whole participates more in political protest activities.	14	68
I thought: If I take part in demonstrations, etc. now, I personally can make a difference.	29	54
Norms		
I thought: Now I am obligated to do something for changes in the GDR in order to keep even more people from leaving.	29	48

charismatic leaders who no longer had the chance to influence events in the GDR? Hirschman (1993) talks about a "vacuum of leadership" through forced exit. This idea appears implausible to us. In chapter 7 we described in detail the problems and insignificance of the opposition due to the government's repressive apparatus and despite the relative autonomy of the Church. The absence of several hundred intellectuals could hardly have changed the development of the revolution in the GDR. Yet if this is the case, who were the potential charismatic leaders and how could these additional intellectuals have initiated the revolution any earlier? We do not have any answers to these questions.

It often happens that an action becomes less costly if the number of those performing this action increases. This was true for emigration as well. The emigration process probably proceeded according to the threshold model described in chapter 2. Those citizens for whom the advantages of emigration most strongly outweighed the disadvantages left first, which lowered the costs for other GDR citizens so that they emigrated. For example, the pictures in West German television portraying the large numbers of East German citizens crossing the borders into Austria left many remaining citizens with the impression that a border crossing would be relatively safe.

Regime Repression and Fear of a "Chinese Solution"
The internal events include the repressive reactions of the SED regime toward the protests. We already addressed the effects of repression in detail in chapter 9.

The Local Elections on May 7, 1989

A decisive event in the development of the protests was the forging of election results during the local elections on May 7, 1989. The unified list of the SED again received an enormously high number of votes—98.85 percent, according to election officials. Members of the opposition had kept an eye on the public counting of the votes in several polling stations, and they believed the results to be forged. There were mounds of complaints to state offices and reports to the police and, for the first time, manifold protest actions took place in various towns. The election fraud undoubtedly evoked moral indignation and dissatisfaction so that protest norms became increasingly applicable.

Western Television and Contacts with FRG Citizens

The described political events could only change the individual incentives for protest because the GDR citizens were informed about them. The SED regime attempted to prevent the spread of certain information or to spread false information. Yet these attempts failed because most of the population received West German television and radio.

East German citizens also had many opportunities to receive information through contacts with West Germans. The efforts toward political recognition and the provision of loans led the GDR to partly give in to the West German demand that both West and East Germans be allowed to visit each other more easily. On January 3, 1989, the East German news agency ADN reported that 2.79 million visits into West Germany were recorded for 1988 (Brown 1991, 271). There were also various contacts made possible by West Germans visiting the GDR, such as in the case of the Leipzig trade fair: because Leipzig had too few hotels, many fair visitors had to be housed in private households.

In general, the opportunity to be informed was probably an important condition for the change in protest-promoting incentives in 1989. Yet it is uncertain how important this condition was. There was still an opportunity to spread information by word of mouth. Furthermore, other East European revolutions occurred without having any sort of accessible information center such as West Germany.

The Self-Reinforcing Effect of the Protests

The increase in protests may have led many citizens to view the chances for success of both collective action and individual action as greater. If more and more people take action, many citizens will view it as unfair or even immoral not to take action and to simply "leave the work to others." An increase in protests may therefore have caused many individuals who hadn't protested before to view action as a "must."

Many citizens also will encourage their friends and acquaintances to take part when they see that many others have become politically active. The protests therefore had an indirect, reinforcing effect. They altered the incentives for protest, which in turn changed the extent of protest. Perhaps the experience of participation in protests also produced a feeling of personal power and led to the impression that the politicians at least took notice of the will of the people.

Conclusion and Unanswered Questions

Our preceding argument is summarized in figure 4. Figure 2 is one of its building blocks: it is the middle part of figure 4. The bracket underneath the incentives indicates the direct effects described earlier. Furthermore, figure 4 shows the relationships between external and internal events on the one hand and incentives on the other. We also see the effects of protest on incentives symbolized by the respective arrows. Finally, figure 4 shows that the protests also influenced external and internal events.[4]

Our preceding argument raises a number of questions. First, did particular political events have a greater effect on the incentives than did other events? The answer is definitely yes, yet there are no data available to examine how large the effects of which events are. Second, did the described events take effect independently of each other, or did the effects of particular events depend on the occurrence of other events—that is, were there interaction effects? For example, Gorbachev's politics may not have had any great effect if the liberalization in Poland and Hungary had not taken place. Our current data do not allow us to provide satisfactory answers to this question.

Spontaneous Coordination and the Importance of the "Critical Mass"

In explaining the demonstrations prior to October 9, 1989, an important question has remained unanswered. We have already seen that the demonstrations in the GDR prior to October 9 were not organized but, rather, emerged spontaneously (see chapters 1, 2, and 7). Because the Monday demonstrations in Leipzig initiated the upheaval in the GDR, we want to know how it was possible for so many citizens to have gathered in downtown Leipzig on October 9 and earlier without any form of organization.

Let us first examine whether the conditions for the development of spon-

---

4. In both figure 2 and figure 4, relationships between variables mean, first, that attributes of *the same* individuals affect each other (example: dissatisfaction increases protest norms), and second, that attributes of *different* individuals are related (example: protests by particular individuals increase incentives for other individuals). In the text, we attempted to clarify the kind of relationship meant in each case.

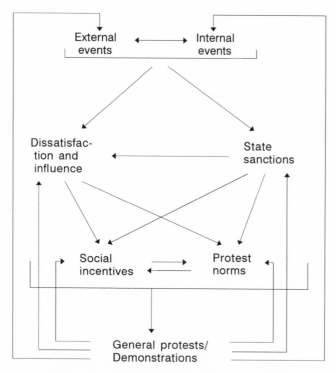

Fig. 4. The dynamics of the revolution in the GDR

taneous cooperation (see chapter 2) were present in Leipzig in autumn 1989. The first prerequisite we mentioned was that citizens must be willing to take part in certain forms of protest. As we saw in this chapter, the incentives for protest increased dramatically after May 7 and in the late summer of 1989. We can therefore assume that the willingness to take political actions against the SED regime was at a high level in summer and autumn 1989. The second condition for the occurrence of spontaneous protests is, as we saw, that citizens believe that no one will organize protests. This condition was also present in the GDR. The third condition was satisfied accordingly: because of the reasons mentioned, no citizen of Leipzig had probably considered organizing a demonstration.

We further saw in chapter 2 that if the mentioned conditions are met, the development of a spontaneous demonstration depends on how citizens solve the problems of coordination and the critical mass. How were these problems solved in summer and autumn 1989?

The Coordination Problem

As is the case for many European cities, Leipzig had a clearly defined city center consisting of Karl-Marx-Platz and its adjacent streets. If one wanted to meet someone without an appointment, one would just go there. At what time would people go? Leipzig citizens knew that peace prayers took place every Monday from 5 to 6 P.M. in the Nikolai Kirche, which is close to Karl-Marx-Platz. The citizens knew about the peace prayers through word-of-mouth communication and the Western media. It was also well known that at least some of those individuals attending the peace prayers would go to Karl-Marx-Platz after the prayer service. Citizens of Leipzig also knew that those attending the peace prayers were critical citizens. Thus, if people who were critical of the SED regime wanted to meet up with like-minded individuals, they would either attend the peace prayers on Mondays or go near the Nikolai Kirche at about 6 P.M.

The peace prayers came into being as a forum for discussion (see Feydt, Heinze, and Schanz 1990 for more details; see also Sievers 1990; Hanisch et al. 1990; Grabner, Heinze, and Pollack 1990) and were not planned to initiate protests or even upheaval. Attendance varied from 10 to 1,000 between 1982 and the beginning of 1989. On September 25, 1989, the first larger demonstration took place in Leipzig after the peace services. On October 2 another church in Leipzig organized peace prayers, and on October 9 two more followed.

The peace prayers can be termed an *institutional incentive*. They were incentives for cooperation among citizens in the form of an opportunity to meet. Due to the strong incentives to protest and the information that critical citizens attended the peace prayers, expectations were created that critical citizens came to a certain place at a certain time. The institution of the peace prayers was a necessary condition for the spontaneous coordination of the protests in Leipzig.

Other events had similar effects as the Monday peace prayers—for example, the festivities on the 40th anniversary of the founding of the GDR on October 7. As we saw earlier, these festivities increased the dissatisfaction of the citizens. Many citizens therefore expected that other citizens also had the need to express their discontent collectively and to also go to public squares in the city centers on that particular day.

The Problem of the "Critical Mass"

The willingness to go to the center of Leipzig on a Monday probably depended on the number of people a person expected to meet. How could a citizen of Leipzig estimate the number of participants? First, a person with many critical friends will estimate the number of participants as relatively high. If demonstrations have taken place already, the estimates for the next demonstration will depend mainly on the number of participants of the prior demonstration. The demonstration on September 25 consisted of approximately 5,000 people. On October 2, approximately 20,000 people took part, and on October 9, at least 70,000. These were the Monday demonstrations. On October 7, a Saturday on which the festivities for the 40th anniversary of the founding of the GDR took place, participation was counted at 10,000. The estimates of the citizens were probably higher than the participant numbers at the prior demonstrations. People probably thought that the increasing dissatisfaction increased other citizens' willingness to participate.

Citizens might also have generalized their own willingness to participate. This may have led them to expect other citizens to participate in the next demonstration as they would themselves. A dramatic overestimate of participant numbers could therefore have developed. This could have caused the expected costs of participation to be highly underestimated. Our data show that the number of participants was *underestimated*. Only 22 percent of our respondents who had participated in at least one demonstration said they had correctly estimated the number of participants when they first participated, while 61 percent had underestimated participants' numbers, and only 17 percent had overestimated them.

In what way do the benefits and costs of participation in a demonstration depend on the *number* of participants? One of the incentives to participate is the expectation of a "critical mass" being present—that is to say, the number of participants sufficient in order to achieve the political goals of a demonstration. The political goals probably varied from participant to participant. The common goal of participants up until October 9 was probably demonstrating to the regime that the population desired reforms. This goal is achieved if a demonstration is considered a protest. In the GDR, a very small number of participants, perhaps 20 to 50, was already sufficient in this regard. The reason is that larger demonstrations were extremely rare and demonstrations with few participants were enough to draw attention. The greater the number of expected participants, the greater is the expected success of protests on the whole. We further hypothesize that the greater the number of participants, the higher is the perceived personal political influence. This may be a result of a process in which individuals attribute the group's success to themselves (see Opp 1978, 86–92; Opp 1989, 229–39). If a large number of participants is expected, participation often becomes a must. In order for a norm of participation to hold, it is often necessary that many people carry out the behavior in question. In this case, moral incentives become relatively strong. Social in-

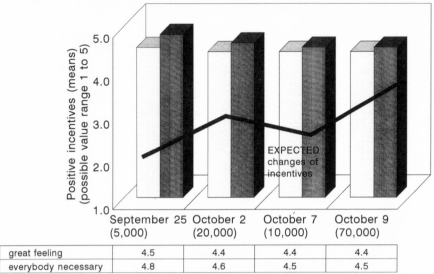

	September 25 (5,000)	October 2 (20,000)	October 7 (10,000)	October 9 (70,000)
great feeling	4.5	4.4	4.4	4.4
everybody necessary	4.8	4.6	4.5	4.5

Dates of Demonstrations

☐ great feeling ■ everybody necessary

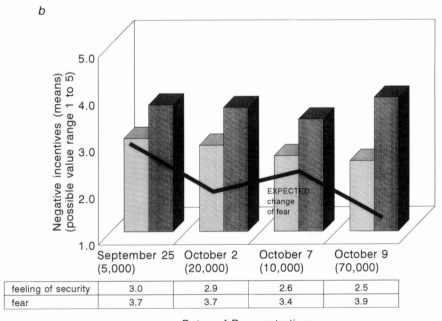

	September 25 (5,000)	October 2 (20,000)	October 7 (10,000)	October 9 (70,000)
feeling of security	3.0	2.9	2.6	2.5
fear	3.7	3.7	3.4	3.9

Dates of Demonstrations

☐ feeling of security ■ fear

Fig. 5. Incentives for four 1989 demonstrations: (*a*) positive; (*b*) negative (value ranges 1–5)

centives developed during the demonstrations as well. In this way, participants of the Monday demonstrations mentioned a feeling of solidarity and felt they had taken part in an important event. Many participants certainly also expected these incentives to arise before they participated, which no doubt contributed to their participation.

Do the costs of participation also depend on the number of participants? It may be argued that when large numbers of people participate, police brutality is expected to be more likely than if participation numbers were small. Yet all demonstrations in the GDR in the past were crushed with the same form of violence, regardless of their size. It is therefore plausible to assume that the participants did not believe the expected number of participants to be correlated with police brutality. It is further plausible that one would feel relatively secure in a large group—that is, the larger the number of participants, the lower the expected probability and fear of repression. Our respondents were presented with the following statement: "If you know that many people will take part in a demonstration, the risk is lower." Among respondents with valid answers, 77.4 percent agreed with this statement.

If these hypotheses are correct, the *positive* incentives should have increased from September 25 to October 2, because there were more participants on October 2 than on September 25. The positive incentives should have decreased from October 2 to October 7 because there were fewer participants on October 7 than on October 2. Finally, because participant numbers were at a peak on October 9, the positive incentives should be highest on this date. The line in figure 5a symbolizes the assumed *changes* of the incentives; it does not represent the size of the means—we used arbitrary values.

In order to test these assumptions, we asked participants how they experienced their first demonstration, and presented them with the following items:

> It was a great feeling to be together with so many people who all wanted the same thing.
> I had the feeling that every single person was necessary in order for anything to be achieved at all.

Figure 5a displays the average agreement for these two statements for those respondents whose first participation was on September 25, October 2, October 7, or October 9. The means for these statements should increase and decrease in the direction symbolized by the line. However, this is not the case: the means hardly differ at all.

With respect to the expected costs (repression) for participation, we expect that at first costs should decrease as the number of participants increases. Then, for October 7, the costs should increase somewhat, whereas there should be a notable decrease for October 9. In order to test these hypotheses we again presented our respondents with two statements referring to their first demonstration:

I was very afraid that the security forces would intervene.
I felt so secure with the many others present that I believed nothing could happen.

With respect to the first statement, the means should be parallel to the line drawn in figure 5b; for the second statement, the line would have to be modified according to our hypotheses. As the figure shows, the means are not consistent with our hypotheses.

Do our findings disprove the hypothesis that incentives correlate with the number of participants? The answers of many respondents to the items mentioned before indicate that the expected number of participants is relevant for the costs and benefits of participation. However, participant numbers were not the main cause for the change in incentives for the various demonstrations. Political events altered incentives to the point that the effects of participant numbers played only a minor role.

The Demonstration Tree

If someone does or does not take part in a demonstration, how high is the probability that this person will take part in the next demonstration, or the one after that? We will first deal with those individuals who did not take part in the demonstration on September 25, and then with those who took part. We will then ascertain for participants and nonparticipants how many individuals took part and did not take part in the following demonstration on October 2, and so on. We will present this information in the form of a "demonstration tree." The demonstration tree for those who did *not* take part in the September 25 demonstration is pictured in figure 6a, whereas figure 6b shows the demonstration tree for those who did take part. The lines in the figures refer to the dates of the different demonstrations. "NO" means "did not participate" and "YES" means "did participate" in the mentioned demonstrations. Below "NO" and "YES" we have written the numbers of respondents belonging to each answer category. For example, 973 of our respondents did not take part in the demonstration on September 25 (fig. 6a). Of these, 850 also did not take part on October 2. The percentages beside the lines refer to respondents who did or did not take part in the next demonstration. For example, out of the 973 nonparticipants for the September 25 demonstration, 87 percent (850 of 973) also did not take part in the October 2 demonstration, whereas 13 percent (123

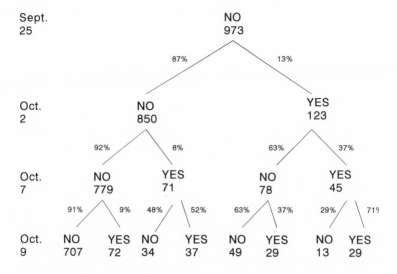

a

		Sept. 25						NO 973						

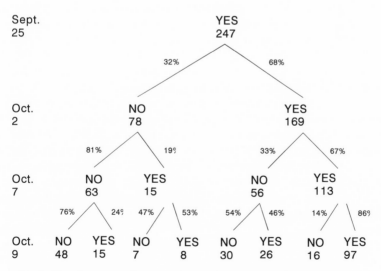

b

Fig. 6. The demonstration tree, September 25, 1989: (a) nonparticipants; (b) participants

of 973) did take part. Therefore, the probability that a nonparticipant from September 25 did not take part in the next demonstration either was .87, and the probability of participation .13.

Let us return to our initial question. If an individual did or did not take part in a demonstration, how probable is participation or nonparticipation in the next and after-next demonstration? The following relationship can be seen immediately:

> *Hypothesis 1*: If a person does *not* take part in a demonstration, the probability of nonparticipation in the next demonstration is higher than the probability of participation.

Among other things, hypothesis 1 implies that if someone did not take part on September 25, the probability is high that this person also did not take part on October 9. We can calculate this probability in the following manner: The number of nonparticipants on October 9 (last line of fig. 6a) is (adding the "NO" responses) 707 + 34 + 49 + 13 = 803. If we divide 803 by the number of nonparticipants on September 25 (973), we get .825, or 82.5 percent. The probability that someone who neither took part on September 25 nor took part on October 9 is thus .825.

Is hypothesis 1 also valid for those who did take part in a demonstration?

> *Hypothesis 2*: If someone *did* take part in a demonstration, the probability that this person will also take part in the next demonstration is higher than the probability of nonparticipation.

Unfortunately, hypothesis 2 cannot be confirmed as well as hypothesis 1 can. It is clearly disproved by those who did not take part on September 25 yet who did take part on October 2 (fig. 6a). According to hypothesis 2, a relatively large percentage of these individuals should have taken part on October 7. Yet in reality, only 37 percent took part on October 7 whereas 63 percent did *not* take part. In two other relationships the percentages indeed tended to be as expected, although differences were not particularly strong. For figure 6a, this is true for those who did not take part on October 2 yet did on October 7: 48 percent of them did not take part on October 9 whereas 52 percent did. Another case is found on the last line of figure 6b (47 percent versus 53 percent).

How can these findings be explained? We proceed from the assumption of our general explanatory model:

> A person will participate in a demonstration if the net utility of participation is greater than the net utility of nonparticipation.

Net utility of an action increases, by definition, to the extent to which the perceived advantages (positive benefits) of an action are greater than the disadvantages (negative benefits or costs). This assumption is equivalent with the following statement: If the net utility of participation becomes greater than the net utility of nonparticipation, the "threshold" for participation is achieved. The more this threshold is exceeded—that is, the greater the net utility surplus (the difference of the net utility of participation minus the net utility of nonparticipation)—the less effect a change of the costs of participation will have on participation. Those individuals with a high net utility surplus will, for example, continue to demonstrate despite increased repression, while those individuals with a low surplus will quit even when costs increase only a little.

We presume that a large number of participants on September 25 had a relatively high net utility surplus of participation. The participants further experienced positive incentives during participation, as we saw earlier. Those individuals with a relatively low net utility surplus were more apt not to take part in the next demonstration. Small cost increases (such as personal ones— one "must" repair one's car or go buy something) suffice to change action.

We further assume that a large number of nonparticipants on September 25 are far below the threshold. The net benefits for only a very few increased so much that the threshold was reached. Thus, only a few would take part in the next demonstration. If the threshold is exceeded at all, the surplus will be low.

Let us turn to the cases where our two hypotheses have not been confirmed. These cases are related to "switchers": if someone participated and then did not, or vice versa, the probabilities of participation or nonparticipation in the next demonstration differ only a little. Yet if someone did or did not take part consistently, for example two times in a row, then the probabilities correspond exactly to our two hypotheses. Three of our problem cases occur *after* the first change from "NO" to "YES," including the case that clearly refutes hypothesis 2. The fourth problem case occurs after a change from "YES" to "NO." We believe that the switchers have a low net utility surplus. This is especially the case for those who did not participate on September 25. If one of these people decided to take part in the next demonstration, then the net utility surplus was probably quite low and thus the probability of switching was probably quite high.

Another explanation for our problem cases could be that the demonstration on October 7 was special and that the respondents were only willing to take part in Monday demonstrations. In order to examine this hypothesis, we calculated the probability of participation and nonparticipation only for the three Monday demonstrations on September 25, October 2, and October 9. We constructed a new demonstration tree out of figures 6a and 6b—not presented here—with only these three demonstrations. There is indeed only one refutation in this new demonstration tree: if someone did *not* take part on September 25 but did on October 2, the chance that this person took part on October 9 is only 0.5. This corresponds to our hypothesis that the nonparticipants from September 25 had a low net utility surplus and thus switched very easily.

Our data do not enable us to test the presumptions made in this section. The findings we presented in the form of a demonstration tree are nevertheless interesting and we believe that it is worth attempting to explain them.

Why Leipzig?

If our explanatory model is correct, the protest-promoting incentives for Leipzig citizens must have been particularly high, because participation there was more extensive and earlier than in other East German cities. To what extent does this hold true? An important condition, which we have already addressed in detail, was the institution of the peace prayers and the clearly structured city center. Such incentives were not present in other cities or areas within the GDR. Furthermore, the dissatisfaction of Leipzig citizens was particularly high (see Hofmann and Rink 1990). We described several events that probably contributed to a high level of dissatisfaction among Leipzig citizens, old and young, in chapter 1. In comparison to all other major cities, Leipzig had the highest level of environmental pollution, the old buildings were in particularly bad condition, and Leipzig had a particularly bad supply position, especially when compared with East Berlin. We have mentioned Leipzig's role as the trade fair city. Citizens were thus able to directly obtain information about conditions in the West, which particularly promoted relative dissatisfaction.

Our theoretical model implies that both moral and social incentives for protest are relatively high when dissatisfaction is high. If we further consider the mentioned institutional incentives, spontaneous protest was most likely to occur in Leipzig on Mondays.

The Situation after October 9, 1989

So far we have focused on the time period between early 1989 and October 9, 1989, because we believe that this is the most interesting period of the GDR revolution. We will therefore only briefly address the period between October 9, 1989, and March 18, 1990. This period is first characterized by the dramatic increase of protests in the entire country between October 9 and November 13. After this date, the protests decreased (see chapter 1). How can this be explained?

The Increase of Protest until the Fall of the Berlin Wall

Because the protests increased between October 9 and November 13, the protest-promoting incentives must have increased more strongly than the negative incentives after October 9. To what extent was this the case? We begin with political dissatisfaction. Repression had become very unlikely after October 9. In this situation, wasn't political dissatisfaction likely to have decreased considerably? We believe that political dissatisfaction hardly changed. The SED and Stasi were still in power. Freedom of travel was now provided, but for how long? On the whole, it seems that GDR citizens still viewed the changes that occurred up to mid-November with skepticism. Our data support this hypothesis. Only one-third of the respondents were satisfied with the political changes between October 9 and March 18.

There were certainly dramatic changes in perceived personal political influence. It was clear after October 9 that political changes had been caused by citizens' protests. Collective protest had thus been successful. The SED leadership's unexpected yielding made further protests appear hopeful. We believe accordingly that each citizen's perceived personal political influence also increased. Our data confirm this. The respondents believed that working in or founding an opposition group, and participating in church activities was more likely to bring about changes after October 9 than before.

According to our previous hypotheses, moral incentives should have been more applicable after October 9. Conditions that limited the applicability of protest norms, such as lacking success of joint protests or repression, no longer existed. Our data confirm this: 47.8 percent of our respondents held the opinion that between October 9 and March 18, citizens felt more strongly than before that they should participate in protest actions, whereas 28 percent perceived no change, and 24 percent said feelings of duty were less strong among citizens.

As was noted earlier, an increase in moral incentives should lead to stronger social incentives: 77.4 percent of the respondents said that their colleagues criticized SED politics after October 9 more than before. Even 79.4 percent said that this was the case with their friends. A person who criticizes the government's politics usually will support protest against this government.

Our respondents thought that their reference persons would value it somewhat more after October 9 if they were to participate in protest actions than before this date. On the respective five-point scales, the mean is 4.0 for the time after October 9 and 3.8 for the period before October 9.

Our data also confirm that the citizens expected less repression after October 9. The average agreement to the item "I was really afraid that the security forces would intervene" was 3.7 for the time prior to October 9 and 2.4 for the time after October 9 (possible values from 1 to 5).

Demonstrations became increasingly organized after October 9. Artists and members of opposition groups called for demonstrations at the same locations where they had originated. Expectations to meet large numbers of people at particular places and times were raised by announcing speakers at the Monday demonstrations. Demonstrations were also organized at other locations in the GDR. Therefore, spontaneous coordination was no longer necessary for the development of protests.

The Decrease in Protests after the Fall of the Wall

From the perspective of a GDR citizen, it seems that the revolution had come to an end after November 9 when the borders to West Germany literally fell down. The political order developed toward a Western democracy. We don't want to describe in detail the events after November 9; the reader can look them up in many published chronicles (see also chapter 11). For our theoretical arguments, it is important that the changes after November 9 caused the incentives for protest to decrease. The reform process, so to speak, continued automatically but was led this time by negotiations between politicians. The revolution from "below" was completed from "above." The goals of the majority of the GDR citizens had been achieved.

Summary

We focused on the question of *why* the revolution in the GDR developed the way it did over time. At the beginning of 1989, political dissatisfaction was relatively high, but perceived political influence was low. This is why political discontent had hardly any protest-promoting effects. Furthermore, protest norms were hardly applicable, and social incentives for protest were also low. Repression was high, and the deterrence effect predominated. The situation changed in the GDR after May 7, 1989, when local election results were forged. This event caused the positive incentives for protest to increase. Repression decreased for participation in general protests but not for participation in demonstrations.

Why did the incentives change in this way? We first showed that the incentives have a causal relationship with each other. Our hypotheses (fig. 2) were confirmed by our survey data (summarized in fig. 3) insofar as the data provided items for the test. We further explained in detail *which* political events changed which incentives in which way. The individual incentives were particularly increased through Gorbachev's reform policies *and* the SED regime's reactions to them, the liberalization in Eastern Europe, the emigration wave, and the repression in the GDR. We further discussed the extent to which emigration weakened the opposition movement and the extent to which the emigration wave caused others to emigrate. Some of these hypotheses could be tested and were confirmed by our data.

The protests had a self-reinforcing effect: people who protested increased the protest-promoting incentives for others. How could the spontaneous demonstrations develop? The three conditions necessary for the development of spontaneous demonstration (chapter 2) were present in the GDR: willingness to take political action against the SED regime in summer and autumn 1989 was high; GDR citizens saw no indication of anyone organizing any protests in summer and autumn 1989; citizens of Leipzig did not consider organizing a demonstration themselves.

If these conditions are present, the development of spontaneous demonstrations depends on how the coordination problem and the problem of the critical mass are solved. The coordination problem in Leipzig was solved by a clearly located city center where one could go to meet others and the institution of the Monday prayers, which caused critical citizens to expect to meet like-minded people on Mondays at the city center near the church.

Regarding the problems of the critical mass, citizens probably assumed that enough other citizens were present for the gathering to be considered a protest by the regime. Yet our data did not confirm the idea that the number of participants is related to the benefits or costs of participation. This finding indicates that the effects of the political events on the changes in incentives were stronger than the number of participants.

An important question regarding the development of the protests arises. If someone does or does not take part in a demonstration, how high is the probability that this person will or will not take part in the next demonstration? We first found that if someone does *not* take part in a demonstration, the probability is high that this person will not take part in the next demonstration, either. Furthermore, if someone takes part in a demonstration, then the probability is high that this person will also take part in the next one. We tried to explain these findings—and some results that were not in line with them.

Why did the protests originate in Leipzig? We argued that not only the institution of the peace prayers, but also other incentives, were important in creating a high level of political dissatisfaction.

We then turned to the period between October 9, 1989, and March 18, 1990. We showed how and why the incentives changed, thus explaining both the increase in protests until mid-November and the decrease thereafter.

CHAPTER 13

Commonsense Explanations of the Revolution

Christiane Gern

In our qualitative interviews, we asked our respondents how they would explain the fall of the GDR and what, in their opinion, the most important factors were that led to these events. In this chapter we want to investigate how our respondents' opinions fit in with our explanatory model.

Why is this question relevant? It is often maintained that the theories sociologists develop are "trivial" in the sense that they only express common knowledge. We would then expect our respondents' own explanations of the GDR revolution to correspond to our explanatory arguments. If this does not hold true, to what extent are our respondents' explanations problematic, for example, in regard to the incomplete explanations discussed in chapter 2? Or do our respondents express interesting new ideas that are not contained in our own explanation but should be a subject of future research? These are the questions this chapter focuses on.

We will show that our respondents' explanations from the qualitative interviews often do not coincide with our own model. We are in no way criticizing our respondents' arguments. It is clear that a person who participated directly in the events in Leipzig does not have the extensive information at her or his disposal as does a group of researchers having studied this subject for a number of years. One must also take into account that the respondents expressed their opinions during a conversation in which not all of the important arguments are normally expressed. This is in part due to the interviewers, who addressed various topics according to the arguments presented by the respondents. Furthermore, the verbal statements of the respondents are not as fully reflected as they would be in written form, and not every element in a chain of thought will have been presented, sometimes because certain facts were presumed self-evident. Nevertheless, we consider it interesting and legitimate to compare our respondents' hypotheses on the revolution in the GDR with our own explanation. We will number the following quotations because we will refer to many of them later.

The qualitative interviews were recorded on audiotape, as explained in the appendix; thus, sentences were sometimes incomplete or grammatically incorrect. In this case we corrected the sentences, as we did in the preceding chapters as well. Because we only quote parts of an interview, it is often necessary to supplement these missing parts. Such supplements were put in brackets.

Dissatisfaction

Almost all our interviewees mentioned the dissatisfaction among the population. They referred to different forms of dissatisfaction. Many people emphasized the *work situation*. For example, when we asked Jochen Läßig about the focal points of dissatisfaction, he answered:

> (1) The most important point was the dissatisfaction in the workplace. I mean, the people just had the feeling that their work had become senseless and ineffective—a waste of time; that engineers did senseless work, for a senseless apparatus. So I really believe the main point was that for most people there was no personal development possible in their work. I think that this was at least the decisive point among the people who started the movement.

Christian Führer, pastor in the Nikolai Kirche, also depicted feelings of working for the "trash can" and professional "dead ends" unless the party was supported. Theologist Detlef Pollack made the following statement:

> (2) Well, the fact that one was not paid for achievements [is a very critical point]. Another critical point for me was that, as a result of this lack of consideration for expert know-how, people were given top positions who [were] not qualified. They were therefore predestined to make bad decisions.

Some respondents mentioned *dissatisfaction with the political system*, such as Mr. Führer:

> (3) Fifty-seven years of bent obedience and tutelage to an overpowering state—first to the fascists and then to the socialists—who in their worldviews were very different, but were very similar in regard to their totalitarianism towards the individual. For me, it was a kind of religious substitute with the accompanying pressure from the cradle to the grave, to the point where the people just didn't want it anymore, although they had of course been masters of accommodation for the last 40 years.

He mentions the travel policies as an example of how the state treated the citizens like little children. Petra Lux from the Neues Forum described these policies as "perversion." Christian Müller of the Neues Forum commented that as far as the political situation was concerned, things had come to a standstill.

Our interviewees responded to questions about the *dissatisfaction with the economic situation* very differently. Theologist Matthias Petzoldt, for example, agrees with Christian Scheibler in regard to the worsening of the economy in 1989. Ms. Lux judges the economic situation from two perspectives: On the one hand, she criticizes the complaints about the economic misery: "I just can't stand how everyone is complaining about how terrible things were and are. We belong to the 'white, European world,' of course, and were a rich country, in this respect." Seen from this perspective, the GDR citizens had little to complain about. Yet Ms. Lux also described another standard, namely the West, the FRG in particular. This other perspective emerged because most of the GDR citizens could receive Western television.

(4) . . . every commercial showed what you could never get in life, even if it was the brand-name laundry detergent Omo. That's perverse. And they had that continually rubbed in their face. And I think that produces a large amount of dissatisfaction.

Yet some interviewees believed that the economic dissatisfaction was not the decisive factor. Pastor Hans-Jürgen Sievers said:

(5) I don't think that the entire movement was initially a question of the standard of living. It was more the fear of not keeping up with the development in the Eastern bloc. . . . You had the impression that all of the upheaval in the Eastern bloc just passed us by; that we just remained an island, an "ice block." And indeed the lack of any form of innovation, or thought, or new perspective within our country left people feeling unbelievably bitter back then.

There is also no consensus among our interviewees about the role of *political dissatisfaction*. Political dissatisfaction is mentioned as an important factor (see quote 5), but theologist Pollack also commented: "Well, I must say that I did notice the aggravation, but there was dissatisfaction for as long as I can remember." (In this case, Mr. Pollack is primarily referring to dissatisfaction with the political system and the work system). Ms. Lux states that the people adapted to the system in the sense that they "had one opinion at home and another in the firm" and dropped opponents of the political system "like a hot potato." She concludes: "I don't think that the citizens were conscious of their political dissatisfaction. People got along well in this schizophrenia. It was an economic dissatisfaction."

Political Events and Increasing Dissatisfaction

Several interviewees mention events *external* to the GDR as causes of increasing dissatisfaction. Mr. Scheibler, for example, points to the impact of the Polish labor union movement and of Gorbachev. This raises the question of how the connection is established between political events on the one hand and, in terms of our theoretical model, incentives to protest (such as political dissatisfaction) on the other (see chapter 2). Mr. Scheibler describes a potential effect of developments in other countries: he argues that these developments contributed to discussing politics in the family and in circles of friends. Mr. Sievers also mentions further effects (quote 5): his statements suggest that dissatisfaction increased because the GDR citizens saw that desired changes were possible in other countries. Other interviewees expressed similar opinions. When asked whether the development in the Eastern European countries also influenced the GDR, Mr. Müller said: "Yes, that was definitely a sign that it is possible [to make changes]." Cabaret performer Bernd-Lutz Lange describes this development vividly:

(6) Many comrades hoped that changes in Moscow would mean changes here. Thus, the changes should come from the Kremlin. Then the changes came. Our hope grew enormously. And then came the shock— the unbelievable consternation: [the GDR leaders] rejected it. Hager said that "if the neighbors decide to wallpaper their rooms that doesn't mean that one must do the same.". . . And then they went as far as to forbid films and the magazine *Sputnik*. That was going too far. They started withdrawing from the German-Soviet friendship. Many said that they did so because they felt ashamed. . . . For the first time, the East German comrade had an argument from the East. Until that time, all of the arguments which were directed against the existing conditions came from Western television and were therefore discredited; they came from the enemy. And after Gorbachev announced his plans, the comrades had an argument from the East for the first time. This was of course actually the beginning of the end.

Mr. Müller and Mr. Lange maintain that the events in other countries encouraged GDR citizens—Lange speaks of the "comrades"—and led them to expect changes in their own country. Ms. Lux and Mr. Petzoldt have similar opinions. Mr. Lange stated that the hope for "changes from above" did not materialize. He also describes the legitimation problems of the GDR government: perestroika and glasnost made it more difficult for GDR leaders to defame critically thinking citizens as "elements controlled by the West" and strengthened their moral position.

Yet our interviewees also mentioned *GDR-internal factors* that heightened the existing dissatisfaction. Dentist Peter Kind mentions the local elections on May 7, 1989, whose results were forged. He also mentions the GDR leadership's reaction to the violent crushing of the Chinese democracy movement.

A number of interviewees mentioned the SED's reactions to the emigration wave. Mr. Kind describes the feelings he believed the SED's reactions evoked in the GDR citizens:

(7) The government's lack of reaction to the mass exit also had a great impact in my opinion. I don't think a person can really suffer any worse punishment than being ignored in this way.

Anger and increased dissatisfaction are thus mentioned as resulting from the government's lack of reaction. Many GDR citizens expected the emigration wave to force the government to introduce changes from above. According to Mr. Müller, the emigration wave had yet another effect: It caused a countermovement to take shape, which announced "We're staying here!" instead of "We want out!" Mr. Sievers comments:

(8) And it was actually clear that these basis groups [the groups that worked under the auspices of the Church] would take advantage of the insecurity caused by the exodus in order to initiate new political developments.

In other words, the emigration wave led on the one hand to increased expectations toward changes in governmental behavior, and on the other hand to political actions by the citizens. Bernd Okun believes that "it wouldn't have gone so far without the emigration wave" and that it was the "opening of the Hungarian border which caused the barrel to overflow." This kind of explanation—when a hole was created in the system by means of external factors, it fell apart—was expressed similarly by other interviewees.

On the whole, our interviewees support a version of the dissatisfaction hypothesis (for a critique see chap. 2). This version often reads: if dissatisfaction reaches a certain level, it explodes into protest. Long-term dissatisfaction, according to some of our respondents, led to resignation, frustration, a "bent back" (quote 3), and "individual depression" (Mr. Scheibler). These explanations are incomplete. It is unclear how such feelings (depression and resignation) are transformed into political action or under what conditions dissatisfaction leads to depression, resignation, or political action.

As we have seen, some of our interviewees also mentioned current external or GDR-internal events that, along with other factors, raised hopes for change and led to the articulation of protest. If we translate the "raised hopes" into the language of our explanatory model, it would supposedly mean that the personal influence to promote change by means of one's own actions was increased by the events that took place.

We argued before, particularly in chapter 12, that in view of the improved chances for the success of political action, a moral obligation for the individual to become active became increasingly applicable. We deemed it important to systematically relate the various external and internal events to incentives to participate. These relationships play a less important role in our interviewees' explanations.

The "Other Side"

A number of interviewees state that two actors were important in the emergence of the revolution: the "population" and the GDR leadership. This change in perspective—that is, looking at both groups of actors and the relations between the actors—is certainly essential in explaining the events in autumn 1989. Mr. Scheibler, for example, spoke about the "senility" of the GDR leaders. In regard to the Stasi, he identified a connection between certain characteristics of an authoritarian state and its resulting inability to function. Mr. Pollack talked about disagreements between "cement-heads" and reformers within the SED, which resulted in a destabilization of the system. Mr. Petzoldt mentioned the weakening of the government due to Erich Honecker's operation on August 21.

In talking about the "other side," some of our interviewees mentioned problems of the "system." Mr. Scheibler, for example, mentioned the "fragility of the socialist system." Such phenomena are usually not related to the individual's actions, yet relating collective phenomena to individual action is necessary in order to explain joint political actions, because a system cannot act. Often, it is also unclear precisely to what characteristics the respective properties of the system refer. For example, what exactly is meant by "fragility" of a system?

Violent suppression of the protests was a behavioral alternative of the GDR government during the tense situation in autumn 1989. How do our interviewees view the importance of repression? For Mr. Petzoldt, Gorbachev again enters the picture. The changes in the USSR gave reason to hope "that the Soviet troops would not intervene if things got serious, such as on June 17th. I think that is a decisive factor. . . ." Mr. Petzoldt is the only interviewee who includes repression as a factor in his explanation. He didn't expect the sanctions to be as harsh as they had been in 1953. In other words, the expected sanctions decreased over time.

The fact that other people do not mention state sanctions in their explanations is probably due to the fact that most people think repression deters people from participation in protest activities; yet when answering our initial question ("How would you personally explain the fall of the GDR?"), the interviewees may have considered only factors that promoted the revolution; factors that adversely affect the revolution are neglected. Yet it is also possible that repression is not mentioned because it is seen as given, as a constant. People might have thought: We always had repression, but then the situation became so unbearable that it didn't matter anymore; one had to take the risk.

The Interplay of Factors

For the explanation presented in this book, interaction effects were important, particularly the multiplicative effect of discontent and perceived personal influence (see chapters 2 and 4). Although all our interviewees mentioned a number of factors relevant for the fall of the GDR, they did not contend that any of these factors had multiplicative effects. Respondents also did not address causal relationships between incentives (see chapter 12).

Why Leipzig?

The following statements by our interviewees were not made in the context of the question "How would you personally explain the fall of the GDR?" but, rather, stem from other parts of the interviews. Regarding the role of Leipzig for the GDR revolution, Mr. Lange refers to Leipzig's history of protest (see chapter 1). All the older citizens, says Mr. Lange, probably never got over the demolishing of the University Church in 1968 and the constant feeling of "unbelievable powerlessness." Yet how exactly this past indignation and the demonstrations could have affected the protests in 1989 remains unclear. Mr. Okun raises another point:

> (9) The movement had a very weak beginning and only became politically effective because the trade fair was in Leipzig. The trade fair in Leipzig meant that the GDR leadership had to refrain from using blatant violence at least once or twice a year. At the trade fair everything took place in front of the cameras of the Western media—in front of the

world, so to speak. Thus, a small group had a huge reinforcing effect. And this was only possible in Leipzig, or maybe in Berlin, but the scene wasn't so developed there.

Mr. Okun sees the importance of the trade fair in the decreased probability of repression, which increased the behavioral opportunities of the citizens. Reports in the media about the trade fair included (at least at the fair in autumn 1989) small protests, which were made known to the public by those reports. Peter Zimmermann indicates another effect of the trade fair:

(10) I think that the everyday life of the people in Leipzig was terrible due to everyday pollution. Then there was this extreme situation twice a year during the trade fair. During the fair, Leipzig was a beautiful city with a lot more to offer. I think it was very open-minded. And then, after the trade fair, Leipzig slumped back into deep provincial life again. The people who lived in and around Leipzig became very sensitive to the economic situation and for the way in which the society was organized, governed, and ruled.

In other words, economic as well as political discontent was increased on account of the trade fair. The citizens saw what they were being deprived of when the trade fair was over and how a twisted picture of true life in the GDR was produced for the world public.

Both effects of the trade fair—the increase in dissatisfaction and the temporary refrain from repression—are certainly very plausible. Open-mindedness, which Mr. Zimmermann mentioned, also emerged through the trade fair because many trade fair guests had to be housed in private homes due to lack of hotel space. Yet how "open-mindedness" could have been relevant for the emergence of protests still remains unclear.

Why Was the Revolution Peaceful?

We asked a special question regarding the nonviolence of the protests in our qualitative interviews. Some of the answers of our interviewees were presented in chapter 6 already. We will now discuss our respondents' explanation of the nonviolent protests more extensively. Some of these explanations include remarks about the behavior of both the demonstrators and the security forces. Let us begin with the reasons for nonviolence of the demonstrators.

Many respondents point to the fact that the demonstrators were in many ways encouraged to act nonviolently. Pastor Harald Wagner, for example, describes the peace prayers as "resting poles . . . where the participants should be inspired not to use violence" (see also chapter 6). The Church's role on the nonviolence is also mentioned by Mr. Sievers, Mr. Walter Köcher, Mr. Okun, and Mr. Petzoldt (see chapters 6 and 8).

Not only the Church, but also the opposition groups propagated nonviolence. Mr. Läßig comments:

(11) . . . we as the New Forum also had weekly crisis meetings back then and considered how we could intervene in order to keep the demonstration peaceful. The most poignant of these meetings was on October 8th, one day before October 9th. It was in the Michaelis church; two meetings, both with over two thousand visitors. And we distributed the appeals on flyers. . . . Thus, we attempted, in an organizational way, to make an impact, but that has not been the only thing because we could never have done it alone. A group of a thousand could never have done it. The nonviolence was partially spontaneous; people just seem to have affected one another spontaneously.

It is interesting to note Mr. Läßig's belief that organized efforts alone would not have been enough and that the nonviolence was also spontaneous. What could have been the reason behind spontaneous nonviolent behavior: the appeals for nonviolence, and the obedience to these appeals? Mr. Wagner attributes nonviolent behavior to the population's massive fear of being injured in the course of their own use of violence. Mr. Petzoldt provides three different reasons:

(12) First, it was certainly the fear. Then there was the rational calculation: If we as demonstrators start using violence, we can surely reckon that this is what they're waiting for. Also, especially the Christians and the churches appealed to nonviolence, which is part of our credo, during the peace prayers and in the distributed flyers.

One reason for the peacefulness is therefore that a peaceful demonstration is viewed as having greater chances for success. Mr. Okun argues similarly:

(13) Yes, I think that the nonviolent nature of the movement was due to what people learned from the events in China. China was, so to speak, the mirror-image of our own future. That could happen to us, but it must not happen. With Krenz at the top, we knew that the leaders were capable of using violence. Thus, if the opposition wanted to make political profit, if they wanted to make a change, they had to think through the basic condition of their actions: no reason to use or provoke violence.

Mr. Petzoldt's third argument is a moral one: the Church represents the principle of nonviolence. Mr. Zimmermann disagrees on this point. He says that there was only a small group that identified with the pacifist tradition. Mr. Scheibler attributes nonviolence norms to another condition:

(14) The socialist ideology actually tried to justify socialism with a positive image of mankind and basic moral values. And one of the most essential ideas was indeed "peace" many years after the cold war. And peace and nonviolence, although not respected by the power apparatus itself, were taught in school and everyday life to the point where an inhibition built up.

If we look at the results of our population survey, we find that it is indeed true that the large majority of GDR citizens rejected violence as a means of political action. Our data do not tell us exactly why this is the case. Yet it seems improbable that this primarily stems from Christian ethics, because many of the GDR citizens were not well acquainted with Christian principles.

What were the reasons for the state's nonviolent reactions? Mr. Scheibler emphasizes the lack of legitimation. In his opinion, the lack of aggression and violence of the citizens forbade the government using violence. The actors would have had to act against their morals. This argument claims that the soldiers' and police officers' moral convictions kept them from attacking their own people. Military State Attorney Köcher, who knew the mood within the police and the army well, expected them to disobey orders:

(15) And when these units were gathered together, there came resistance, especially from the soldiers. They came out and said directly: "We're not going to attack."

Mr. Scheibler's opinion and this quote suggest that an order to attack was not made because the leaders could not rule out refusals to obey orders.

Mr. Pollack believes that the explanation of nonviolence is equivalent with the explanation of the security forces' behavior. He believes that with the lifting of the Breshnev Doctrine, the GDR leadership could no longer reckon with miliary aid from the Soviet Union. In his opinion, the problem with the delegation of decision making to the local level was that these groups were not used to making decisions. Then there was the division between the "reformers and the cement-heads" so that the leadership was characterized by a certain inability to function. Mr. Läßig said the following:

(16) The leaders were already senile. They didn't have things under control anymore. This is exemplified by their reaction to the opening of

the borders, which happened without their really taking notice. . . . But there were enough people on the level below who knew that the reaction in China just would not work in a country on the border to the West. Thus, it was clear to them that they would stay maybe two more years in office if they started a bloodbath, but whoever analyzed the mass emigration movement in summer would actually have had to know that there was no hope for the future. . . . Enough people knew that and that's why almost no one made this decision. There were certainly hardliners, but they faded into the background because they supported an offside position.

On the one hand, Mr. Läßig talks about the legitimation problem. In contrast to the legitimation toward its own population, Mr. Läßig argues that the use of violence would have caused a legitimacy problem on the international political level. On the other hand, he argues that the refrain from violence was due to the conviction that violence would bring only temporary success, at the cost of massive suffering among the population.

Finally, Mr. Kind states that the police officers had expected a demonstration of 7,000 but not 70,000. In his opinion, the police officers would themselves have been in danger of being injured.

In summary, although every explanation by itself is incomplete, we find all of the factors we consider relevant when we look at all of them together. In our analysis of the nonviolent behavior of the demonstrators, we found that the fear of injury, normative motives, social incentives, and the greater prospects of success were important. For the repression apparatus, the lack of legitimacy and prospects for success, moral considerations, unclear orders, and possibly the risk of endangering themselves played a role in this regard. Here our own explanation differs from that of our interviewees (see chapter 11).

The opinions on the causes of nonviolence expressed in our interviews give rise to a point that is not addressed in chapter 6. In this chapter, the calls for nonviolence—the social incentives—were considered an independent factor next to the motive of success probability and moral incentives. In this section, we have mentioned a number of times that not only the peaceful behavior as such, but also the calls for nonviolence, must be explained. Social incentives certainly contribute to the explanation of the demonstrator's behavior, yet we must also explain why these appeals were made. We saw in this section that moral and pragmatic reasons led the initiators to propagate nonviolence. According to this hypothesis, on the one hand, these incentives led directly to nonviolent behavior; on the other hand, they also led to appeals to refrain from violence, which had the effect of keeping things peaceful.

Spontaneous Cooperation

A number of our interviewees mentioned that the demonstrations in the GDR were not organized prior to October 9, 1989, or described the events as "spontaneous" or "as if they happened on their own accord." These statements were usually not made when we asked interviewees to explain the fall of the GDR; rather, they came up in discussions of other topics (with the exception of Mr. Petzoldt's account.) Both Mr. Lange and Mr. Okun commented on the fact that Leipzig has a clearly defined city center, which, as Mr. Lange continued, made communication easier: you always met someone in the city and could exchange information. Mr. Lange emphasized that there were no people or groups that started or organized the revolution. Mr. Petzoldt described in detail how the spontaneous cooperation functioned. He begins with the peace prayers. When not only citizens who were willing to emigrate voiced their views, but also the call "We're staying here!" could be heard, this is what happened:

> (20) And that caused . . . the citizens of Leipzig, who stood there by the thousands looking on, to identify with the people who were demonstrating in this way. And even before October 9th, there were larger and larger gatherings, even demonstrations which went down to the train station. They were always dissolved by force. This led to the ritual of people coming together. You didn't need to put an announcement in the paper or distribute flyers . . . it was a kind of self-functioning. A sort of ceremony or ritual emerged in Leipzig which always recharged itself until October 9th, by which time we didn't know what was coming.

Mr. Petzoldt's description is very enlightening at first glance and resembles our own account. We went a bit farther, however, by asking how the estimated participant numbers could have influenced the willingness to participate, for we assumed that the willingness to take risks differs from person to person and that the expectation of low participant numbers would cause few people to participate. The decisive question is thus: how could this "recharging" that Mr. Petzoldt mentions occur? Although Mr. Petzoldt's description contains important elements—such as the spontaneous character of the protests, their "process" character, and the structural condition of the peace prayers—it is still incomplete compared to our own account (chapter 12). In his explanation, we find characteristics of some commonsense theories in chapter 2. For example, the events are not explicitly connected to the behavioral alternatives of the actors, and the separate steps of decision making are not explicitly specified. As we mentioned before, it is quite understandable that such detailed chains of thought are not expressed in an interview.

Summary

Our interviewees attribute the fall of the GDR to a number of factors. Because not only long-term dissatisfaction, but also current crisis factors were taken into consideration, many of their explanations have a dynamic character.

Relevant factors are not only mentioned in regard to the conditions and developments of the GDR itself, but also in regard to external factors— principally Gorbachev and his politics. Many interviewees refer to two groups of actors in their explanations: the GDR leadership and the population. The explanation suggested in this book differs from the interviewees' explanations in regard to the following points:

1. Some initially plausible assumptions that maintain, for example, that dissatisfaction leads to protest behavior, prove to be problematic upon closer scrutiny.
2. Interaction effects and causal relationships between incentive variables are not mentioned by the interviewees.
3. The effects of political events on perception of behavioral alternatives and incentive variables were left open by the interviewees.
4. Some factors, such as personal influence and sanctions, are given greater emphasis in our own model. One reason might be that factors that promote protests are often ignored in commonsense explanations, an example being repression, whereas attention focuses on factors promoting protest.

If we compare the commonsense theories of the revolution with our own explanation, we conclude that our own theoretical explanations are in no way "trivial" in the sense that they only reiterate the obvious. We certainly find many interesting elements in the commonsense explanations, yet our suggested explanatory model goes beyond these explanations in important respects. Nonetheless, the interviewees' statements suggest a modification of our explanation in one point: Moral and other incentives can both directly and indirectly—via the calls for nonviolence—explain the nonviolent behavior of the demonstrators. We did not address this set of effects in chapter 6. It would be interesting to test these effects in future research.

In everyday life, not every theory can be thoroughly tested as is done through scientific enquiry. Yet scientific theories are based on everyday life observations, and we therefore included our interviewees' observations in our own explanation of the GDR revolution in 1989 in many sections of this book.

CHAPTER 14

Some Conditions for the Emergence of Spontaneous, Nonviolent Revolutions

Karl-Dieter Opp

This book focuses on explaining how the revolution in the German Democratic Republic emerged. Yet social scientists are not simply interested in the explanation of isolated cases, but in the formulation of theories as well. A theoretical question starting from the "case of the GDR" could be: under what conditions would a revolution originate that resembles the revolution in the GDR? Before we can answer this question, we must clarify what we mean by a revolution that "resembles" the revolution in the GDR. The revolution in the GDR is so fascinating because it both occurred spontaneously and ensued nonviolently. Thus, an interesting theoretical question we will address in this chapter is: under what conditions do spontaneous and nonviolent revolutions emerge? We define a *revolution* as the replacement of the elite and the introduction of a new political or economic order after (violent or nonviolent) protests by the population. A revolution is *spontaneous* if the protests are not organized. We assume that the country in question is governed by an authoritarian regime.

We do not "generalize" the results of our explanation of the revolution in the GDR. Rather, we use our research results as a source of speculation about general conditions of spontaneous, nonviolent revolutions. Therefore, the following hypotheses are in no way "proven" by the revolution in the GDR. We cannot even use the revolution in the GDR to confirm our hypotheses because they were formulated on the basis of the revolution in the GDR. Thus, the hypotheses we present must be tested by analyzing other concrete revolutions.

The Willingness to Take Action against the Regime

Our explanation proceeds in several steps—see figure 1. We first assume that an individual's intention to take part in protests depends, among other things, on *positive* incentives to protest: dissatisfaction, influence, moral and social

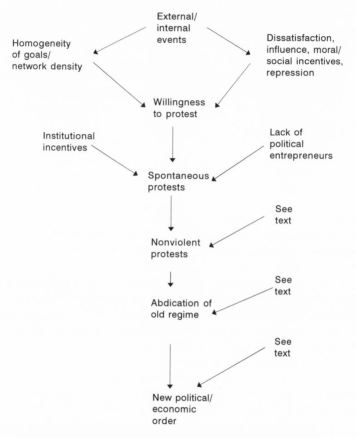

Fig. 1. The emergence of spontaneous, nonviolent revolutions

incentives. In order for a relatively large number of citizens to take part in protests against the regime, a high *homogeneity*, or similarity, of political goals and types of dissatisfaction must be present. This was the case in the GDR. For example, almost all citizens were similarly dissatisfied with political conditions. If homogeneity is present, a change in political events will simultaneously increase the willingness to protest for a relatively large number of citizens.

Positive incentives include, as was noted before, social incentives. The more contact between the citizens—that is, the larger the *network density*—the stronger the incentives. We mentioned the importance of personal networks for the revolution in the GDR. Yet close contacts between citizens alone do not promote protest. The citizens must also be critical of the regime—that is, dissatisfied.

Negative incentives include *repression* (see chapter 9 for more details). If repression is on the upward sloping (left-hand) part of the inverted U-curve (see fig. 3 in chapter 9), then the likelihood of protests is relatively high. Deterrence effects will be low if positive incentives are strong.

Is the *speed of political changes* relevant for the extent of protest? The positive incentives for protest will be relatively high if changes occur quickly, because quick and strong changes attract more attention. Citizens will talk about them and encourage each other to "take action." Protest norms also become applicable. These effects are weaker when changes are slow.

The incentives we have described will be affected by *internal and external events*, which will be unique in each country. These events and their relationships to incentives must thus be researched empirically.

Spontaneous Protests

The willingness to take part in protests will be relatively high if the positive incentives clearly outweigh the negative ones. Additional incentives must be present for "spontaneous" protests to occur. In chapters 2 and 12, we dealt with the conditions for the emergence of spontaneous protest in detail. Figure 1 in this chapter identifies institutional incentives and the lack of political entrepreneurs as particularly important in this regard.

Nonviolent Action

The most important conditions for spontaneous protests to be nonviolent were discussed in chapter 6. Whether or not citizens take nonviolent action depends on the extent to which they believe they can achieve their political goals by means of nonviolent protest. The greater the expected repression and the less the opposition is organized, the more citizens will believe they will have success when taking nonviolent political action. Citizens then assume that an all-powerful government can presumably not be crushed by means of unorganized, violent civil action. Yet they believe that, if anything, nonviolent forms of resistance might be successful.

Second, the more one expects and fears an increase in repression when violence is used, the more likely the use of nonviolent tactics. Third, the more moral ideas rejecting violence as a form of political action are accepted, the more probable the use of nonviolent actions. Finally, incentives against violence in specific situations are very important in preventing violence. The more similar these views among the population are (i.e., low perceived effectiveness and strong, moral rejection of violence) the greater the probability that protests will remain nonviolent.

Demonstrators and security forces face each other at spontaneous protests. We believe that another important condition for nonviolent protests is that security forces do not use violence against demonstrators.

The Abdication of the Old Regime

Under what conditions does a regime resign? We saw in chapter 11 that every dictatorship is confronted with problems of information and repression. These problems can vary in degree. If, for example, a relatively small percentage of the population, such as a group of dissidents, shows a high willingness for protest, the information problem is not as serious as if almost the entire population were willing to take action against the regime. The repression problem is less serious, for example, if the army is largely shielded from the population and is therefore falsely informed by propaganda about the protest motives.

First, the more regimes are surprised by protests from the population, and the more extensive the protests by the population are, the greater the probability that a regime will resign. In the GDR, the information about the population's willingness to protest was grossly distorted, whereas the regime's perceived ability to stay in power was low due to the protests' extensiveness. Second, spontaneous and nonviolent protests cause a regime to view its chances for holding onto power as relatively low. The repression problem also increases. An army will be less willing to shoot at hundreds of thousands of nonviolent, average citizens than at a group of dissidents who use violence. Third, the greater a regime views the repression problem to be, the greater the probability of its resignation. If, for example, the willingness of the army and police to intervene is viewed as high, we can expect that an attempt will be made to crush protests. Finally, a regime will also consider its relations with other countries. The more a regime expects military support from other countries, the greater the probability that it will not resign.

The New Order

The resignation of a regime does not imply anything about which new order will replace the old one. If, for example, the opposition groups in the GDR could have designed the new order, it certainly would have been very different from the present-day order. What determines whether a new order is really new, compared to the existing order? One condition is the degree of dissatisfaction with the old order. If the citizens were highly dissatisfied with many aspects of the old order—that is, not dissatisfied with only the current government's actions—we can expect that the new order will be very different from the old order.

What new order will prevail? This depends on the citizens' ideas about what order serves their needs best. Such ideas originate from information that citizens gather from the mass media and personal discussions with other citizens. On the basis of this information, many people develop ideas about the kind of political order that is more or less "good" for them. In the Eastern European countries, the citizens apparently had clear ideas about the kind of order that was superior to a communist dictatorship with a centrally planned economy: a Western-style democracy with a market economy.

A new political order does not emerge spontaneously but, rather, is "created." Who enforces the new order? In the phase following the collapse of a regime, the available incentives in the form of prestige, power, and income are so large that a large number of people will actively work toward the realization of the new order. Citizens belonging to the opposition, or who at least did not support the old order, initially belong to the circle of individuals having the largest support from the population. If the new order is a democracy, those who can best represent the will of the voters will "get through." These do not have to be the people who initiated the revolution.

CHAPTER 15

Theories of Revolution and the Fall of the GDR

Karl-Dieter Opp

The extensive literature about the causes of revolutions include Marxist, structuralist, and system-theoretical or functionalist explanations, as well as deprivation theories and the rational actor model.[1] Explanations dealing with protest behavior could also be added to this list because protests are often the beginning of a revolution. In the face of the plethora of theories, the following question arises: to what extent can the events in the GDR in 1989 be explained, and perhaps better, by theories other than the rational actor model, which we used in this book? This question is the focus of the present chapter.

Revolution and Rationality

Explanations of revolutions that apply the rational actor model are rare. Until now, Samuel L. Popkin (1979) is the only one who has undertaken an extensive attempt to explain a particular revolution, namely the revolution in Vietnam. Clausjohann Lindner (1972) formulated a stage model of revolutions based on a variant of the rational actor model applied here. Gordon Tullock's theory of revolution (1974) is the most well-known and, thus, the "standard" theory based on the rational actor model that is sometimes also called the "economic" model of man—therefore the name "economic" theory of revolution.

The "Economic" Standard Theory of Revolution

Gordon Tullock's theory (1974; see also Silver 1974 and Tietzel, Weber, and Bode 1991) is based on Mancur Olson's theory of collective action (1965; see also Tullock 1974, 42) which we presented in chapter 2. Tullock's initial hypothesis is adopted from Olson: Within a large group (such as the GDR),

---

1. Especially Salert (1976) provides an excellent account and criticism of major theories of revolution.

preferences for public (or, equivalently, collective) goods are not causes for contributing to the provision of such public goods. The reason is that a single individual usually has no influence on the provision of public goods and, by not participating, spares the costs of participation.

Tullock then introduces an assumption about the distribution of preferences for the public good: The public good is one "for the entire society" (1974, 42). Tullock also adopts Olson's second basic idea: if people contribute to the provision of a public good, it is because they are interested in selective incentives such as money, power, or a better professional position. Thus, if public goods are produced, they are only by-products of revolutionary actions.

Tullock formalized his theory in the form of two equations. The first equation defines the total benefits that originate if a person does not take part in the revolution (P_{In}). The total benefits equal the benefit of the public good which the participants of a revolution desire (P_g). Yet a citizen receives the public good only if the revolution is successful. The greater the likelihood of success (L_v), the greater the total benefits the citizens expect from the revolution if they do not take part. If L_v is equal to zero, the public good will not be produced.

The second equation defines the net benefits of participating in revolutionary actions (P_r), such as demonstrations. The greater the preference for the public good (P_g), and the higher the likelihood of revolutionary success (L_v), the greater the net benefits. If Tullock had left it at that, the benefits of inactivity and participation would be identical. Yet if the probability that the public good will be offered increases through a person's participation (L_i), the benefit of participation will also be greater. L_i represents the personal influence to lessen dissatisfaction by means of participation.

Gordon Tullock's theory of revolution:

$$P_{In} = P_g \cdot L_v$$

Total Payoff to Inaction
= Public good generated by successful revolution
· Likelihood of revolutionary victory assuming subject is neutral

$$P_r = P_g \cdot (L_v + L_i)$$

Total Payoff to subject if he or she joins revolution
= Public good generated by successful revolution
· (Likelihood of revolutionary victory assuming subject is neutral
+ Change in probability of revolutionary success resulting

from individual participation in
revolution)

$+ R_i \cdot (L_v + L_i)$ + Private reward to individual for
his or her participation in revolu-
tion if revolution wins
· (see before)

$- P_i \cdot [1 - (L_v + L_i)]$ − Private penalty imposed on individual for participation in revo-
lution if revolution fails
· [1 − (see before)]

$- L_w \cdot (I_r + E)$ − Likelihood of injury through
participation in revolution—for or
against
· (Injury suffered in action
+ Entertainment value of participation)

Selective incentives are personal rewards (R_i) such as an office in the
new government if the revolution is successful. If one increases the revolution's success by taking part (L_i), one increases the chances of receiving
personal rewards.

Yet participation in a revolution is also associated with a risk in the form
of punishment (P_i) if the revolution fails. The greater the probability of a
revolution's success and personal influence $(L_v + L_i)$, the lower the probability of punishment. Thus, the expression $(L_v + L_i)$ must be subtracted from
1 because probabilities can vary only between 0 and 1. The minus sign before
this term of the equation says that in general, personal punishment lowers the
benefits of participation.

There is always a chance of being injured or killed at revolutionary
activities. The more probable (L_w) and the worse (I_r) an injury, the lower the
benefits of participation become. Finally, according to Tullock, participation in revolutions has an entertainment value (E): Participation is fun in itself (39).

A person will take part in revolutionary actions if P_r is greater than P_{In}.
The size of the net benefit for participation in revolutionary actions results
from subtracting the first equation from the second (if $P_r > P_{In}$, then it
follows: $P_r - P_{In} > 0$).

Tullock introduces another assumption. He maintains that L_i is close to
zero—that is, participation or nonparticipation of an individual does not
influence the probability of the success of a revolution. Therefore, L_i in the
equation can be eliminated.

Along with inactivity or participation in revolutionary activities, Tullock
addresses a third behavioral alternative: one could side with the government.

Generally, GDR citizens did not appear to consider this alternative, and thus we will not address this point any further.

The main causes for the participation in revolutionary activities are thus the personal rewards and punishments as well as the danger of injury during the participation in the protests. The entertainment value, contends Tullock, plays no role if the risks are high. One does not go to a demonstration for amusement if one could be seriously injured.

Tullock also addresses the government members' behavior. Although Tullock's hypotheses contain a number of ideas that also apply to the GDR, he nevertheless does not formulate an explanatory model applicable to the situation in the GDR. Therefore, we will no further discuss these ideas.

A Critique

Tullock assumes that the preferences for all members of a society are equal. Yet since preferences are irrelevant in Tullock's explanation of revolutions, this assumption is not needed. Here is an important difference between Tullock's explanation and our own: we saw that the intensity and distribution of public good preferences in a society play a major role for participation in revolutionary activities. Even if we assume that the single citizen has no political influence—which is incorrect—*dissatisfaction* has *indirect* effects on the participation in protests because it increases other incentives for protest.[2]

Let us now turn to the factor *probability of success* of the revolution. According to the "objectivist" version of the rational actor model, which is standard in economics, this should be an objective probability rather than an individually perceived probability. Tullock does not specify which type is meant or how it should be ascertained. It is by far more plausible that the success of collective action *perceived* by the citizens is important for the participation in a revolution.

---

2. Tullock asks why explanations of revolutions by means of public goods preferences are so widespread (1974, 39–41). He argues that revolutionaries want to show themselves in a favorable light and therefore present their participation in a revolution as a fight for public goods. Tullock also could use this argument against our own research: maybe those of our respondents who took part in the protests also mentioned "noble" motives for participation in order to be looked upon favorably. However, we did not ask directly about the motives for participation in protest, but instead asked generally about the extent of political dissatisfaction. We asked both participants and nonparticipants of protests the same questions. The answers to the questions on participation in protests were given in written form so that the interviewers could not see the answers. Because the survey was anonymous, there was no chance to be "looked upon favorably." But let's assume that the respondents really wanted to show themselves in a favorable light and that this was possible by expressing high dissatisfaction. If this were the case, we would expect that both the participants and the nonparticipants would make an attempt at this, and we would not have found any relationship between dissatisfaction and participation. Yet such a relationship did exist. On the subject of social desirability, see also the introduction of this book.

Furthermore, the *distribution* of the mentioned subjective probabilities—and of other incentives—is important in explaining the participation in revolutionary activities. If, for example, incentives are concentrated in certain groups of individuals, it is much more likely that at least some participate than if, for example, for some individuals incentive *A* and for others incentive *B* is high.

The first equation has another flaw: A number of "soft" incentives are missing. In the last phase of the revolution in the GDR, inactivity was certainly associated with negative sanctions from neighbors and friends.

Tullock assumes that political influence (L_i) is close to zero. Our data clearly refute this assumption, and we saw that perceived political influence is an important factor for participation in the general protests and demonstrations.

It is also questionable whether L_v and L_i should be added rather than multiplied (see chap. 2 and Finkel, Muller, and Opp 1989). If we add L_v and L_i, public good preference would be an incentive even if one perceives no personal influence. Yet this is implausible. Why would someone take part if one views one's own participation as superfluous while believing that the protest will be successful on the whole?

In regard to private rewards, Tullock mentions incentives such as a position in the new government. Material incentives certainly didn't motivate GDR citizens to protest, because up to October 9 and presumably even up to the fall of the Berlin Wall on November 9, 1989, no one imagined that the socialist government would fall apart.

Tullock argues that in the case of low success probability of a revolution, the probability of punishment is high. This hypothesis is not very plausible. Dissidents often serve their long jail terms before a revolution is successful. Dissidents are only then let out of jail, trials are terminated, and rehabilitation follows.

Both terms in the equation that refer to private penalty and injury (P_i and L_w) during participation in revolutionary actions have a negative sign, that is to say, an increase in these variables has a deterrence effect. Tullock's model does not include hypotheses about radicalizing effects.

There are two other differences between Tullock's theory and our own:

1. Tullock's theory does not contain any hypotheses about why incentives change.
2. Tullock does not address the interdependence of incentives (see chapter 12, in this volume).

Our conclusion from the preceding discussion is that a relatively restrictive rational actor model, which does not consider perceptions and soft incentives, cannot explain the protests in the GDR. Yet this does not mean that

Tullock's theory does not apply to other revolutions. Tullock himself indicates the kinds of revolutions which his model can explain (1974, 44 ff.): There must be groups who expect great benefits or who themselves can strongly influence the result of the revolution by participating in it. These are often members of the government or military leaders. Tullock maintains accordingly that (44) "revolutions tend to be run by prime ministers, crown princes, and ministers of war." He continues (47), " true revolutions (uprisings from *outside* the government apparatus) are extremely rare and perhaps nonexistent." Yet the revolution in the GDR was a revolution from "outside the government apparatus"; it was a revolution "from below." Tullock's theory is probably not appropriate for the explanation of such revolutions.

The Resource Mobilization Perspective

In this section we will present the basic ideas of the resource mobilization (RM) perspective—one of the most intensively discussed theories of political protest and social movements in sociology. We then explore the extent to which this perspective is appropriate in explaining the revolution in the GDR.

Theory

As summaries of the resource mobilization perspective exist (see Jenkins 1983; Knoke 1990; for criticism see McAdam 1982, Piven and Cloward 1991), we will concentrate on its basic ideas.

> *Hypothesis 1*: In order to achieve their goals, groups attempt to expand the resources at their disposal—that is, to mobilize new resources.

Because resources are scarce, hypothesis 1 implies that groups are in competition for scarce resources.

> *Hypothesis 2*: Formation, development, and success of a social movement or political group in general depend on the resources the actors have at their disposal.

Hypothesis 2 is formulated on the *macrolevel*, the units are collectives (groups, societies, and so on). Supporters of the RM are also interested in the explanation of individual behavior—that is, in statements on the *microlevel*:

> *Hypothesis 3*: The political participation of people depends on the resources at their disposal.

In the RM, the term *resources* is used in a very broad sense. It includes financial means, access to media, support from sympathizers, loyalty of members or groups, rights, space, knowledge, and skills at the actors' disposal (see Gamson 1968, 94; Jenkins 1983, 533; Oberschall 1973, 28). In other words, resources are goods (everything that is beneficial or costly to the actors) at the actors' disposal. Put differently, resources are opportunities or restrictions of action. *Mobilization* of resources means the process in which a group obtains control over resources (see Jenkins 1983, 532; Tilly 1978, 7; see also other definitions, such as Oberschall 1973, 28; Etzioni 1968, 243).

Advocates of the RM differ according to the role that dissatisfaction among the population plays (see the discussion by Jenkins 1983, 530–32). Some supporters of the RM argue that deprivation is so widespread that it only slightly helps, if at all, to explain political participation (McCarthy and Zald 1977, 1215). Other RM supporters emphasize, on the other hand, that deprivations play a central role. This is particularly the case in more recent research (see Walsh 1981; Walsh and Warland 1983; Useem 1985). In these cases, deprivation is viewed as an important determinant of political participation but one that takes effect only if protest-promoting structures are present.

What is the relationship between these assumptions of the RM and the rational actor model? The most important RM supporters use the rational actor model as a theoretical basis. Oberschall (1973, 29) writes that "individuals . . . make rational choices based on the pursuit of their selfish interests in an enlightened manner. They weigh the rewards and sanctions, costs and benefits, that alternative courses of action represent to them." (See also Jenkins 1983, 538; McCarthy and Zald 1977, 1216.)

Not all advocates of RM will agree that their underlying theory is the rational actor model. This goes for Fireman and Gamson (1979), for example, who criticize this model. If we compare the model, which these and other authors criticize, with the theoretical model used in this book, we come to the following conclusion: the mentioned authors criticize a model that has very little to do with the model used in this book and by other advocates of RM (see Opp 1989, chap. 2 for more details). In their criticism, the authors proceed from neoclassical economics, in which only "hard" incentives are allowed and in which other, very restrictive assumptions (complete information, no transaction costs, and so forth) are made.

Can the Resource Mobilization Perspective Explain the Revolution in the GDR?

The Lack of an Explanatory Model of Individual Action

Most often, RM doesn't deal with the incentives underlying individual behavior in detail, although Klandermans (1984) presented an explanatory model of individual action, which is similar to ours, for the purpose of providing RM with an individualistic basis. This and other "micromodels" at hand are not applied systematically and explicitly by advocates of RM.

The treatment of dissatisfaction presents a particular problem. If we proceed from the more recent research mentioned previously, the contended effects of dissatisfaction correspond to the rational actor model. Yet hypotheses about the effects of other incentives are not formulated and tested in detail. Hypotheses about the indirect effects on dissatisfaction are missing.

How Do Resources Change Individual Action?

Since an explanatory model of individual action is lacking, assumptions about what external or internal events change the individual incentives for protest in what way are also lacking.

Proponents of RM will probably consider an explanatory model of individual action unnecessary, insisting that the RM is a macrotheory. This contention yields the following major problem: the hypothesis that a change in resources leads to a change in political action can only be applied to explain political action if (1) the exact meaning of the term *resources* is more clearly specified, and (2) if it is clarified what changes in resources lead to which form of political action. For example, does the change in Gorbachev's politics or the opening of the Hungarian borders represent an increase in resources? Is the institution of peace prayers a resource? Did the GDR government's public support of China's crushing the democratic movement decrease the population's resources? And if Gorbachev's politics provide additional resources, are they resources for violent or nonviolent political action? Such questions cannot be answered clearly because the term *resources* is not sufficiently clear and because there is no specification as to what changes in resources lead to which forms of behavior.

The "Market Model" of the Resource
Mobilization Perspective

An important flaw of RM is the following assumption about the origin of social movements: there is a *market for resources* where the various actors compete for the use of resources. This basic assumption may be accurate in Western democracies, but it is not applicable in situations in which governmental repression is so strong that a competition for resources is not possible. Thus, hypotheses about the origin of spontaneous protests are missing in the RM.

When Are Protests Successful?

Although there is some research that deals with the success of social movements, there is no theory that, for example, can be applied to the reactions of the GDR government. This is because the RM deals with groups and only rarely "goes down" to the level of the individual actor.

Structural Explanations

Many social scientists believe that structural explanations are most appropriate for explaining revolutions. How does a structural explanation differ from our own? To what extent are structural approaches problematic? We will address these questions in the following sections.

What Is a Structural Explanation?

Theda Skocpol's book *States and Social Revolutions: A Comparative Analysis of France, Russia, and China* (1979) is considered one of the major works of a modern, purely structural explanation of revolutions. To understand what is meant by a *structural explanation*, it is useful to begin with Skocpol's account of structural explanations. In explaining social revolutions, the author demands that, first, the emergence of a revolutionary situation within the regime be viewed as a problem (18). Then, maintains Skocpol, it is necessary to analyze complex, institutionally determined situations and relations between different groups that influence the revolutionary process and bring forth a new regime. It is necessary to simultaneously concentrate on the relations among societies within world-historically developing international structures. In doing this, an "impersonal and nonsubjective viewpoint" must be taken. Thus, groups and societies, not individuals, are the units of analysis. Skocpol writes (13) that her method is based on Marxist ideas in which relations between social classes and objective conditions such as productive forces and relations of production play a role in the emergence of a revolution.

Skocpol rejects a "voluntaristic" perspective—that is, the idea that human behavior is goal oriented. The rational actor model contains such a voluntaristic perspective, because it maintains that preferences (certain goals) are a determinant of individual action.

How does a structural explanation differ from our own model of explanation? The differences are depicted in figure 1.[3] In a structural explanation, factors such as productive forces and relations of production are related to other macrofactors such as revolutions. Thus, it is maintained that certain structural factors have structural effects. These are propositions referring to the macrolevel—see arrow 1 in figure 1.

Our own explanatory model could be termed *structural-individualistic*

---

3. Similar diagrams are used by Coleman (1990) to describe relationships between the "collective" and "individual" level.

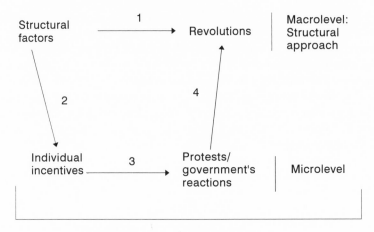

Structural-individualistic approach

Fig. 1. Structure, incentives, and revolutions

(Opp 1978, chap. 2). To be sure, it includes structural hypotheses (arrow 1 in fig. 1), such as hypotheses on the effects of political events on the emergence of demonstrations in the GDR. In contrast to a purely structural explanation, however, a structural-individualistic explanation proceeds from the assumption that revolutions and other collective phenomena are the result of actions taken by individual actors (arrow 4 in fig. 1). A second assumption is that certain individual incentives are important for these actions to be carried out (arrow 3 in fig. 1). Finally, assumptions are made regarding the manner in which structural factors influence the individual incentives (arrow 2 in fig. 1).[4]

Thus, structural and structural-individualistic approaches do not contradict each other in a strict sense, yet a structural-individualistic approach does not stop with the relationships on the structural level. The structural-individualistic model asks, moreover, why such relationships exist. Thus, from the perspective of a structural-individualistic approach, a structural explanation is incomplete.

Why Are Structural Explanations Inadequate?

Skocpol's first argument for a purely structural perspective (1979, 16–18) is that a voluntaristic perspective requires that in a society, the existing social order is based on a consensus of the majority that its needs are to be satisfied.

---

4. For a more elaborate description of the way a structural-individualistic model works, see Coleman 1987, 1990; Opp 1988b; Wippler and Lindenberg 1987.

Only when the majority withdraws its support for the government will a government be overthrown. A voluntaristic perspective would view this as the "ultimate and sufficient condition for revolution." However, a rational actor model allows the formulation of very different models about the emergence of revolutions. In no way has the assumption criticized by Skocpol to be made within any model based on the theory of rational action. It is indeed surprising that Skocpol says nothing about whether the hypothesis she criticizes follows from a voluntaristic perspective.

According to Skocpol, a second argument is more important (1979, 16–18): the voluntaristic perspective strongly suggests that revolutionary movements mobilize the masses and consciously "make" revolutions. Yet this, says Skocpol, is incorrect (17):

> . . . revolutionary situations have developed due to the emergence of politicomilitary crises of state and class domination. And only because of the possibilities thus created have revolutionary leaderships and rebellious masses contributed to the accomplishment of revolutionary transformations.

This is again the aged misunderstanding that a voluntaristic model must assume that individuals consciously strive toward the outcome of joint action. Indeed, one of the strengths of a structural-individualistic approach is that it can show how collective action may lead to outcomes that were in no way planned or intended. The standard example is Adam Smith's argument in his work *An Inquiry into the Nature and Causes of the Wealth of Nations* (1776). He says that the subjects of the economy are only interested in their own welfare, but that this in turn contributes to the general welfare. The revolution in the GDR is another example of this because, as we showed earlier, it was not planned by the participants.

Again Skocpol does not show how the assumption she criticizes is derived from a voluntaristic model, for example, from the rational actor model. Important works in this tradition dealing with political processes such as Downs 1957, Olson 1965, and Tullock 1974 had already been published by the time Skocpol's book went into print in 1979. An analysis of the way the rational actor model has been used and may be used in explaining political phenomena would have made it clear that her arguments are untenable.[5]

We believe there are three arguments that speak *against* a structural

---

5. This criticism of Skocpol does not insinuate that her explanations for the revolutions in France, Russia, and China are wrong. Yet they are incomplete in that references to the individual actors are missing (see fig. 1). For a discussion of Skocpol's theory from a rational actor perspective, see Taylor 1988.

perspective and *for* a structural-individualistic perspective. First, proponents of structural explanations continually refer to individual actors when they explain or interpret their hypotheses. This applies to Skocpol, as Taylor (1988) shows, and as we will see further, also to Karl Marx, a main advocate of structural explanations. If the structuralists implicitly apply a structural-individualistic model, one could ask why they don't formulate such a model explicitly. This would clarify their arguments and make them empirically testable.

The "reversion" of proponents of the structural perspective on the level of the individual actors shows that they are also not content with a purely structuralist perspective. They also want to know why a structural hypothesis is valid. For example, why should a "contradiction" between forces and relations of production lead to revolutions? Revolutions are the result of individual actions. How does the mentioned "contradiction" influence the citizens' behavior so that revolutions develop? Structural-individualistic models attempt to answer such questions. They allow us to more deeply understand what happens on the structural level.[6] This is the second major argument for a structural-individualistic explanation.

The third argument that speaks against a purely structural explanation is that structural hypotheses are only valid if certain characteristics of individual actors are given (Malewski 1967, Opp 1979). For example, whether or not an extremely unequal distribution of wealth and income leads to a revolution depends on (1) which and how many individual actors view such a distribution as a collective evil, and (2) the extent to which actors believe that protests could change the distribution (see Lichbach 1989, 1990). Thus, structural hypotheses are only valid under specific conditions, which can by ascertained by systematically applying a rational actor model.

Political "Opportunities" as Causes of Revolutions

A new explanatory model for protests and revolutions is becoming more and more popular among sociologists and political scientists: it is argued that the development of protests and revolutions is due to changing "opportunities" or "opportunity structures." Tarrow (1991a, 13, see also Tarrow 1991b) summarizes the central hypothesis:

> Mass outbreaks of collective action are best understood as the collective responses of citizens, groups and elites to an expanding structure of political opportunities.

---

6. On the "depth" of an explanation in general, see Popper 1972, chap. 5.

Tarrow claims that this hypothesis is an alternative to the resource mobilization perspective (1991a, 14). He does not discuss, however, what the relationship is between this hypothesis and the rational actor model.

Does the described hypothesis contradict our own explanatory model? The answer is definitely no. Among other things, the rational actor model contends that preferences and constraints determine behavior (see chapter 2). *Constraints* are defined as opportunities or limitations for action—that is, events that make possible or restrict the realization of individual goals. If we compare the "new" opportunity proposition with the rational actor model, we find that the former rules out preferences as explanatory factors. The opportunity structure thus seems to be an incomplete rational actor model. Proponents do not seem to realize this as they do not refer to the rational choice literature. This may suggest that the term *opportunities* is used differently in this literature than in the rational actor model. Tarrow (1991a, 15) writes:

> The onset of a wave of mobilization can be seen as a collective response to generally expanding political opportunities in which the costs and risks of collective action are lowered and the potential gains increase.

Thus, *political opportunities* are to be understood as events that change the benefits and costs of collective political action (also see Amenta and Zylan 1991, Kitschelt 1986). This corresponds exactly to what we described as internal and external events (see in particular chapter 12).

Although political opportunities are contained in our own explanatory model, the political opportunity model and our own model differ because the opportunity model is restricted to structural hypotheses (arrow 1 in fig. 1). Thus, there are no propositions specifying the various benefits and costs of political action (arrow 3 in fig. 1). There are therefore no hypotheses about which opportunities change which types of costs and benefits (arrow 2), and how collective action of actors (the citizens and the state) produces a "revolution" (arrow 4). The opportunity model is therefore an incomplete explanation of revolutions.

The danger of such an incomplete explanation is that events are considered opportunities arbitrarily, when they occur prior to the phenomenon to be explained. It is not clear whether the events are in fact opportunities or how these events change the actors' costs and benefits. In the quoted article by Tarrow on the explanation of the Eastern European revolutions, for example, the Helsinki Final Act is deemed an opportunity because opposition groups could appeal to it during confrontations with the government. It remains unclear to what extent the Helsinki Final Act corresponds to what is meant by "opportunity." Which individual incentives to act were changed by the Final Act?

Marx's Theory of Revolution

To what extent can Marx's theory of revolution[7] explain the revolution in the GDR? There are two possible answers to this question. The first is that Marxist theory is not at all applicable for explaining the revolution in the GDR because Marx did not address the development of revolutions in socialist societies. We should note here that this implies that Marx's theory cannot be disproven by the upheaval in Eastern Europe, either.

The second answer proceeds from the assumption that Marx formulated general conditions for the emergence of revolutions. If these conditions are not given, revolutions should not arise. Therefore, Marxist theory can be used to explain the revolution in the GDR. This second answer is far more plausible than the first because Marx saw the communist social order as the way out of the "contradictions" of capitalism: no revolutions can arise in a communist order because the conditions for revolutions are no longer present. Therefore, Marx has formulated general conditions for the emergence of revolutions.

Marx expected capitalism to be destroyed by a *violent* takeover of power by the proletariat. Thus, Marx probably saw revolutions as violent overthrows of governments. Therefore, it could be contended that no revolution took place in the GDR at all because this revolution was peaceful. Again, this would lead to the conclusion that Marx's theory would not be applicable to the GDR revolution, this time for a different reason. It may be possible that the conditions Marx deemed necessary for the development of violent upheavals also lead to the development of peaceful changes—that is to say, Marx could have characterized the circumstances to be explained inaccurately. This can be tested by applying the theory to the GDR revolution, which we will now do.

According to Marx, the main causes for the fall of capitalism are its inherent contradictions. The basic contradiction can be characterized in the following manner:[8] on the one hand, production is done socially: the workers manufacture products together. On the other hand, there is private ownership of the means of production—that is, only a few "capitalists" appropriate the products. This basic contradiction between productive forces (social production) and relations of production (private ownership) creates insolvable conflicts. These conflicts finally prompt the proletariat to organize and violently

---

7. For an account of this theory with further references, see Cohan 1975 and Salert 1976.

8. On this subject, see in particular Friedrich Engels, *Die Entwicklung des Sozialismus von der Utopie zur Wissenschaft* [The development of socialism from utopia to science], reprinted, for example, in Fetscher 1966.

take over power, that is, a revolution originates. In the new order, those contradictions are absent. Accordingly, there can be no revolution in a society without the mentioned basic contradiction.

The emergence of the GDR revolution contradicts Marx's ideas. It is irrelevant whether the GDR was a "true" communist society or not. According to Marx, the decisive causes of the revolution lie in the development of forces and relations of production. The "contradictions" of capitalist production were not present in the GDR.

Although Marx is considered a representative of a structural explanation, he, like many other structuralists, leaves this level of analysis as he deals continually with individual actors, such as in the work *Ludwig Feuerbach und der Ausgang der klassischen deutschen Philosophie* [Ludwig Feuerbach and the origin of classic German philosophy] by Friedrich Engels (reprinted, for example, in Fetscher 1966), which contains an excellent characterization of the structural-individualistic research program (see Fetscher 1966, 212–13 and 226–27). In the *Manifest der Kommunistischen Partei* [Communist manifesto], Marx characterizes, for example, the serious woes of the citizens caused by the capitalist forces of production that contribute to the development of a revolution. Accordingly, one could also view Marx as a "theorist of deprivation" who maintains that high dissatisfaction leads to the organization of the workers and finally to the takeover of power. Yet Marx is in no way an advocate of a pure dissatisfaction hypothesis. Rather, he mentioned a number of other conditions leading to the consolidation of workers and finally to a revolution. Yet Marx did not recognize the free-rider problem, as Olson (1965, chapter 4) shows in particular.

The conclusion we draw is that the Marxist theory of revolution cannot contribute to explaining the revolution in the GDR. Depending on its interpretation, this theory is either inapplicable or wrong.

Deprivation: The Classic Explanation of Revolutions

In this section, two questions will be answered: (1) To what extent can the hypotheses of some important representatives of the theory of deprivation explain the revolution in the GDR? (2) To what extent are these hypotheses in accordance with the rational actor model? This section expands on our account and critique of deprivation theory in chapter 2.

Can "Dissatisfaction" Explain the Revolution in the GDR?

The basic hypotheses of the main advocates of deprivation theory, James C. Davies (1962) and Ted Robert Gurr (1970), are clearly disproven by the revolution in the GDR. Gurr summarizes his theory in the following manner (1970, 12–13):

> The primary causal sequence in political violence is first the development of discontent, second the politicization of that discontent, and finally its actualization in violent action against political objects and actors. Discontent arising from the perception of relative deprivation is the basic, instigating condition for participants in collective violence.

According to Gurr, "political violence" also encompasses "revolutions" (3–4). *Revolution* is defined as "fundamental sociopolitical change accomplished through violence." Thus, Gurr argues that dissatisfaction leads to *violent* political activity. Yet this was not the case in the GDR.

Dissatisfaction is often also viewed as the cause of *non*violent political action (see Gurney and Tierney 1982; Opp 1988a; Opp and Roehl 1990a). If dissatisfaction causes citizens to take political action, why should they then only choose violent forms of political action?[9] Is such a modified dissatisfaction hypothesis valid for the GDR? As we saw earlier, dissatisfaction increased during 1989 and went hand in hand with an increase in protests. This is in accordance with the dissatisfaction hypothesis.

After October 9, dissatisfaction decreased, although probably to no great extent (see chapter 12). In particular, political repression decreased and the GDR citizens could leave their country. According to the dissatisfaction hypothesis, a decrease in protest should have occurred. Yet the opposite was the case, as we saw earlier. This increase in protests would correspond to Alexis de Tocqueville's hypothesis that reforms often lead to an increase in political activity. Yet the protests did decrease later on. Many of the citizens' demands had been satisfied. This again confirms the prior mentioned dissatisfaction hypothesis, which says that a decrease in dissatisfaction leads to a decrease in protest.

A problem with the dissatisfaction hypothesis surfaces at this point. If increasing satisfaction sometimes leads to an increase and sometimes to a decrease in political activity, this hypothesis loses its explanatory power to a large extent: it can only predict that political action is not stable if dissatisfaction changes. The question arises what the conditions are that determine when an increase or decrease in satisfaction increases or decreases protest.

James C. Davies (1962) provides such a condition. He contends that revolutions arise if, after a long period of social and economic improvements, a short period of sharp reversal in the form of a worsening of the situation

---

9. Even if we assume frustration-aggression theory is valid, as does Gurr, this does not mean that nonviolent forms of reactions to frustration are excluded. Frustration can lead to very different reactions.

occurs. Regardless of what is meant by "long" and "short" periods and a "sharp reversal," the revolution in the GDR did not develop after a period of social and economic improvements. Thus, Davies's theory is not applicable to explaining the revolution in the GDR.

In Gurr's work and in other works *relative deprivation* is viewed as the cause of revolutions. Are our arguments against a dissatisfaction explanation also valid for "relative" dissatisfaction? Gurr defines this expression in the following manner (1970, 13)

> Relative deprivation is defined as a perceived discrepancy between men's value expectations and their value capabilities. Value expectations are the goods and conditions of life to which people believe they are rightfully entitled. Value capabilities are the goods and conditions they think they are capable of attaining or maintaining, given the social means available to them.

For instance, if people think they are entitled to a monthly income of $3,000, but in a given situation cannot earn this money, they are "relatively deprived." Accordingly, GDR citizens could have been relatively deprived in that they felt entitled to democracy and free traveling but were not able under the given circumstances to realize these goals.

Our theoretical model does not differentiate between various types of discontent. Thus, according to the rational actor model, any type of dissatisfaction is relevant for protest activity, as long as people think protest can reduce this type of discontent. As relative dissatisfaction is a certain type of dissatisfaction, its effect should be similar to other types of discontent. We surmise that for many, perhaps even for the majority of GDR citizens, we did in fact measure "relative" dissatisfaction in the sense defined by Gurr. Many citizens presumably believed themselves entitled to political freedoms and an environment that is not detrimental to their health. Accordingly, our critique of discontent explanations also holds true for relative dissatisfaction.

The term *relative discontent* often has another meaning: people might be discontented because they compare themselves with a group that is better off. Discontent in this case stems from a comparison with a group. According to the rational actor model, the effect of dissatisfaction is not dependent on how discontent *originates*. Whether it increased by factual changes—such as a nuclear power accident—or by comparison with a group is irrelevant as far as the effect of discontent is concerned.

Deprivation theory has another weakness: It cannot explain the reactions of authoritarian regimes such as the decision to use repression,[10] and neither

---

10. Although such hypotheses are discussed in the quoted work of Gurr, they are not derived from propositions about deprivation.

does it contain hypotheses about the *indirect* effects of discontent, which we dealt with in chapter 12 in particular.

When Does Increasing Satisfaction Increase Political Action?

Is the rational actor model capable of explaining Alexis de Tocqueville's ([1856] 1978) hypothesis, which says that the improvement of a situation, such as the introduction of political reforms, makes protests more likely? According to our model, a decrease of discontent leads to an increase in protest if a decrease in dissatisfaction leads to a strong increase in positive incentives to protest. We presented a similar argument in our explanation of why the protests increased in the GDR after October 9, 1989 (see chapter 12). Silver (1974) also maintains that reforms raise certain incentives for participation in a revolution. These incentives are identical to factors mentioned in equation 2 of Tullock's theory. Coleman (1990, chap. 18) argues similarly in his analysis of theories of revolution. The rational actor model is thus capable of specifying conditions for increasing discontent to increase political action.

Problems and Further Research

The hypotheses in this book give rise to a number of questions, which will be discussed in this section.

The Revolutions in Eastern Europe and Other Countries

Although an increasing amount of work has been done on the Eastern European revolutions, detailed explanations are still rare. It would be interesting to apply our own explanation of the revolution in the GDR to other Eastern European countries. We believe that the incentives mentioned in our model were also effective in these other revolutions. This is also the case for social incentives, although the sources of these incentives were different. Opposition groups or the Church played different roles in Poland or Czechoslovakia than in the GDR. Repression in other Eastern European countries was also probably ineffective or had radicalizing effects. The internal and external events that caused the changes in incentives were certainly different than those in the GDR. Poland and Hungary, as the forerunner countries, had only the Soviet Union as a source of change in protest-promoting incentives. Possibly internal events were more important in these countries for changing incentives.

There was empirical research in all Eastern European countries before the breakdown of communist rule. Since the fall of the GDR, data sets have been made available to the public, particularly through the Zentralarchiv für Empirische Sozialforschung [Central archive for empirical social research] in Cologne, Germany. It would be worth it to take a look at the available empirical studies in other Eastern European countries and see if they are appropriate for testing hypotheses that explain the revolutions in the different countries.

Because the revolutions took place several years ago, a detailed questionnaire such as the one we used for the GDR in winter 1990 would no longer be appropriate. Yet because of the importance of the revolutions for the lives of the citizens, many of them may still be able to remember many facts connected to the revolutionary events. We need to see what still lies firm in their memories. Perhaps surveys could still be conducted today, with which some of the hypotheses presented here or even new ones could be tested.

Our explanatory model could be applied to other countries in which dictatorships were replaced by democracies. Examples include Spain, Portugal, Greece, and Peru. Is our incentive model also valid for these countries? What internal and external events were important for the changes in incentives? Were there spontaneous protests? Apparently, spontaneous protests took place quite frequently throughout history (see Rudé 1964). Does our explanation of the emergence of spontaneous protests also hold for other countries?

Problems of the Rational Actor Theory in Explaining Revolutions

Although we believe that the rational actor model is superior to other theories, this does not mean that this model is flawless. One problem is that different *forms of dissatisfaction* have different effects (chapter 4). According to the rational actor model, perceived influence is important for the effect of dissatisfaction. We explained the irrelevance of economic dissatisfaction by arguing that the citizens above all believed they would achieve political reforms by means of their protest. Yet we were not able to test this. To what extent is our presumption valid?

A further problem is the relatively small *interaction effect of discontent and influence*. According to the rational actor model, the effect of dissatisfaction depends on the perceived influence. Our data do confirm this hypothesis, but we expected the interaction effect to be far greater. This concern is valid for both this study and others. How can this relatively low interaction effect be explained?

An important part of our explanatory model was the *explanation of the changes in incentives* through external and internal events. Most of these changes were ascertained using items in a questionnaire. It would be better if we had theories at our disposal with which the changes in incentives by political events could be explained, yet such theories are mostly missing.

Developing New Models to Explain Revolutions

For a proponent of the theory of rational action, available theories of revolution cannot explain the revolution in the GDR. This is not surprising because different processes of revolutionary events, or only rebellions without changes of the economic or political order, or even political inactivity, are to be expected in different social situations. Since all revolutions are different, many social scientists refrain from proposing general propositions about revolutions. Instead they analyze single revolutions and focus on particular facts that they see as causes for the particular revolution. No reasons are given why these factors rather than others were singled out.

The structural-individualistic approach works differently. The theoretical core is the rational actor theory, which is enhanced by various additional assumptions. These assumptions refer, among other things, to the conditions under which the explanandum emerges. This procedure is called *model building*. Chapter 14 contains an example. First, the problem to be explained was formulated: the conditions leading to spontaneous, nonviolent revolutions. The theoretical core for solving this problem is the rational actor model. Then a number of assumptions were made—that is, we described a situation in which particular actors have particular goals and also face certain restrictions. The result of the joint actions is a spontaneous, nonviolent revolution.

It is important to note that this procedure does not yield a single theory explaining all forms of revolutions. Rather, certain sets of conditions are described under which certain forms of revolutions develop. The history of revolutions shows that these conditions can be very different. Model building takes account of this fact: it allows us to explain which forms or revolutions develop or do not occur in which situations.

Explaining revolutions by means of model building based on the rational actor model has only begun. The explanation of the Eastern Europe revolutions seems particularly pressing. Because they occurred recently, we have the unique opportunity to gather data in order to examine different models.

The Integration of Theoretical Explanations

Not much work has been done that systematically compares competing explanations. To make progress in the explanation of revolutions, it is important to conduct more comparative theoretical research. It would be most productive if the explanatory power of the various approaches would be discussed on the basis of concrete revolutions.

Summary

Are there other theories that can better explain the revolution in the GDR than our own? We first asked whether the GDR revolution can be better explained by an "economic" model of man, a version of the theory of rational action that does not take perceptions into account but instead proceeds from "objective" factors and uses only "hard" material incentives in explanations. We discussed the most well known of such theories suggested by Gordon Tullock and showed in detail that it cannot explain the revolution in the GDR.

The resource mobilization perspective proved to have the following problems when applied to the revolution in the GDR:

1. There is no explanatory model of individual action.
2. There are, accordingly, no hypotheses about which resources change the individual incentives in what way.
3. The proponents of this perspective assume a market model in which political actors compete for limited resources; there was no such situation in the GDR.
4. Detailed statements regarding the conditions under which protest leads to revolutionary changes are missing.

"Structural" explanations are widely used to explain revolutions. They only address collective, and not individual, actors. We discussed why such explanations are insufficient and how they must be complemented by connecting them to an individual level. We criticized arguments made by Theda Skocpol, one of the main representatives of structural explanations. We then argued for a structural-individualistic approach as we used it in this book.

A new version of structural explanations is emerging that deals with opportunity structures. *Opportunities* are, along with preferences, a determinant of action, according to the rational actor model. Proponents of this approach thus use an incomplete rational actor model, apparently without realizing it. Some other problems of this approach are discussed in the text. Karl Marx is one of the classic advocates of a structural explanation. We argued that Marxist theory either cannot be used to explain the GDR revolution or is clearly disproven by the events in the GDR.

Continuing our earlier discussion about the discontent hypothesis (chapter 2), we discussed the most well known versions stemming from Ted Robert Gurr and James C. Davies. The hypothesis that increasing dissatisfaction leads to violence is disproven by the events in the GDR. Another variant of the discontent hypothesis maintains that increasing satisfaction, such as the introduction of reforms, leads to revolutions. Yet such a hypothesis is not very informative as decreasing dissatisfaction either increases or decreases protests. Davies also contends that revolutions emerge if, after a long period of social and economic improvements, a short period of sharp reversal occurs in the form of a worsening of the situation. There was no such situation in the GDR.

Deprivation theory also maintains that *relative* deprivation leads to revolutions. Whatever the form of dissatisfaction, it takes effect only when accompanied by perceived influence and other incentives, according to our model. We showed, finally, that the rational actor model can explain that increasing dissatisfaction sometimes increases protests.

At the end of this chapter we discussed problems for future research on explaining revolutions. Important directions for further research include the application of the explanatory model developed in this book to the revolutions in Eastern Europe, eliminating some problems of rational actor explanations, and systematic comparisons of theoretical approaches to explain revolutions.

Appendix

Christiane Gern

In the first part of the Appendix we will describe the data sets we used in this book, and we will discuss some aspects of data validity in more detail than in the introduction. The second part is devoted to the construction of the scales.

1. The Data

The Representative Population Survey

The survey of 1,300 representative Leipzig residents took place between November 4, and December 21, 1990, about a year after the decisive demonstrations in October 1989. A pretest was carried out by five interviewers of the survey institute who interviewed 30 people between September 24 and October 5, 1990.

Who Conducted the Survey?
The institute USUMA (Unabhängiger Service für Umfragen, Methoden und Analysen [Independent service for surveys, methods and analyses]) in East Berlin conducted the survey. The USUMA was founded in the beginning of 1990. We decided in favor of an East German institute because we presumed that the Leipzig residents would react to West German interviewers more skeptically than they would to East German ones. According to an assessment of the ZUMA (Zentrum für Umfragen, Methoden und Analysen [Center for surveys, methods and analyses]) in Mannheim, West Germany, a good survey quality would be ensured by the USUMA, which meets West German standards.

How Were the Respondents Selected?
Our goal was to carry out a survey representative of Leipzig. Respondents were first selected by randomly drawing addresses from the municipal registration office. Two thousand addresses from citizens age 14 and older were acquired this way. The selected persons were mailed a letter with information on the purpose of the study asking them to participate. The aspired number of 1,300 interviews could not be realized from the address sample due to a low response rate (we will come back to this problem). In the meantime, unification had taken place and another address sample could not be utilized because of legal reasons. Therefore, the USUMA employed the random route

procedure: The city of Leipzig was divided in 60 zip code–based sample points with approximately the same number of inhabitants. Interviewers were assigned a starting point and followed a prescribed route—for example, turn left on the second corner, walk to the third house on the left side—which led them to certain households. If a household was comprised of more than one person, a household member was selected according to a given key.

We tested whether respondents differed according to which selection procedure was employed. We compared the means of the two groups for various demographic variables (see chapter 10) as well as for the variables used in our models—participation in general protests, participation in demonstrations, public goods motivation for general protests and demonstrations, protest norms, membership in protest-encouraging groups, expectations of reference persons, number of critical friends, probability and fear of sanctions, sanction experience—and found that there were no substantive and few statistically significant differences: Eta-coefficients were .06 or smaller. We also computed correlations between the aforementioned model variables for the two groups separately. In most cases, correlations were identical. Where there were differences, they were nonsystematic: some correlations were larger in the address sample, some in the random route sample.

Why Was the Response Rate So Low?
Table A1 displays the return rate. In total, 1,314 interviews were conducted. Fourteen of them could not be used—primarily because the questionnaire was not completed—so that our sample consists of 1,300 respondents. Normally, survey return rates are roughly 60 percent. Thus, compared to other studies, our response rate of about 40 percent is rather low. What could be the reason for this? The USUMA reported that at that time, a high nonresponse rate was common for surveys. People were afraid of dubious door-to-door traders and felt insecure because of growing crime rates, the USUMA told us. Also, people were distrustful because of their experience with the state security. According to the USUMA, this explains the higher nonresponse rate of the address sample. The USUMA also suspects that the large number of people who could not be contacted for the address sample can partly be accounted for by wrong addresses.

Is the Population Survey Representative of Leipzig?
First, it is important to note that the relatively low response rate of 40 percent is not equivalent with nonrepresentativity. Rather, it is important that the nonreturns are random for all groups in the population. We will examine several characteristics of the population to see if this is the case.

Sex
Official statistics describe the structure of the population of Leipzig according to sex and age. While 14-year-olds are included in our study, the official data lump people 14 and younger together, so that we had to exclude the 14-year-olds when we compared our sample to the population with respect to age and sex.

According to the official data for 1990, 54.4 percent of the Leipzig population 15 years and older is female, which leaves 45.6 percent for the men. In our data, the males are slightly overrepresented: 48.5 percent are male, and "only" 51.5 percent are

TABLE A1. Response Rates of the Samples

	Address Sample	Random Route Sample	Total Sample
Original sample	2,000 (100%)	1,260 (99.9%)	3,260 (100%)
Nonrespondents			
No contact possible	796 (39.8%)	236 (18.7%)	1,032 (31.7%)
Decline of interview	508 (25.4%)	406 (32.2%)	914 (28.0%)
Interview conducted	696 (34.8%)	608 (49.0%)	1,314 (40.3%)

female. Since these differences are rather small, the sexes can be said to be represented well in our sample.

Age

Figures A1 and A2 show how the age structure of our sample compares to the age structure of Leipzig. Since official data were already categorized, we adopted the same class boundaries in order to be able to compare the figures. We looked at the figures for

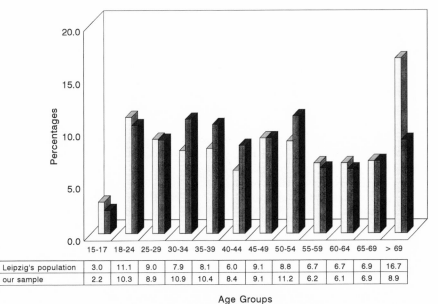

	15-17	18-24	25-29	30-34	35-39	40-44	45-49	50-54	55-59	60-64	65-69	> 69
Leipzig's population	3.0	11.1	9.0	7.9	8.1	6.0	9.1	8.8	6.7	6.7	6.9	16.7
our sample	2.2	10.3	8.9	10.9	10.4	8.4	9.1	11.2	6.2	6.1	6.9	8.9

Age Groups

☐ Leipzig's population ■ our sample

Fig. A1. The age structure of Leipzig's female population and of our sample, 1990 (population information compiled from data collected by the authors and *Statistisches Jahrbuch Leipzig* 1992 [Statistical Yearbook of Leipzig])

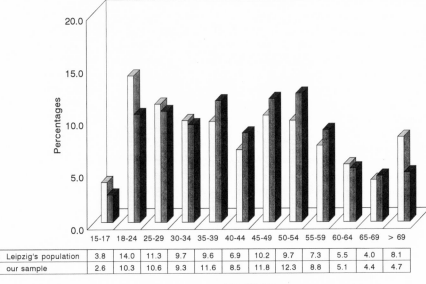

	15-17	18-24	25-29	30-34	35-39	40-44	45-49	50-54	55-59	60-64	65-69	> 69
Leipzig's population	3.8	14.0	11.3	9.7	9.6	6.9	10.2	9.7	7.3	5.5	4.0	8.1
our sample	2.6	10.3	10.6	9.3	11.6	8.5	11.8	12.3	8.8	5.1	4.4	4.7

Age groups

☐ Leipzig's population ■ our sample

Fig. A2. The age structure of Leipzig's male population and of our sample, 1990 (population information compiled from data collected by the authors and *Statistisches Jahrbuch Leipzig* 1992 [Statistical Yearbook of Leipzig])

women and men separately because the sexes' age structure is different and there might be differences within the sexes that neutralize each other and therefore would not be discovered if the sexes were analyzed together.

For the women, the figures for the age group 70 years and older are fairly discrepant. According to the official data, 16.7 percent of the female population (15 years and older) were age 70 and older in 1990. In our sample, only 8.9 percent of the women belonged to this age category. The other differences are much less pronounced.

For the men, the group represented least exactly in our sample is the one for age 18 to 24. While in the general population 14 percent of the males belong to this category, it is only 10.3 percent in our sample. Paralleling the women, the oldest group of 70 and older is underrepresented: it is 8.1 percent in the general population, but only 4.6 percent in our sample. Again, this is not a dramatic difference.

The figures thus show that residents 70 years and older are slightly underrepresented in our sample. One reason for this finding may be, as was reported by the USUMA's interviewers, that old people refused to be interviewed more often than others. But we think that all in all, the age structure of Leipzig's inhabitants is sufficiently well represented in our survey.

SED Membership

With respect to the subject of our study, it is definitely a decisive criterion for the representativity of the sample whether people associated with the political institutions and parties in the GDR are represented proportionally to their number in the Leipzig population. Therefore, we checked whether the number of people who said they were a member of the SED corresponds to the respective number for Leipzig as a whole. Since one had to be 18 years old to become a member of the SED, we considered only those respondents who were at least 18 years old and gave a valid answer to the respective question. Out of these 1,244 people, 21 percent—262 respondents—said they were a party member before October 9, 1989. According to the chair of the PDS, the legal successor of the SED, there were about 80,000 SED members in Leipzig in 1989. Since the adult population in 1989 amounted to 425,381, the percentage of SED members in Leipzig was 18.8 percent. SED members are thus represented very well in our study. Since nationwide about 20 percent of the population held a membership in the SED, Leipzig is not atypical of the country as a whole.

Church Membership

We also examined the degree to which members of the church are represented in our sample. According to the theologian Detlef Pollack of Leipzig University, the Protestant church in Leipzig had a total of 61,150 members in 1989. This number is based on church tax cards that were set up for each member after confirmation. Based on the Leipzig population who were 14 and older, 13.9 percent of the city's residents held a membership in the Protestant church. Out of 1,276 respondents in our sample who indicated their church affiliation, 18.2 percent said they were a member of the Protestant church. This means that members of the Protestant church are overrepresented in our sample. Mr. Pollack reported the membership of the Catholic Church to amount to roughly 3 to 5 percent of the population of large towns. Since the percentage of Catholics in our sample is 4.9 percent, this group is adequately represented in our sample.

Participation in Demonstrations

In spite of generally good representativity with respect to demographic criteria, respondents indicated to have participated more often in demonstrations up to October 9, 1989, than was to be expected given the estimated figures. Out of Leipzig's 530,010 residents, 440,156 were at least 15 years old in 1989.[1] For the period from September 25 to October 9, the estimated number of participants is 105,000. Thus, 23.9 percent of the citizens are estimated to have participated in the demonstrations, while 76.1 percent supposedly had remained inactive.[2] Our survey gives a higher percentage of

---

1. In our sample, the youngest respondents were 14 years old. As was already mentioned, official statistics available to us do not list this age group separately. Therefore, we have to exclude this age group. Although some demonstrators may have been 14 and younger, their total number was probably so low that it is defensible to treat them as nondemonstrators in this context.

2. The demonstrations did not draw Leipzig citizens exclusively; other people from the area participated as well. Since our survey is restricted to Leipzig inhabitants, it follows that the demonstrators may be even more overrepresented because the percentage of non-Leipzig demonstrators is not known.

participants, namely 39 percent, whereas only 61 percent indicated they did not take part in the demonstrations. What could be the reason(s) for this discrepancy?

One reason may be that people who actively took part in the events of autumn 1989 also took a greater interest in the subject of this study and thus participated more often. However, our analyses described previously suggest that our respondents are representative of the population. Memory failures could play a role. For instance, it is difficult to say exactly when something happened that dates a year back (see Brown, Shevell, and Rips 1986). Also, experiencing similar events several times—like going to several demonstrations—may lead to a general memory, leaving the single event less clear (Strube 1987). Although October 9, a well-known landmark, was chosen to demarcate two periods of time, we cannot completely rule out the possibility that wrong dating occurred.

One could go to the city center for various reasons: with the intention to demonstrate or out of curiosity. One could pull back if trouble should arise. Surely, some people joined the demonstration spontaneously. Sometimes, it might thus have been unclear whether a person took part in a demonstration or just watched it. Given social desirability (see the introduction), people who just watched what was happening might well remember that they actually participated in the demonstration.

We cannot be sure why there are "too many" demonstrators in our survey. All three reasons mentioned might have a part in it. However, it is not very likely that they led to an overrepresentation as strong as it is.

Up to this point we assumed that the estimates of demonstration participation are correct. However, this assumption is definitely wrong. We showed in chapter 1 that at least on October 9, 1989, the figure estimated is way too low. Accordingly, demonstration participants may not be overrepresented, as the estimated figures are wrong.

However, let's assume participants are in fact overrepresented. Would this fact have an impact on the results of our statistical analyses? To answer this question, we weighted the respondents in our survey according to the estimated percentage of demonstration participants, which is 23.9 percent, and nonparticipants, which is 76.1 percent, in the Leipzig population.[3] Inactive respondents were thus given more weight, while active ones received less weight. The total number of 1,300 respondents remains unchanged.

We calculated regression models with the following independent variables (for details, see the section on scale construction later in this chapter): protest norms, public goods motivation, probability and fear of sanctions, number of critical friends, expectations of reference persons, and membership in protest-encouraging groups. The dependent variable was "participation in demonstrations." All scales refer to the period up to October 9, 1989.

The regression models were calculated both for the weighted and the unweighted data. The coefficients were very similar; the largest difference was found for public goods motivation: The standardized regression coefficient was .37 for the unweighted

---

3. Demonstrators were weighted by .607 to achieve a percentage of 23.9 for 1,300 respondents. Nondemonstrators were weighted by 1.255. In absolute numbers, weighting resulted in lowering the original number of 512 to 311 participants, whereas the number of nonparticipants was raised from originally 788 to 989.

data, but only .33 for the weighted ones. The explained variance is .20 for the unweighted and .15 for the weighted data.

We further compared the means of the incentive variables of the weighted and the unweighted data. We expected the means of the weighted sample to be lower because the incentives are more pronounced for demonstration participants, but this group of people was weighted less. The data confirm this expectation, but the differences are small. There are no differences for fear of sanctions. There is a difference of .01 for probability of sanctions (value range: .1 to .8); for protest norms and expectations of reference persons (value range: 1 to 5) it is .06 for each scale. The largest difference of 1.06 was found for public goods motivation (value range: 1 to 25).

These analyses allow the following conclusions. The variables in the weighted and the unweighted model have very similar effects. In the weighted model, however, we can explain a larger amount of variance. The descriptive results in this book are based on the unweighted data, the values of which are slightly higher than those of the weighted data. However, the differences are so small that this does not affect the validity of our accounts.

To What Point in Time Do the Answers Refer?
Our questions in the questionnaire refer to two time periods, before and after October 9, 1989. Respondents may have changed some attitudes within these intervals. Perceived political influence, for example, on the average was probably lower at the beginning of 1989 than in October. How did respondents react to interview questions when attitudes or opinions changed *within* one of the time periods? We believe that respondents reported the attitudes or opinions they held at the end of the respective period. This assumption is supported by the answers of the respondents. It is unlikely that the perceived influence in May was already as high as our data show.

Memory
We mentioned in the introduction that we asked the respondents how well they remembered the events of autumn 1989. We tested whether the results of the statistical analyses differ for those who claimed to have a very good memory and those who admitted that some things had already slipped their minds. Due to small numbers (N = 21) we excluded the third group (1.6 percent of respondents, who said they had forgotten everything) from these analyses.

First we tested whether the means of the most important variables differ for these two groups. It turned out that the respective eta-coefficients were generally low: Six out of 11 coefficients were smaller than .10; the other five were between .12 and .16. Those who said they remembered things well were relatively active, were confronted with positive incentives to a relatively high degree, and expected, feared and were exposed to repression to a relatively high extent. This does not come as a surprise: the results mean that those who participated in the revolution to a high degree are the ones who remember it well.

Did they also give more reliable answers? If this holds true, random measurement errors for those with a good memory should be fairly low. Thus, the correlations among the incentive variables or of the incentive variables with the protest variables should be higher for the ones with a good memory than for the ones with a moderately good memory. This is not the case: most of the correlations we calculated for the variables mentioned are very low. The few correlations that are relatively high—differences between significant correlations are .11 at the most—do not show a pattern: sometimes the correlations are higher for those with a good memory, whereas for other variables the opposite is the case.

The Opposition Sample

In addition to the representative sample of Leipzig citizens, 209 members of the opposition movement were interviewed using the same questionnaire. We were interested to find out whether or to what degree the members of the opposition movement differed from the average population. Since those members are a rather small group and may therefore not be present in our sample to an extent to allow statistical analyses, we decided to draw a special sample. The opposition sample is not a representative survey. The goal was to cover a spectrum of the opposition movement.

To qualify for this sample, potential respondents should have been a member of an opposition group. Interviewees were selected according to the snowball principle: In the Haus der Demokratie [House of democracy] in Leipzig and through the Protestant church the interviewers tried to establish contacts. These persons then mentioned others to the interviewers, who in turn named others, and so on. Interviewers were instructed to find two "representatives" of each of the following groups: Bürgerinitiative Leipzig [Citizen's initiative Leipzig], Demokratie Jetzt [Democracy now], Demokratischer Aufbruch [Democratic awakening], Freie Initiative 89 [Free initiative 89], Grüne Partei Leipzig [Green party of Leipzig], Initiative für Frieden und Menschenrechte [Initiative for peace and human rights], Neues Forum [New forum], Sozialdemokratische Partei Deutschlands, or SPD [Social democratic party of Germany], and Vereinigte Linke [United leftists]. Additionally, two interviewees from other groups could be selected.

However, when checking the data, it turned out that only 80 out of the interviewed 209 people considered themselves a member of at least one of those groups. One explanation for this low number may be that a formal membership was hardly known. Since we had no additional information, we decided to label only those 80 people "members of the opposition movement." This data set is primarily used in chapter 10.

The Qualitative Interviews

The authors of this study conducted extensive qualitative interviews with 19 Leipzig residents. One of these talks was a group discussion with three students, the other 16 were on a one-to-one basis. Most of the people we talked to were particularly involved in the events of autumn 1989. Among them are theologians and pastors, representatives of dissident groups like the Neues Forum and the Demokratischer Aufbruch, a former military prosecutor, and average citizens critical of the regime without ties to opposition groups.

The talks were carried out along the lines of a loosely structured outline that contained the central subjects dealt with in the standardized questionnaire. Additionally, these talks provided us with in-depth information on complex matters. For example, we were interested in the interviewees' own account of the revolution in 1989. Sometimes, the outline was disregarded in favor of an in-depth discussion of specific themes. The interview with a former military prosecutor, for instance, focused on the role of the police and the military in autumn 1989. These qualitative interviews were recorded and transcribed. In contrast to the representative survey, excerpts from these interviews serve only illustrative purposes.

2. Scale Construction

Procedure

Unless indicated otherwise, we replaced the missing values of single items by the mean of the respective item if the number of missing values does not exceed 5 percent. The replacement of missing values has the advantage that statements based on statistical analyses always refer to the same number of respondents. Replacement does *not* lead to better confirmation of our hypotheses; often the opposite is the case. For each item, we will specify how many respondents did not answer the respective item.

Usually, the scales are constructed additively. After adding the single values, the scale is divided by the number of indicators in order to have the same value range for the scale as for the single items.

The Scales

For every single indicator and scale we give the mean (M), the standard deviation (S), and the number of missing values (MV) if there are any.

Participation in General Protests and Demonstrations
For the construction of the scale *participation in general protests before October 9*, see the introduction. The means, standard deviations, and missing values for the actions 1 to 4 (see the introduction) are: 1. M = 1.33, S = .65, MV = 32; 2. M = 2.14, S = 1.07, MV = 43; 3. M = 2.15, S = 1.25, MV = 70; 4. M = 1.94, S = 1.10, MV = 23. The scale's mean is 1.89, the standard deviation .71 (value range 1 to 4; no missing values). Reliability (alpha) is .65. Eliminating any of the indicators does not improve alpha. A factor analysis yielded a single factor with an explained variance of 50.4 percent.

In our questionnaire we determined the willingness to engage in *other* protest actions, for example: "writing letters to representatives or the media," "wearing badges, stickers and other 'signs of recognition' (e.g., white cloth on cars)," "organization of or participation in demonstrations." We had assumed when phrasing these items that the context made it clear that the items referred to protest actions directed against the SED regime. However, statistical analyses indicated that these items correlated differently with dissatisfaction and other incentive variables. This suggested that respondents, for instance, checked "organization of and participation in demonstrations" also if they participated in demonstrations organized by the SED. We therefore included only those actions in our scale that were clearly protest actions directed against the SED regime.

Regression analyses with the most important incentive variables were also run with *another dependent variable*, namely with an additive scale of the mentioned protest items 1 to 4 where for all items the answer categories "was out of the question" and "considered, but not carried out" were coded 0 and the other two categories 1 and 2. The results of these analyses were very similar to those with the scale we used in this book. For theoretical reasons, we prefer the scale used throughout the book because benefits and costs of an action also play a role for taking an action into account.

In the scale *participation in general protests after October 9*, we only included the following two actions:

> Working with or founding of an opposition group (opposition movement, citizens' initiative) (M = 1.40, S = .69, MV = 65); participation in peace prayers and other church events (M = 1.75, S = 1.06, MV = 57); scale "participation in general protests after October 9" (M = 1.58; S = .72).

The construction of the scale *participation in demonstrations before October 9* is described in the introduction. We would like to add the following: Since this scale consists of four dichotomous variables with the answer categories no and yes, we replaced the missing values not by the mean but by the mode—that is, nonparticipation. The scale's mean is .84 and its standard deviation 1.27, and the value range is from 0 to 4.

For *participation in demonstrations after October 9*, we asked our respondents how often they participated after October 9. Answer categories were coded from 0 to 3 and read "not participated," "participated once," "participated twice or three times," "participated more than three times." Since this variable is close to being an interval scale, the nine missing values were replaced by the mean, being 1.18. The standard deviation is 1.23.

Discontent

Respondents were presented a list of problems and asked to indicate "how content or discontented they were with what is in the list." The degree of discontent could be expressed by choosing among five answer categories, from 1 meaning "very discontented" to 5 meaning "very content."

The items were factor-analyzed (ULS, varimax rotation). Four factors were extracted, with one factor showing a high loading of only one item (which refers to the efficiency of the health system). An imposed three-factor solution revealed a high loading of this indicator on one of the three factors while the factorial structure remained unchanged otherwise. Together, the three factors explain 35 percent of the variance (factor 1: 24.8 percent, factor 2: 6.7 percent, and factor 3: 3.5 percent). Items with high loadings on the first factor refer to the political situation; the second factor is characterized by high loading items mentioning aspects of the social situation such as provision of child care; and items mentioning economic aspects loaded on the third factor. Accordingly, we constructed three scales: political dissatisfaction, social dissatisfaction, and economic dissatisfaction.

We included only those indicators with loadings of at least .50. This criterion resulted in a one-indicator scale for economic dissatisfaction. For theoretical reasons, the items were inverted, meaning that now value 5 means "very discontented" and 1 "very content." High values thus indicate a high level of discontent.

Scale *political dissatisfaction* (M = 4.32, S = .66). Discontent with: the degree the SED dictated what to do (M = 4.30, S = .93, MV = 13); the possibilities to freely say one's opinion (M = 4.26, S = .97, MV = 3); the degree one could expect a fair political trial in court (M = 4.33, S = .88, MV = 88); the environment in the GDR (M = 4.45, S = .83, MV = 2); the degree of Stasi surveillance (M = 4.28, S = .91, MV = 42).

Scale *social dissatisfaction* (M = 2.39, S = .74). Discontent with: child care (M = 1.98, S = .87, MV = 37); the degree to which equality of the sexes was accomplished (M = 2.68, S = .97, MV = 19); the educational possibilities (M = 2.58, S = 1.06, MV = 12).

Scale *economic dissatisfaction* (M = 4.26, S = .86). Discontent with the choice of commodities in the shops (M = 4.26, S = .86, MV = 2).

Influence

We measured perceived influence separately for each protest action. The reason for this measurement is that, according to the theory applied in this book, people tend to perform those actions they consider effective. Our influence scales thus refer to those actions included in our protest scales. Accordingly, we asked respondents how they perceived their personal chances to change the political and economic situation in the GDR via various actions. Answer categories ranged from "very unlikely" (code 1) to "very likely" (code 4).

Scale *personal influence by general protests before October 9* (M = 2.01, S = .63). Working with or founding of an opposition group (M = 2.06, S = .88, MV = 16); refusal to take part in political elections, or cast an invalid vote (M = 1.84, S = .91, MV = 9); refusal to become a member of the SED, the union, or similar political groups (M = 1.82, S = .91, MV = 23); participation in peace prayers and other church events (M = 2.32, S = .93, MV = 12).

The influence scale referring to the scale *participation in demonstrations before October 9* consists of two statements, referring to two situations: the emigration wave and the liberalization in Eastern Europe. Respondents were presented with these situations and then asked to indicate for each the extent to which they agreed with the statement: "I thought: If I take part in demonstrations and similar actions now, I personally can make a difference," with answer possibilities from "does not hold true at all" (code 1) to "holds completely true" (code 5).

In regard to the emigration wave, the introductory phrase read: "What did you think when you got to know that more and more GDR citizens were fleeing to the West?" The statistical measures are: M = 3.40, S = 1.41, MV = 18. The liberalization in Eastern Europe was exemplified in the following manner: "e.g., the legalization of the union Solidarity and the first free elections in Poland; demonstrations took place in Hungary and other East-European states." The statistical measures for this item are: M = 3.22, S = 1.37, MV = 17. The scale *personal influence by demonstrations before October 9* has a mean of 3.31 and a standard deviation of 1.29.

Effectiveness of collective protests (M = 3.86, S = 1.20) was measured by the following item, which refers to respondents' reaction to the emigration wave: "It was clear to me that there was now a definite opportunity to make a difference if the population as a whole participates more often in protest activities." Originally, there were 12 missing values.

Belief in the unity principle (M = 4.27, S = 1.02) was ascertained by this item: "Every single member is necessary for the success of a political group, regardless of the size of the group." Twenty-seven missing values were replaced by the mean.

Public Goods Motivation: Discontent and Influence
Theoretical considerations and empirical research (see chapter 2) indicate that discontent and perceived personal political influence, group influence, belief in the unity principle, and perceived obligation to protest have a multiplicative effect on political protest. We only combined those variables multiplicatively that had the strongest effects on the dependent variables in our logged models. These variables are political discontent and perceived personal influence. We constructed two scales, one for general protests and one for participation in demonstrations. For general protests, we constructed the scale "collective goods motivation for participation in general protests" (with a mean of 8.76 and a standard deviation of 3.27, value range from 1 to 20). This scale consists of the multiplied scales "political discontent" and "personal influence by general protests before October 9." For participation in demonstrations, we constructed the scale "collective goods motivation for participation in demonstrations," (with a mean of 14.61 and a standard deviation of 6.57, value range from 1 to 25). This scale consists of the multiplied scales "political discontent" and "personal influence by demonstrations before October 9."

Protest Norms
The following list encompasses the indicators measuring the degree to which respondents felt obligated to protest before October 9. We differentiated between protest norms and norms referring to the use of violence. For protest norms, we further distinguished several types.

There were five answer categories for each item, ranging from "doesn't hold true at all"—or, depending on the question, "fully disagree"—to "holds completely true" or "fully agree." All items were coded in a way that a high value indicates a high level of obligation. Some of the following indicators are starred (*), which means that the values referring to the phrasing in the questionnaire were inverted in order to have high values denoting a high level of obligation. The scales and the respective items are:

Discontent orientation: "If a citizen is very dissatisfied with the government's policies, she or he should do something against it, such as demonstrate" (M = 3.91, S = 1.18, MV = 8).
Protest orientation due to external events: (a) impact of the emigration wave: "I thought: Now I'm obligated to do something for changes in the GDR in order

to keep even more people from leaving" (M = 3.27, S = 1.33, MV = 16); (b) impact of liberalization in Eastern Europe: "I thought: Now I'm actually obligated to do something to contribute to changes in the GDR" (M = 3.23, S = 1.22, MV = 17).

Success neutrality: * "A citizen should only engage in political action if she or he believes to be able to make an impact" (M = 2.27, S = 1.30, MV = 11).

Risk orientation: * "Nobody can be expected to take part in a political action if she or he might be sent to prison for it" (M = 2.59, S = 1.30, MV = 23); "If one is convinced to effect something through a demonstration, one should not shrink from high risk" (M = 3.79, S = 1.12, MV = 13); "If discontent is very high among the population, one has to participate in political actions even if this is accompanied by personal disadvantages" (M = 3.71, S = 1.10, MV = 12).

Willingness of others to participate: * "I feel that I should be politically active only if there are sufficient others" (M = 3.07, S = 1.43, MV = 16).

General protest orientation: * "Politics should be left to the elected representatives" (M = 3.75, S = 1.35, MV = 14).

We constructed a scale *protest norms* by adding three of the aforementioned scales and dividing the sum by three: *discontent orientation, risk orientation,* and *general protest orientation* (M = 3.68, S = .76). These three types of norms have fairly high means, and their effects on the two protest scales are fairly high if all of the aforementioned norms scales are included in regression analyses as independent variables and the two protest scales as dependent variables.

As already mentioned, we also ascertained the extent to which respondents considered the use of violence justified. The following items are included in the scale *violence orientation* (M = 1.54, S = .63):

"Violence against *objects* (such as setting a car on fire) can be morally justified" (M = 1.13, S = .53, MV = 6); "Violence against *persons* can be morally justified" (M = 1.17, S = .59, MV = 6); "If a government suppresses civil rights, the use of violence by citizens can also be justified" (M = 2.33, S = 1.41, MV = 11).

Expectations of Reference Persons
Expectations of reference persons were measured the following way: "If you think of those people whose opinion is particularly important to you, e.g., your spouse, friends, co-workers or other people: if you had taken part in a political action, such as a demonstration, how would these people have reacted to that?" Possible answers ranged from "very negatively" (code 1) to "very positively" (code 5); M = 3.80, S = .99, MV = 25.

Integration in Social Networks
Three types of social relationships were investigated: memberships in groups, networks of critical friends, and networks of critical coworkers.

In order to measure *group membership*, respondents were presented a list with types of groups, such as "church group" or "block party." Further memberships could be added. The interviewees indicated, for each group type, whether they were a member prior to October 9. Those 698 respondents who held at least one membership were then asked: "Were you encouraged to participate in demonstrations and similar actions aiming at change of the political situation, or was this not the case?" In response, 122 indicated encouragement of protest actions in at least one group.

In our scale *group encouragement of protest actions before October 9*—occasionally, we also refer to *membership in protest-encouraging groups*—all respondents are included. Those 1,178 people, including those with no group membership, who were not encouraged were assigned code 0, while those 122 encouraged to participate in protest actions received code 1.

Regarding our respondents' *friends*, we first asked respondents to estimate how many of their friends criticized the conditions in the GDR. Answer categories were "none" (code 1), "some" (code 2), "many" (code 3), and "almost all" (code 4). Those who said they had no friends answered "does not apply." There were 92 missing values, including 80 respondents without friends. This item's mean is 3.27 and the standard deviation .84. We also asked how many friends participated in demonstrations, peace prayers, and similar activities. Again, answer codes ranged from "none" (code 1) to "almost all" (code 4). Missing values were assigned to 129 respondents who said they didn't know. The mean is 2.46, the standard deviation .88, and there are 221 missing values, including those who had no friends. The scale *number of critical friends* (M = 2.99, S = .64, MV = 235) consists of the additive combination of the two indicators described previously divided by two. The higher the values of the scale, the stronger the integration into a critical and active network of friends. We did not replace the missing values because most of them are due to the fact that people didn't have friends or didn't know about their protest behavior.

The questions referring to *coworkers* correspond to those asked in regard to friends. We ascertained the number of colleagues who criticized the conditions in the GDR (M = 3.19, S = .85, MV = 220) and carried out protest actions (M = 2.30, S = .79, MV = 336). The answer categories are the same as well, except that "does not apply" in this context means that there were no coworkers. We posed an additional question asking how close relations with coworkers were (M = 3.06, S = .77, MV = 178); this was not done with respect to friends because relationships are close by definition. Answer categories were "very distant" (code 1), "rather distant" (code 2), "rather close" (code 3), and "very close" (code 4). The scale *number of critical coworkers* was constructed—analogous to the friends scale—by adding the two items mentioned first and dividing the sum by two. This term was then multiplied by the value of the item "closeness to colleagues." This procedure is based on the assumption that attitudes and behavior of colleagues should only matter if contacts are fairly close (M = 8.88, S = 3.12, MV = 375), with a value range from 1 to 16.

There were 163 people saying they had no fellow employees, and 148 said they didn't know about their protest activity. Again, we didn't replace the missing values. The higher the values of the scale, the more respondents are integrated in close, critical, and active networks of coworkers.

State Sanctions

Probability of Sanctions

We asked respondents "how probable they personally thought state sanctions occurred if one took part in a demonstration before October 9." One of the four consequences mentioned read: "I could have been arrested." Four answer categories were provided: "highly improbable," "improbable," "probable," and "highly probable." Since probabilities can be viewed as numbers varying from 0 to 1, we coded "highly improbable" as .2, "highly probable" as .8, and the other two answers as .4 and .6. Respondents were assigned 0 if the respective consequence could not occur—that is, if they did not work or if they were single and didn't have a family. We presented four consequences (C1, C2, C3, C4):

> C1: "I could have been arrested" (M = .68, S = .15, MV = 19); C2: "At the demonstration, I could have been injured by security forces" (M = .65, S = .15, MV = 15); C3: "There could have been problems at my workplace" (M = .50, S = .28, MV = 18); C4: "There could have been problems for my immediate family (spouse, children)" (M = .52, S = .27, MV = 18).

These four items comprise the additive scale *probability of sanctions before October 9* (M = .59, S = .15, value range .10 to .80). The higher the values, the more probable the respondents considered the sanctions to be.

Fear of Sanctions

We also investigated how severe respondents judged the priorly mentioned consequences to be if they had occurred. This time we presented three answer codes, namely "not so severe" (code 1), "severe" (code 2), and "very severe" (code 3). If a consequence did not apply, respondents were assigned code 0, which means that they were indifferent with respect to this particular consequence. The statistical indices of the four consequences are: C1: M = 2.46, S = .67, MV = 19; C2: M = 2.51, S = .60, MV = 20; C3: M = 1.79, S = 1.06, MV = 17; C4: M = 2.29, S = 1.04, MV = 13. *Fear of Sanctions before October 9* (M = 2.26, S = .56) is an additive scale with a value range from .5 to 3. The higher the values, the more severe respondents would have judged the consequences to be had they occurred.

Experience of Sanctions

We ascertained whether respondents in fact had had contact with the police or security agencies due to political activity. This was the case for 150 interviewees, while 1,150 hadn't experienced sanctions. We asked whether respondents had been observed, interrogated, indoctrinated, or arrested. It should be noted that we didn't ask how often each type of sanction was experienced, but rather whether respondents suffered several *types* of sanctions. The scale *experience of state sanctions before October 9*, or simply: "experience of sanctions" ranges from "no experience" (code 1) to "four experiences" (code 2). One, two, and three types of experience were assigned the values 1.25, 1.50, and 1.75. The scale's mean is 1.05, the standard deviation .16.

Demographic Variables

Age. Age was coded in years and varied from 14 to 87 years (M = 43.7, S = 16.37).

Sex. Value 1 denotes men, value 2 women (M = 1.52).

General education. This variable comprises four categories: "not finished 8th grade" (code 1), "not finished 10th grade" (code 2), "finished 10th grade" (code 3) and "finished Abitur/finished Abitur and vocational degree" (code 4) (M = 2.67, S = .93).

Professional education. There are six categories: "no vocational training" (code 1), "semi-skilled worker" (code 2), "skilled worker" (code 3), "technical college degree" (code 4), "Meister"; "master or technician degree" (code 5) and "university degree" (code 6) (M = 3.59, S = 1.32).

Income. The monthly household net income was measured in 16 categories. The highest category, referring to "more than 6.000 DM" [about $ 3,750, assuming a current exchange rate of 1.60 DM per Dollar] per month, was not mentioned by respondents (M = 5.50, S = 1.32).

Marital status. Code 1 refers to people who are married and live with their spouse, code 0 refers to everybody else (M = .62, S = .49).

Number of children. This variable measures the number of children under 18 who live with the respondent. The value range is from 0 to 5 (M = .63, S = .91).

Bibliography

Ajzen, Icek. 1988. *Attitudes, Personality, and Behavior.* Pacific Grove, Calif.: Brooks-Cole.

Ajzen, Icek, and Martin Fishbein. 1980. *Understanding and Predicting Social Behavior.* Englewood Cliffs, N.J.: Prentice Hall.

Alchian, Arman A., and William Allen. 1974. *University Economics: Elements of Inquiry.* London: Prentice Hall.

Amenta, Edwin, and Yvonne Zylan. 1991. "Political Opportunity, the New Institutionalism, and the Townsend Movement." *American Sociological Review* 56: 250–65.

Andert, Reinhold, and Wolfgang Herzberg. 1990. *Der Sturz: Erich Honecker im Kreuzverhör.* Berlin and Weimar: Aufbau-Verlag.

Arnold, Michael, and Berndt Schirmer. 1990. *Gesundheit für ein Deutschland.* Köln: Deutscher Ärzte Verlag.

Ash, Timothy Garton. 1990. *The Magic Lantern: The Revolution of '89 Witnessed in Warsaw, Budapest, Berlin, and Prague.* New York: Random House.

Banac, Ivo, ed. 1992. *Eastern Europe in Revolution.* Ithaca, N.Y., and London: Cornell University Press.

Baumgärtner, Theo. 1991. *Die Determinanten politischen Protests: Eine Untersuchung bei Landwirten in der Bundesrepublik Deutschland.* Hamburg: Kovac Verlag.

Bauß, Gerhard. 1977. *Die Studentenbewegung der sechziger Jahre in der Bundesrepublik und Westberlin: Handbuch.* Cologne: Pahl-Rugenstein.

Becker, Gary S. 1976. *The Economic Approach to Human Behavior.* Chicago and London: University of Chicago Press.

Bernholz, Peter, and Friedrich Breyer. 1984. *Grundlagen der Politischen Ökonomie.* Tübingen: Mohr.

Biermann, Wolf. 1990. "Über das Geld und andere Herzensdinge." *Die Zeit*, no. 47 (16 November).

Boettcher, Erik. 1974. *Kooperation und Demokratie.* Tübingen: Mohr.

Bohley, Bärbel. 1989. "Vierzig Jahre Warten." In Bärbel Bohley et al., eds., *40 Jahre DDR: Und die Bürger melden sich zu Wort*, 5–11. Frankfurt am Main: Carl Hanser Verlag.

Bohley, Bärbel, et al., eds. 1989. *40 Jahre DDR: Und die Bürger melden sich zu Wort.* Frankfurt am Main: Carl Hanser Verlag.

Brand, Karl Werner. 1990. "Massendemokratischer Aufbruch im Osten: Eine Herausforderung für die NSB-Forschung. *Forschungsjournal Neue Soziale Bewegungen* 3, no. 2: 9–16.

Brewer, William F. 1986. "What is Autobiographical Memory?" In David C. Rubin, ed., *Autobiographical Memory*, 25–49. Cambridge: Cambridge University Press.

Brown, J. F. 1991. *Surge to Freedom: The End of Communist Rule in Eastern Europe.* Twickenham, England: Adamantine Press.

Brown, Norman R., Steven K. Shevell, and Lance, J. Rips. 1986. "Public Memories and Their Personal Context." In David C. Rubin, ed., *Autobiographical Memory*, 137–58. Cambridge: Cambridge University Press.

Brunner, Karl. 1987. "The Perception of Man and the Conception of Society: Two Approaches to Understanding Society." *Economic Enquiry* 25: 367–88.

Chalmers, A. F. 1982. *What is This Thing Called Science?* St. Lucia, Queensland: University of Queensland Press.

Chong, Dennis. 1991. *Collective Action and the Civil Rights Movement.* Chicago: University of Chicago Press.

Cohan, A. S. 1975. *Theories of Revolution: An Introduction.* London: Nelson.

Coleman, James S. 1987. "Microfoundations of Macrosocial Behavior." In Alexander, Jeffrey C., et al., eds., *The Micro-Macro Link*, 153–73. Berkeley: University of California Press.

Coleman, James S. 1990. *Foundations of Social Theory.* Cambridge, Mass. and London: Belknap Press of Harvard University Press.

Czollek, Michael. 1990. "Entlarvt." In Thomas Blanke and Rainer Erd, eds., *DDR— Ein Staat vergeht*, 65–70. Frankfurt am Main: Fischer Taschenbuch Verlag.

Dähn, Horst. 1985. *Das politische System der DDR.* Berlin: Wissenschaftlicher Autoren-Verlag.

Damm, Fritz. 1990. *Wir dekorieren! 40 Jahre politischer Witz in der DDR.* Frankfurt am Main: Fischer Taschenbuch Verlag.

Davies, James C. 1962. "Toward a Theory of Revolution." *American Sociological Review* 27:5–19.

de Tocqueville, Alexis. [1856] 1978. *Der alte Staat und die Revolution.* Reprint, Munich: Deutscher Taschenbuch Verlag.

de Wroblewsky, Clement. 1990. *Wo wir sind ist vorn: Der politische Witz in der DDR.* Hamburg: Rasch und Röhring.

Döhnert, Albrecht, and Paulus Rummel. 1990. "Die Leipziger Montagsdemonstrationen." In Wolf-Jürgen Grabner, Christiane Heinze, and Detlef Pollack, eds., *Leipzig im Oktober: Kirchen und alternative Gruppen im Umbruch der DDR: Analysen zur Wende*, 147–58. Berlin: Wichern-Verlag.

Downs, Anthony. 1957. *An Economic Theory of Democracy.* New York: Harper and Row.

East, Roger. 1992. *Revolutions in Eastern Europe.* London: Pinter Publisher.

Elvers, Wolfgang, and Hagen Findeis. 1990. "Die politisch alternativen Gruppen im gesellschaftlichen Wandel: Eine empirische Studie zu ihrem Selbstverständnis." In Wolf-Jürgen Grabner, Christiane Heinze, and Detlef Pollack, eds., *Leipzig im Oktober: Kirchen und alternative Gruppen im Umbruch der DDR: Analysen zur Wende*, 97–111. Berlin: Wichern-Verlag.

Etzioni, Amitai. 1968. "Mobilization as a Macrosociological Conception." *British Journal of Sociology* 19:243–53.

Falcke, Heino. 1990. "Kirche und christliche Gruppen. Ein nötiges oder unnötiges Spannungsfeld?" In Detlef Pollack, ed., *Die Legitimität der Freiheit.* 103–13. Frankfurt am Main: Peter Lang.

Feather, Norman T., ed. 1982. *Expectations and Actions: Expectancy-Value Models in Psychology.* Hillsdale, N.J.: Lawrence Erlbaum.

Festinger, Leon. 1957. *A Theory of Cognitive Dissonance.* Stanford: Stanford University Press.

Fetscher, Iring, ed. 1966. *Marx-Engels I. Studienausgabe.* Frankfurt: Fischer Bücherei.

Feydt, Sebastian, Christiane Heinze, and Martin Schanz. 1990. "Die Leipziger Friedensgebete." In Wolf-Jürgen Grabner, Christiane Heinze, and Detlef Pollack, eds., *Leipzig im Oktober: Kirchen und alternative Gruppen im Umbruch der DDR: Analysen zur Wende*, 123–35. Berlin: Wichern-Verlag.

Finkel, Steven E., and Karl-Dieter Opp. 1991. "Party Identification and Participation in Collective Political Action." *Journal of Politics* 53:349–71.

Finkel, Steven E., Edward N. Muller, and Karl-Dieter Opp. 1989. "Personal Influence, Collective Rationality, and Mass Political Action." *American Political Science Review* 83:885–903.

Fireman, Bruce, and William Gamson. 1979. "Utilitarian Logic in the Resource Mobilization Perspective." In Mayer N. Zald and John McCarthy, eds., *The Dynamics of Social Movements*, 8–44. Cambridge, Mass.: Winthrop.

Fischer Weltalmanach 1990. 1990. Frankfurt: Fischer Taschenbuch-Verlag.

Förster, Peter, and Günter Roski. 1990. *DDR zwischen Wende und Wahl: Meinungsforscher analysieren den Umbruch.* Berlin: LinksDruck Verlag.

Freud, Sigmund. 1985. *Der Witz und seine Beziehung zum Unbewußten.* Leipzig and Weimar: G. Kiepenheuer.

Frey, Bruno S. 1980. "Ökonomie als Verhaltenswissenschaft. Ansatz, Kritik und der europäische Beitrag." *Jahrbuch für Sozialwissenschaft* 31:21–35.

Frey, Bruno S. 1992. *Economics as a Science of Human Behavior.* Boston: Kluwer.

Frohlich, Norman, and Joe A. Oppenheimer. 1978. *Modern Political Economy.* Englewood Cliffs, N.J.: Prentice-Hall.

Frohlich, Norman, Joe A. Oppenheimer, and Oran R. Young. 1971. *Political Leadership and Collective Goods.* Princeton, N.J.: Princeton University Press.

Funk, Uwe. 1990. "Die Existenz sozialethischer Gruppen in der evangelischen Kirche der DDR als gesellschaftswissenschaftliches Problem." In Detlef Pollack, ed., *Die Legitimität der Freiheit*, 81–102. Frankfurt am Main: Peter Lang.

Gamson, William A. 1968. *Power and Discontent.* Homewood, Ill.: Dorsey.

Gamson, William A. 1975. *The Strategy of Social Protest.* Homewood, Ill.: Dorsey.

Gensicke, Thomas. 1992. *Mentalitätsentwicklungen im Osten Deutschlands seit den 70er Jahren. Vorstellung und Erläuterung von Ergebnissen einiger empirischer Untersuchungen in der DDR und in den neuen Bundesländern von 1977 bis 1991.* Speyer: Forschungsinstitut für Öffentliche Verwaltung.

Gerechtigkeit-Frieden-Bewahrung der Schöpfung. 1990. Leipzig: St. Benno-Verlag.

Gill, David, and Ulrich Schröter. 1991. *Das Ministerium für Staatssicherheit. Anatomie des Mielke-Imperiums*. Berlin: Rowohlt.

Glaeßner, Gert-Joachim. 1989. *Die andere deutsche Republik. Gesellschaft and Politik in der DDR*. Opladen: Westdeutscher Verlag.

Glotz, Peter. 1992. "Die Einheit und die Spaltung Europas. Die Auswirkungen der mitteleuropäischen Revolution von 1989 auf Gesamteuropa." *Aus Politik und Zeitgeschichte: Beilage zu Das Parlament* no. B 6/92, 50–61.

Goldfarb, Jeffrey C. 1978. "Social Bases of Independent Public Expression in Communist Societies." *American Journal of Sociology* 83:920–39.

Goldfarb, Jeffrey C. 1982. *On Cultural Freedom: An Exploration of Public Life in Poland and America*. Chicago and London: University of Chicago Press.

Goldfarb, Jeffrey C. 1992. *After the Fall: The Pursuit of Democracy in Central Europe*. New York: Basic Books.

Grabner, Wolf-Jürgen, Christiane Heinze, and Detlef Pollack, eds. 1990. *Leipzig im Oktober: Kirchen und alternative Gruppen im Umbruch der DDR: Analysen zur Wende*. Berlin: Wichern-Verlag.

Granovetter, Mark. 1978. "Threshold Models of Collective Behavior." *American Journal of Sociology* 83:1420–43.

Granovetter, Mark. 1986. "Economic Action and Social Structure: The Problem of Embeddedness." *American Journal of Sociology* 91:481–510.

Gurney, Joan N., and Kathleen Tierney. 1982. "Relative Deprivation and Social Movements: A Critical Look at Twenty Years of Theory and Research." *Sociological Quarterly* 23:33–47.

Gurr, Ted Robert. 1970. *Why Men Rebel*. Princeton, N.J.: Princeton University Press.

Gwertzman, Bernard, and Michael T. Kaufman, eds. 1990. *The Collapse of Communism*, 1st ed. New York: Random House.

Gwertzman, Bernard, and Michael T. Kaufman, eds. 1991. *The Collapse of Communism*, 2d ed. New York: Random House.

Hanisch, Günter et al., eds. 1990. *Dona nobis pacem: Fürbitten und Friedensgebete Herbst '89 in Leipzig*. Berlin: Evangelische Verlagsanstalt.

Hardin, Russell. 1982. *Collective Action*. Baltimore and London: Johns Hopkins University Press.

Heinze, Christiane, and Detlef Pollack. 1990. "Zur Funktion der politisch alternativen Gruppen im Prozeß des gesellschaftlichen Umbruchs in der DDR." In: Wolf-Jürgen Grabner, Christiane Heinze, and Detlef Pollack, eds., *Leipzig im Oktober: Kirchen und alternative Gruppen im Umbruch der DDR: Analysen zur Wende*, 82–90. Berlin: Wichern-Verlag.

Hempel, Carl G. 1965. *Aspects of Scientific Explanation and Other Essays in the Philosophy of Science*. New York and London: Free Press.

Hirschman, Albert O. 1970. *Exit, Voice, and Loyalty: Responses to Decline in Firms, Organizations, and States*. Cambridge, Mass.: Harvard University Press.

Hirschman, Albert O. 1993. "Exit, Voice, and the Fate of the German Democratic Republic: An Essay in Conceptual History." *World Politics* 45 (January): 173–203.

Hofmann, Michael, and Dieter Rink. 1990. "Der Leipziger Aufbruch 1989: Zur Genesis einer Heldenstadt." In Wolf-Jürgen Grabner, Christiane Heinze, and Detlef

Pollack, eds., *Leipzig im Oktober: Kirchen und alternative Gruppen im Umbruch der DDR: Analysen zur Wende,* 114–22. Berlin: Wichern-Verlag.

Hoppert, Leo. 1990. *Egon reiß die Mauer ein Leipziger DEMO-Sprüche.* Münster: Coppenrath Verlag.

Janning, Josef, Hans-Josef Legrand, and Helmut Zander, eds. 1987. *Friedensbewegungen: Entwicklung und Folgen in der Bundesrepublik Deutschland, Europa und den USA.* Cologne: Verlag Wissenschaft und Politik.

Jenkins, J. Craig. 1983. "Resource Mobilization Theory and the Study of Social Movements." *Annual Review of Sociology* 9:527–53.

Joas, Hans, and Martin Kohli, eds. 1993. *Der Zusammenbruch der DDR.* Frankfurt: Suhrkamp.

Karklins, Rasma, and Roger Petersen. 1993. "Decision Calculus of Protesters and Regimes: Eastern Europe 1989." *Journal of Politics* 355:3588–614.

Kirchgässner, Gebhard. 1980. "Können Ökonomie und Soziologie voneinander lernen?" *Kyklos* 33:420–48.

Kirchgässner, Gebhard. 1991. *Homo Oeconomicus: Das ökonomische Modell individuellen Verhaltens und seine Anwendung in den Wirtschafts- und Sozialwissenschaften.* Tübingen: J. C. B. Mohr.

Kitschelt, Herbert. 1986. "Political Opportunity Structures and Political Protest: Anti-Nuclear Movements in Four Democracies." *British Journal of Political Science* 16:57–85.

Klandermans, Bert. 1984. "Social Psychological Expansions of Resource Mobilization Theory." *American Sociological Review* 49:583–600.

Klier, Freya. 1991. *Lüg Vaterland: Erziehung in der DDR.* Munich: Kindler.

Knoke, David. 1988. "Incentives in Collective Action Organizations." *American Sociological Review* 53:311–29.

Knoke, David. 1990. *Political Networks: The Structural Perspective.* Cambridge: Cambridge University Press.

Köhler, Anne. 1991. "Die Umfrageforschung in der DDR—vor und nach der 'Wende.'" In Karl Furmaniak and Hartmut Kiock, eds., *Programmforschung in der und über die (ehemalige) DDR,* 115–34. Munich: Gesellschaft für Programmforschung in der öffentlichen Verwaltung e.V.

Krusche, Günter. 1990. "Gemeinden in der DDR sind beunruhigt. Wie soll die Kirche sich zu den Gruppen stellen?" In Detlef Pollack, ed., *Die Legitimität der Freiheit,* 57–62. Frankfurt am Main: Peter Lang.

Kuhn, Ekkehard. 1992. *Der Tag der Entscheidung: Leipzig, 9 Oktober 1989.* Berlin: Ullstein.

Kuran, Timur. 1989. "Sparks and Prairie Fires: A Theory of Unanticipated Revolutions." *Public Choice* 61:41–74.

Kuran, Timur. 1990. "Now out of Never: The Element of Surprise in the East European Revolution." *World Politics* 44:7–48.

Kuran, Timur. 1991. "Cognitive Limitations and Preference Evolution." *Journal of Institutional and Theoretical Economics* 147:241–73.

Langguth, Gerd. 1976. *Die Protestbewegung in der Bundesrepublik Deutschland 1968–1976.* Cologne: Verlag Wissenschaft und Politik.

Leif, Thomas. 1987. "Die professionelle Bewegung—zentrale Entscheidungsgremien und Meinungsführer." In Josef Janning, Hans-Josef Legrand, and Helmut Zander, eds., *Friedensbewegungen. Entwicklung und Folgen in der Bundesrepublik Deutschland, Europa und den USA*, 54–63. Cologne: Verlag Wissenschaft und Politik.

Lemke, Christiane. 1991. *Die Ursachen des Umbruchs 1989*. Opladen: Westdeutscher Verlag.

Lichbach, Mark. 1989. "An Evaluation of 'Does Economic Inequality Breed Political Conflict?' Studies." *World Politics* 41:431–70.

Lichbach, Mark. 1990. "Will Rational People Rebel against Inequality? Samson's Choice." *American Journal of Political Science* 34:1049–76.

Lieberwirth, Steffen, ed. 1990. *Wer eynen spielmann zu tode schlaegt . . . Ein mittelalterliches Zeitdokument anno 1989*. Leipzig: Edition Peters, Militzke Verlag.

Lieser-Triebnigg, Erika. 1985. *Recht in der DDR: Einführung und Dokumentation*. Cologne: Verlag Wissenschaft und Politik.

Lindner, Bernd. 1990. "Soziologie der Losungen." In Wolfgang Schneider, ed., *Leipziger Demontagebuch*, 169–73. Leipzig and Weimar: G. Kiepenheuer.

Lindner, Bernd, and Ralph Grüneberger, eds. 1992. *Demonteure. Biographien des Leipziger Herbst*. Bielefeld: Aisthesis.

Lindner, Clausjohann. 1972. *Theorie der Revolution. Ein Beitrag zur verhaltenstheoretischen Soziologie*. Munich: Goldmann.

Loest, Erich. 1979. *Es geht seinen Gang*. Rudolstadt: Greifenverlag.

Lorenz, Günter, and Hartmut Lorenz. 1990. "Eine Chronik der Ereignisse." In Jörg Swoboda, ed., *Die Revolution der Kerzen*, 7–68. Wuppertal and Kassel: Onckenverlag.

Löscher, Lutz, and Jürgen Vogel. 1990. "Leipziger Herbst." In Stefan Heym and Werner Heiduczek, eds., *Die sanfte Revolution: Prosa, Lyrik, Protokolle, Erlebnisberichte, Reden*, 127–45. Leipzig and Weimar: Gustav Kiepenheuer Verlag.

Maaz, Hans-Joachim. 1990. *Der Gefühlsstau: Ein Psychogramm der DDR*. Berlin: Argon.

Malewski, Andrzej. 1967. *Verhalten und Interaktion*. Tübingen: Mohr.

Marwell, Gerald, and Ruth E. Ames. 1979. "Experiments on the Provision of Public Goods: I. Resources, Interest, Group Size, and the Free-Rider Problem." *American Journal of Sociology* 84:1335–60.

Marx, Karl, and Friedrich Engels. 1966. *Ausgewählte Schriften in zwei Bänden*, Band 1. Berlin: Dietz Verlag.

Mayer, Hans. 1991. *Der Turm von Babel. Erinnerungen an eine Deutsche Demokratische Republik*. Frankfurt am Main: Suhrkamp Verlag.

McAdam, Doug. 1982. *Political Process and the Development of Black Insurgency 1930–1970*. Chicago and London: University of Chicago Press.

McCarthy, John D., and Mayer N. Zald. 1977. "Resource Mobilization and Social Movements." *American Journal of Sociology* 82:1212–41.

McLean, Ian. 1987. *Public Choice: An Introduction*. New York: Blackwell.

Meckling, William H. 1976. "Values and the Choice of Model of the Individual in the Social Sciences." *Schweizerische Zeitschrift für Volkswirtschaft und Statistik* 112:545–59.

Menge, Marlies. 1990. *Ohne uns läuft nichts mehr: Die Revolution in der DDR.* Stuttgart: Deutsche Verlags-Anstalt.

Merton, Robert K. 1957. *Social Theory and Social Structure.* Glencoe, Ill.: Free Press.

Mitchell, Robert C. 1979. "National Environmental Lobbies and the Apparent Illogic of Collective Action." In Clifford S. Russell, ed., *Collective Decision Making: Applications from Public Choice Theory*, 87–136. Baltimore and London: Johns Hopkins University Press.

Mitter, Armin, and Stefan Wolle, eds. 1990. *Ich liebe euch doch alle! Befehle und Lageberichte des MfS Januar–November 1989.* Berlin: BasisDruck.

Moe, Terry M. 1980. *The Organization of Interests: Incentives and the Internal Dynamics of Political Interest Groups.* Chicago and London: University of Chicago Press.

Mueller, Dennis C. 1989. *Public Choice II.* Cambridge: Cambridge University Press.

Mühler, Kurt, and Steffen H. Wilsdorf. 1991. "Die Leipziger Montagsdemonstration—Aufstieg und Wandel einer basisdemokratischen Institution des friedlichen Umbruchs im Spiegel empirischer Meinungsforschung." *Berliner Journal für Soziologie* 1:37–45.

Mühler, Kurt, and Reinhart Wippler. 1994. Die Vorgeschichte der Wende in der DDR: Versuch einer Erklärung." *Kölner Zeitschrift für Soziologie und Sozialpsychologie* 45:691–711

Muller, Edward N. 1979. *Aggressive Political Participation.* Princeton, N.J.: Princeton University Press.

Muller, Edward N., and Karl-Dieter Opp. 1986. "Rational Choice and Rebellious Collective Action." *American Political Science Review* 80:471–89.

Müller-Enbergs, Helmut, Marianne Schulz, and Jan Wielgohs, eds. 1991. *Von der Illegalität ins Parlament: Werdegang und Konzept der neuen Bürgerbewegungen.* Berlin: LinksDruck.

Musiolek, Berndt, and Carola Wuttke, eds. 1991. *Parteien und politische Bewegungen im letzten Jahr der DDR (Oktober 1989 bis April 1990).* Berlin: BasisDruck.

Naimark, Norman M. 1992. "'Ich will hier raus': Emigration and the Collapse of the German Democratic Republic." In Ivo Banac, ed., *Eastern Europe in Revolution*, 72–95. Ithaca, N.Y. and London: Cornell University Press.

Neubert, Ehrhart. 1991. "Protestantische Kultur und DDR-Revolution." *Aus Politik und Zeitgeschichte: Beilage zu "Das Parlament"* 19:21–29.

Neues Forum Leipzig, ed. 1990. *Jetzt oder nie—Demokratie: Leipziger Herbst '89.* Leipzig, Munich: Bertelsmann.

Oberschall, Anthony. 1973. *Social Conflict and Social Movements.* Englewood Cliffs, N.J.: Prentice Hall.

Olson, Mancur. 1965. *The Logic of Collective Action.* Cambridge, Mass.: Harvard University Press.

Opp, Karl-Dieter. 1978. *Theorie sozialer Krisen: Apathie, Protest und kollektives Handeln.* Hamburg: Hoffmann and Campe.

Opp, Karl-Dieter. 1985. "Konventionelle und unkonventionelle politische Partizipation." *Zeitschrift für Soziologie,* 14:282–96.

Opp, Karl-Dieter. 1986. "Soft Incentives and Collective Action: Participation in the Anti-Nuclear Movement." *British Journal of Political Science* 16:87–112.

Opp, Karl-Dieter. 1988a. "Grievances and Participation in Social Movements." *American Sociological Review* 53:853–64.

Opp, Karl-Dieter. 1988b. "The Individualistic Research Program in Sociology." In Gerard Radnitzky, ed., *Centripetal Forces in the Sciences,* vol. 2, 208–24. New York: Paragon House.

Opp, Karl-Dieter. 1990a. "Postmaterialism, Collective Action, and Political Protest." *American Journal of Political Science* 34:212–35.

Opp, Karl-Dieter. 1990b. "Testing Rational Choice Theory in Natural Settings." In J. J. Hox and J. de Jong-Gierveld, eds., *Operationalization and Research Strategy,* 87–102. Amsterdam and Lisse: Swets and Zeitlinger.

Opp, Karl-Dieter. 1991a. "Processes of Collective Political Action: A Dynamic Model and the Results of a Computer Simulation." *Rationality and Society* 3:215–51.

Opp, Karl-Dieter. 1991b. "DDR '89. Zu den Ursachen einer spontanen Revolution." *Kölner Zeitschrift für Soziologie und Sozialpsychologie* 43:302–21.

Opp, Karl-Dieter. 1992a. "Spontaneous Revolutions: The Case of East Germany in 1989." In Heinz D. Kurz, ed., *United Germany and the New Europe.* Cheltenham: Elgar.

Opp, Karl-Dieter. 1992b. "Legaler und illegaler Protest im interkulturellen Vergleich." *Kölner Zeitschrift für Soziologie und Sozialpsychologie,* 44:436–60.

Opp, Karl-Dieter. 1993. "Politischer Protest als rationales Handeln: Eine Anwendung des ökonomischen Ansatzes zur Erklärung von Protest." In Bernd-Thomas Ramb and Manfred Tietzel, eds., *Die ökonomische Logik des menschlichen Verhaltens.* Munich: Vahlen.

Opp, Karl-Dieter. 1994. "Repression and Revolutionary Action: East Germany in 1989." *Rationality and Society* 6:101–38.

Opp, Karl-Dieter, and Christiane Gern. 1993. "Dissident Groups, Personal Networks, and Spontaneous Cooperation: The East German Revolution of 1989." *American Sociological Review* 58:659–80.

Opp, Karl-Dieter, and Wolfgang Roehl. 1990a. *Der Tschernobyl-Effekt: Eine Untersuchung über die Determinanten politischen Protests.* Opladen: Westdeutscher Verlag.

Opp, Karl-Dieter and Wolfgang Roehl. 1990b. "Repression, Micromobilization, and Political Protest." *Social Forces,* 69:521–48.

Opp, Karl-Dieter, et al. 1984. *Soziale Probleme und Protestverhalten: Eine empirische Konfrontierung des Modells rationalen Verhaltens mit soziologischen Hypothesen am Beispiel von Atomkraftgegnern.* Wiesbaden: Westdeutscher Verlag.

Opp, Karl-Dieter, in collaboration with Peter and Petra Hartmann. 1989. *The Rationality of Political Protest. A Comparative Analysis of Rational Choice Theory.* Boulder, Colo.: Westview Press.

Piven, Frances Fox, and Richard A. Cloward. 1977. *Poor People's Movements: Why They Succeed, How They Fail.* New York: Random House.

Piven, Frances Fox, and Richard A. Cloward. 1991. "Collective Protest: A Critique of

Resource Mobilization Theory." *International Journal of Politics, Culture and Society* 4:435–58.

Pollack, Detlef. 1990. "Ursachen des gesellschaftlichen Umbruchs in der DDR aus systemtheoretischer Perspektive." In Wolf-Jürgen Grabner, Christiane Heinze, and Detlef Pollack, eds., *Leipzig im Oktober: Kirchen und alternative Gruppen im Umbruch der DDR: Analysen zur Wende*, 12–23. Berlin: Wichern-Verlag.

Popkin, Samuel L. 1979. *The Rational Peasant: The Political Economy of Rural Society in Vietnam.* Berkeley: University of California Press.

Popkin, Samuel. 1988. "Political Entrepreneurs and Peasant Movements in Vietnam." In Michael Taylor, ed., *Rationality and Revolution*, 9–62. Cambridge: Cambridge University Press.

Poppe, Ulrike. 1990. "Das kritische Potential der Gruppen in Kirche und Gesellschaft." In Detlef Pollack, ed., *Die Legitimität der Freiheit*, 63–79. Frankfurt am Main: Peter Lang.

Popper, Karl R. 1972. *Objective Knowledge: An Evolutionary Approach.* Oxford: Oxford University Press.

Prosch, Bernhard, and Martin Abraham. 1991. "Die Revolution in der DDR: Eine strukturell-individualistische Erklärungsskizze." *Kölner Zeitschrift für Soziologie und Sozialpsychologie* 43:291–301.

Protokoll eines Tribunals: Die Ausschlüsse aus dem DDR-Schriftstellerverband 1979. 1991. Reinbek: Rowohlt Taschenbuch Verlag.

Rein, Gerhard, ed. 1989. *Die Opposition in der DDR. Entwürfe für einen anderen Sozialismus.* Berlin: Wichern-Verlag.

Rein, Gerhard. 1990. *Die protestantische Revolution 1987–1990.* Berlin: Wichern-Verlag.

Reißig, Rolf. 1991. "Der Umbruch in der DDR und das Scheitern des 'realen Sozialismus.'" In Rolf Reißig and Gert-Joachim Glaeßner, eds., *Das Ende eines Experiments: Umbruch in der DDR und deutsche Einheit*, 12–59. Berlin: Dietz Verlag.

Richter, Johannes. 1989. "Wir sind Sachsen!" In Gerhard Rein, ed., *Die Opposition in der DDR: Entwürfe für einen anderen Sozialismus*, 182–87. Berlin: Wichern-Verlag.

Riker, William H., and Peter C. Ordeshook. 1968. "A Theory of the Calculus of Voting." *American Political Science Review* 65:25–42.

Riker, William H., and Peter C. Ordeshook. 1973. *An Introduction to Positive Political Theory.* Englewood Cliffs, N.J.: Prentice Hall.

Rudé, George. 1964. *The Crowd in History: A Study of Popular Disturbances in France and England 1730–1848.* New York: Riley.

Salert, Barbara. 1976. *Revolutions and Revolutionaries. Four Theories.* New York: Elsevier.

Schabowski, Günter. 1990. *Das Politbüro: Ende eines Mythos.* (Eine Befragung, edited by Frank Sieren and Ludwig Koehne). Reinbek: Rowohlt Taschenbuch Verlag.

Schabowski, Günter. 1991. *Der Absturz.* Berlin: Rowohlt.

Schäuble, Wolfgang. 1991. *Der Vertrag: Wie ich die deutsche Einheit verhandelte.* Stuttgart: Deutsch Verlags-Anstalt.

278   Bibliography

Schell, Manfred, and Werner Kalinka. 1991. *Stasi und kein Ende: Die Personen und Fakten*. Frankfurt: Ullstein.

Schelling, Thomas C. 1960. *The Strategy of Conflict*. Cambridge: Harvard University Press.

Schmid, Josef. 1991. "Die politische Rolle der Evangelischen Kirchen in der DDR in den achtziger Jahren." In Helmut Müller-Enbergs, Marianne Schulz, and Jan Wielgohs, eds., *Von der Illegalität ins Parlament: Werdegang und Konzept der neuen Bürgerbewegungen*, 342–65. Berlin: LinksDruck.

Schneider, Wolfgang, ed. 1990. *Leipziger Demontagebuch*. Leipzig and Weimar: G. Kiepenheuer.

Schorlemmer, Friedrich. 1991. *Bis alle Mauern fallen: Texte aus einem verschwundenen Land.* Berlin: Verlag der Nation.

Schüddekopf, Charles, ed. 1990. *Wir sind das Volk: Flugschriften, Aufrufe und Texte einer deutschen Revolution*. Reinbek: Rowohlt.

Schulz, Marianne. 1991. "Neues Forum—Von der illegalen Opposition zur legalen Marginalität." In Helmut Müller-Enbergs, Marianne Schulz, and Jan Wielgohs, eds., *Von der Illegalität ins Parlament: Werdegang und Konzept der neuen Bürgerbewegungen*, 11–104. Berlin: LinksDruck.

Schwarz, Norbert. 1990. "Assessing Frequency Reports of Mundane Behaviors. Contributions of Cognitive Psychology to Questionnaire Construction." *Review of Personality and Social Psychology: Research Methods in Personality and Social Psychology* 11:98–119.

Scott, John. 1991. *Social Network Analysis: A Handbook*. London: Sage.

Sievers, Hans-Jürgen. 1990. *Stundenbuch einer deutschen Revolution*. Göttingen: Vandenhoeck & Ruprecht.

Silver, Morris. 1974. "Political Revolution and Repression: An Economic Approach." *Public Choice* 17:63–71.

Skocpol, Theda. 1979. *States and Social Revolutions: A Comparative Analysis of France, Russia and China*. Cambridge: Cambridge University Press.

Smith, Adam [1776] 1970. *An Inquiry into the Nature and Causes of the Wealth of Nations*. Hormondsworth, England: Penguin Books.

Sontheimer, Kurt. 1990. *Deutschlands Politische Kultur*. Munich: Piper.

Staritz, Dietrich. 1990. "Ursachen und Konsequenzen einer deutschen Revolution." In *Der Fischer Weltalmanach*, 13–44. Frankfurt: Fischer Taschenbuch-Verlag.

Statistisches Jahrbuch der DDR '90. 1990. Berlin: Rudolf Haufe Verlag.

Strohmeyer, Arn. 1990. *Visa frei bis Hawaii: Neue DDR-Witze & Demo-Sprüche*. Frankfurt am Main: Eichborn.

Strube, Gerhard. 1987. "Answering Survey Questions: The Role of Memory." In H. J. Hippler, N. Schwarz, and S. Sudman, eds., *Social Information Processing and Survey Methodology*, 86–101. New York: Springer.

Swoboda, Jörg, ed. 1990. *Die Revolution der Kerzen*. Wuppertal and Kassel: Onckenverlag.

Tarrow, Sidney. 1991a. "Understanding Political Change in Eastern Europe." *PS: Political Science and Politics*, March 1991, 12–20.

Tarrow, Sidney. 1991b. *Struggle, Politics, and Reform: Collective Action, Social Movements, and Cycles of Protest*. Ithaca, N.Y.: Cornell University Press.

Taylor, Michael. 1988. "Rationality and Revolutionary Collective Action." In Michael

Taylor, ed., *Rationality and Revolution*, 63–97. Cambridge: Cambridge University Press.

Tetzner, Reiner. 1990. *Leipziger Ring: Aufzeichnungen eines Montagsdemonstranten. Oktober 1989 bis 1. Mai 1990*. Frankfurt: Luchterhand.

Thaysen, Uwe. 1990. *Der Runde Tisch, Oder, Wo blieb das Volk: Der Weg der DDR in die Demokratie*. Opladen: Westdeutscher Verlag.

Tietzel, Manfred, Marion Weber, and Otto F. Bode. 1991. *Die Logik der sanften Revolution*. Tübingen: Mohr-Siebeck.

Tillock, Harriet, and Denton E. Morrison. 1979. "Group Size and Contributions to Collective Action: An Examination of Olson's Theory Using Data from Zero Population Growth Inc." *Research in Social Movements, Conflicts and Change* 2:131–58.

Tilly, Charles. 1978. *From Mobilization to Revolution*. New York: Random House.

Todorova, Maria N. 1992. "Improbable Maverick or Typical Conformist? Seven Thoughts on the New Bulgaria." In Ivo Banac, ed., *Eastern Europe in Revolution*, 148–67. Ithaca, N.Y. and London: Cornell University Press.

Tullock, Gordon. 1971. "The Paradox of Revolution." *Public Choice* 11:88–99.

Tullock, Gordon. 1974. *The Social Dilemma: The Economics of War and Revolution*. Blacksburg, Va: University Publications.

Tullock, Gordon. 1987. *Autocracy*. Dordrecht: Kluwer.

Uhlaner, Carole. 1989. "Rational Turnout: The Neglected Role of Groups." *American Journal of Political Science* 33:390–422.

Useem, Bert. 1980. "Solidarity Model, Breakdown Model, and the Boston Anti-Busing Movement." *American Sociological Review* 45:357–69.

Useem, Bert. 1985. "Disorganization and the New Mexico Prison Riot of 1980." *American Sociological Review* 50:677–88.

Walsh, Edward J. 1981. "Resource Mobilization and Citizen Protest in Communities around Three Mile Island." *Social Problems* 29:1–21.

Walsh, Edward J., and Rex H. Warland. 1983. "Social Movement Involvement in the Wake of a Nuclear Accident: Activists and Free Riders in the TMI Area." *American Sociological Review* 48:764–80.

Weber, Hermann. 1991. *DDR. Grundriß der Geschichte 1945–1990*. Hannover: Fackelträger.

Weede, Erich. 1992. *Mensch und Gesellschaft: Soziologie aus der Perspektive des methodologischen Individualismus*. Tübingen: J. C. B. Mohr.

Weiß, Robert. 1990. *Chronik eines Zusammenbruchs: Der heiße Herbst und seine Folgen in den Ländern des Warschauer Paktes*. Berlin: Dietz Verlag.

White, James W. 1988. "Rational Rioters: Leaders, Followers, and Popular Protest in Early Japan." *Politics and Society* 16:1–34.

Wielepp, Christoph. 1990. "Montags abends in Leipzig." In Thomas Blanke and Rainer Erd, eds., *DDR—Ein Staat vergeht*, 71–78. Frankfurt am Main: Fischer Taschenbuch-Verlag.

Wilkening, Christina. 1990. *Staat im Staate: Auskünfte ehemaliger Stasi-Mitarbeiter*. Berlin and Weimar: Aufbau-Verlag.

Winkler, Gunnar, ed. 1990. *Sozialreport 90. Daten und Fakten zur sozialen Lage in der DDR*. Berlin: Die Wirtschaft.

Wippler, Reinhard, and Siegwart Lindenberg. 1987. "Collective Phenomena and Rational Choice." In Jeffrey C. Alexander et al., eds., *The Micro-Macro Link*, 135–52. Berkeley: University of California Press.

Wuttke, Carola, and Bernd Musiolek, eds., 1991. *Parteien und politische Bewegungen im letzten Jahr der DDR*. Berlin: BasisDruck.

Zanetti, Benno, ed. 1991. *Der Weg zur deutschen Einheit: 9.November 1989–3.Oktober 1990 mit den wichtigsten Reden*. Munich: Goldmann.

Date Due

OCT 2 97			
DE1 2 97			
DE1 7 97			
APR 1 1 '89			